D1279755

Sociology of Education

SUNY Series in Urban Public Policy
James Bohland and Patricia Edwards, Editors

Sociology of Education

Emerging Perspectives

EDITED BY

Carlos Alberto Torres
and
Theodore R. Mitchell

State University of New York Press

Published by
State University of New York Press, Albany

© 1998 State University of New York

For information, address State University of New York
Press, State University Plaza, Albany, N.Y., 12246

Production by Diane Ganeles
Marketing by Anne Valentine

Library of Congress Cataloging-in-Publication Data

Sociology of education : emerging perspectives / Carlos Alberto Torres
and Theodore R. Mitchell, editors.
    p.   cm.
    Includes bibliographical references and index.
    ISBN 0–7914–3755–8 (hc : alk. paper). — ISBN 0–7914–3756–6
(pbk. : alk. paper)
    1. Educational sociology.   I. Torres, Carlos Alberto.
II. Mitchell, Theodore R.
    LC191.S6619   1998
306.43´2—dc21   97–35891
                                                    CIP

10 9 8 7 6 5 4 3 2 1

Contents

1

Introduction

❑

Carlos Alberto Torres and Theodore R. Mitchell

Why Emerging Perspectives and New Departures?

The title of this book does not pretend to be pompous but just to recognize the reality of drastic departures in sociology of education today. What marks the development of the discipline of sociology of education is a large number of emerging perspectives resulting from the growing scholarship of class, race, ethnicity, and gender. However, we decided against coining a catchy term to encapsulate with elegance and precision these new departures because we are not in the business of creating another cottage industry in sociology of education. Yet, we are witnessing the emergence of various different theoretical and methodological strands in sociology of education which drastically depart from the established tradition. Philosophically, one may argue that these new perspectives criticize the old perspectives, retain what is valuable, and improve their analysis, in a kind of sociological *Aufhebung*,[1] marking the latter part of this century.

Three elements stand out in these new departures and emerging perspectives. First, in sociology of education there is the emergence of new epistemological approaches which differ sharply from positivism and empiricism. Second, the sociology of education is pressed to confront the dilemmas posed by the dichotomy between modernism and postmodernism, or poststructuralist forms of theoretical representation, and its implications for the scholarship of class, race, and gender. Finally, the sociology of education

1

is asked to confront the new risks and challenges that these new theoretical developments pose for educational research, and particularly for the future of public education in the United States and elsewhere. Hence, this introduction serves the dual purposes of outlining these problems and introducing the different chapters of the book.

The Logic of Explanation in the Sociology of Education: New Departures?

Sociology of education has come a long way from the Durkheimian foundational suggestion that to study education is to study how the older generations transmit the culture to the new generations. It has also moved beyond the new sociology of education approach inspired by the reception of Karl Mannehim's critique of knowledge as "a tool in the struggle for status and power" (Wexler 1987, 26). The new perspectives are also moving beyond the question of school knowledge, linking the sociology of knowledge tradition with the classroom-based "pedagogical interest of the curricularists in both classroom interaction and school knowledge" (Wexler 1987, 35). The task has been magnified. The functions traditionally assigned to education—particularly to the schooling of promoting skills, cognitive training, and preparation for citizenship—are either becoming obsolete in the view of some scholars or at least put into question by changes in the process of work and key dynamics in educational environments (Aronowitz and DiFazio 1994).

Additionally, the emerging perspectives in sociology of education have left the bedrock of the East-West confrontation (that marked so much of the scholarship in sociology during the 1940s, 1950s, and 1960s) where Marxism and neo-Marxism were seen as challengers to the established positivist and structural-functionalist paradigm. Indeed, the new perspectives in sociology of education have also come a long way in understanding the limitations of the normal positivist science implied in much of the traditional number-crunching and hypothesis-testing scholarship. There is still an important gap between the new perspectives in sociology of education and its ability to impact educational policy formation and the practices in school settings. But there is always a beginning for everything.

From The Logic of Positivism in Educational Planning to Emerging Perspectives in the Sociology of Education

The logic of educational planning is closely linked with the model of normal social science, dominated by the epistemological paradigm of positivism (Wallerstein 1991a; Morrow and Brown 1994). Explanations are based on the possibility that establishing regularities can be differentiated from accidental generalizations or laws. However, work in the social sciences shows that the social sciences, in sharp contrast with the natural sciences, face a principle of ambiguity. Many events, given the open-ended and eventual idiosyncratic nature of social life, do not conform to a rule of universality and hence invalidate the rule, or at least do not make the notion of universality a precondition for scientific work but another "contested terrain." To account for this, conventional sociology of education has resorted to statistical probabilistic models rather than generalization of laws or law-like explanations. Laws, and law-like models of explanations, should be differentiated from merely empirical generalizations which address the issue of how to move from empirical observations to definitions of causality.

The problem is how to identify causal explanations without relying on interpretations. The simple approach to this problem is to think of theoretical statements as hypothetical deductive postulations; that is, logical constructions rather than real entities (Bredo and Feinberg 1982, 21). The question then is whether it is possible to sharply differentiate, as a logical distinction, between theory and observation, a principle which has been challenged in the most recent work in sociology of education. Likewise, how to differentiate theory from method, considering that a great deal of the empirical work that is being developed in the recent perspectives in sociology of education is theory-driven research, relying on case studies.

The new scientific models in sociology of education do not consider scientific work as separated from its theoretical foundations and universally applicable. The debates among paradigms and approaches, ranging from modernist to postmodernist perspectives and structuralists to poststructuralist models, indicate that any pretension to establish a sense of certainty and analytical precision in a world, which is increasingly unpredictable and imprecise, may be pompous and even naive (Samoff 1990; Morrow and Torres 1995; Morrow and Torres, in press). Indeed, if anything, the new perspectives in sociology of education address the understanding of reality as a concrete totality with a great degree of variability and volatility. Hence, the challenge is to traditional notions of linear and evolutionary concepts of knowledge, around which not only deterministic inferences and deductive conclusions are based, but also empirical foundations are organized.

In addition to a more flexible and even playful notion of science, empirical events, and theoretical analysis, the new perspectives in sociology of education tend to downplay the normative distinction between value judgments and empirical judgments. The new emerging perspectives employ more open-ended scientific models, trying to search less for patterns of regularity, universality, and reproducible results than for representations of the dynamics of transformation of complex totalities that cannot be parceled out into distinct domains. Hence, the new perspectives in sociology of education, despite their reliance on case studies and theory-driven methodologies, are heavily interdisciplinary and comparative. In this context, there is no specific call for specialized methods or means to identify laws or law-like processes.

To be sure, there is an understanding that reality shows some recurrent patterns and regularities. These patterns and regularities can be studied at different levels which cannot be easily dissociated, including meta-theories, middle-range theories, and empirical research. None of these levels of scientific work can be easily differentiated, nor can they be pursued as totally independent instances. They are, however, moments in the division of labor of the research process where grand-theorizing, specific, context-bound theories, data collection, and data analysis of discrete data can be singled out as discrete steps in the research process. Yet, there is a constant iteration in all these moments, with the "empirical" moment deconstructing the "meta-theoretical" or "theoretical" moment and vice versa, in an endless succession of iterations and revisions throughout the whole research process. Contrary to the old scientific tendency, which emphasizes disciplinary rather than interdisciplinary or transdisciplinary work, the new perspectives in sociology of education tend to be interdisciplinary, transdisciplinary, and comparative in nature (Morrow and Torres 1995; Liebman and Paulston 1994; Paulston and Liebman 1994).

These new emerging perspectives in sociology of education consider that reality is constituted through nonlinear events and through profound discontinuities in real life phenomena. This, of course, questions traditional notions of objectivity. In the new and emerging perspectives, the notion of social objectivity is not a premise of "good" research, but an agonic process to be hoped for; it involves in a dialectical process both the researchers and the so-called research object. Objectivity becomes another goal to be achieved through processes of iteration, multiple checks and balances throughout the whole research process, multiple processes of intersubjective exchanges among researchers and population "studied," and the quality of the intellectual analysis in decodifying the different processes of representation (and hence, languages, voices, identities) of the people involved in the research.

Broadening the notion of objectivity includes a critical reconsideration of the notion of subjectivity as an asset rather than a liability in the research project. The subjectivity and singularity of the researcher cannot be ignored when attempting to achieve a notion of a universal, clearly established, and procedurally bound notion of social objectivity which can be easily attained through the implementation of methodological rules—as if the subject matter will remain unpolluted. In short, in social research there are not ready-made "recipes" which can be thought of as simple, easy to apply, and universal; a set of hygienical rules which, in turn, can be implemented in a laboratory-like, environmentally controlled model.

An important example of these dilemmas is the discussion on race in educational research. Research shows that race is difficult to talk about, especially in large groups and for fear of being misconstrued (Cooper et al. 1994). Investigating race relations involves questions of power, that is, not only the differential power of researchers over the researched population, but also the differential power of university researchers from different races, ages, and occupational positions (Gitlin 1994). All make the discussion on race (and undoubtedly any discussion involving class and gender themes) more complex (Cooper et al. 1994). Self-reflective behavior by researchers, addressing how difficult it is to investigate issues of race, even when the research team is made of multicultural perspectives and experiences, leads a group of researchers to spell out their own dilemmas about race, gender, age, and reputation and how that affects the methodology and substantive part of their own research (Cooper et al. 1994). Some findings from the literature suggest that for the study of nonsensitive, nonracial issues, the race of the researcher matters very little, and has no bearing on the research quality of outcomes. Yet, some argue, for instance, that "White researchers tend to use a methodological approach that is hierarchical. Their approach manipulates those being interviewed as objects and dictates that there should be as little human contact as possible and no emotional involvement. The danger of this approach to research lies in the feelings of exploitation it creates within minority communities and the distorted knowledge that results" (Cooper et al. 1994, 7).

These are some of the reasons that when trying to understand reality "as it is" or as it "appears to be," the practitioners of these emerging perspectives in sociology of education are more skeptical than their more conventional counterparts in assuming that science and ideology are clearly distinct, potentially antagonistic, and certainly irreconcilable practices in research. On the contrary, while agonizing to establish as many checks and balances as possible to understand reality as a social construction, they do not deposit their trust in scientific practices which are clearly differentiable and discernible through the systematic application of the scientific method and certain ethical and epistemological precepts regarding the separation of value judgments and empirical judgments. The notion of the "empirical" reality thus appears as a much more complex theoretical notion for sociologists employing these emerging perspectives in sociology of education.

There are, of course, several policy implications related to this new epistemological criteria. Educational planners schooled in the positivistic social sciences argue that there is a fundamental social order underlying the dynamic of things themselves. This order is discernible through the methodical and rigorous application of a specific method of social science. This method must reflect the premises of all scientific methods according to the model of natural sciences; that is, a method based on foundationalism, objectivity, the search for control and manipulation of variables, experimentalism (or quasi-experimentalism), universality, and rationality (Silos 1995). This scientific method permits the discovery of regularities which can be measured and quantified, applied in experimental or quasi-experimental analyses, or used to study correlations, causalities, or manipulated (controlled) in future analyses. The goal of social science is to develop a set of arguments which study causal relations, and, when possible, these detected patterns or regularities can be applied like laws or empirical guidelines. These laws can be summed up in brief, concise, simple phrases; they can even be presented mathematically and used—previous to empirical exam and proof and subject to the falsifiability of the hypothesis—to manipulate and indeed plan the process of development of social reality. More complicated analyses trying to understand the historical nuances of things, their interrelations, and the theoretical multidisciplinary analysis of numerous observations which may make the analysis problematic, tentative or uncertain, are rejected as unnecessary (Samoff 1990). Or, if they are considered pertinent in theoretical terms, they are considered lacking usefulness for planning, which is based on well-defined problems, with a sense of urgency and immediacy, and motivated not by theoretical reasons, but by actions which quickly and efficiently resolve specific and pressing problems (Torres 1996[a]).

A central claim of the new perspectives in sociology of education is the need to think of reality as ever changing with a number of dimensions or layers which constitute independent spheres but share intertwined dynamics. Hence, the emphasis on the scholarship of class, race, and gender as an integrated set of theories is not only facing the challenge of postmodernism, but also moving beyond the political immobilism of many postmodernist positions.

The Scholarship of Class, Race, and Gender: Integrated Perspectives?

R. Morrow and C. A. Torres' work (Morrow and Torres 1995) advanced the proposition that the scholarship of race, class, and gender as integrated perspectives has emerged from the tradition of critical modernism, and, as such, constitutes a response to the excesses of postmodernism.

As it has been discussed elsewhere (Torres 1996[c]; Morrow and Torres 1995), postmodernism argues that there is a "new" epoch in society and thus a new cultural paradigm. Some of the key sociological implications of postmodern society and culture can be summarized as involving various processes of fragmentation as follows: (1) a decentering and fragmentation of power that calls into question theories of domination and hegemony; (2) an uncoupling of material interests and subjective expressions in collective action, resulting in the shift of the demands of social movements from distributional to cultural-ethical issues; (3) the emergence of heterogeneity as opposed to the homogenization that has been previously characteristic of the world system; and (4) a growing distrust and disillusionment with democracy, resulting from the fragmentation of political communities and identities.

Hence, postmodernism argues that power has become decentered and fragmented in contemporary societies. Thus, to suggest the notion of a ruling elite, conducting its business with decisive

influence in the formulation of public policy or education, will obscure—in a postmodern view—the multiplicity of powers that interact in society and its policy outcomes (Bowles and Gintis 1986). How
does one define power that is fragmented and lacking an unifying
principle? Does this undermine the nonsynchronous, parallelist conception of the relations of class, gender, and race in cultural reproduction? Does, in short, the fragmentation of power undermine
conceptual frameworks and "grand narratives" such as of hegemony
and domination (Torres 1996[c])?

The so-called death of grand narratives poses political and epistemological questions. For Michel Foucault, truth depends on strategies of power rather than epistemological criteria. This is a central
concern for a theory of the state and power. Does this mean that if we
rely on skeptical poststructuralist accounts we cannot define some
"master signifier," that helps us to ground, ethically and politically
political action? Otherwise we cannot validate ex ante any policy recommendation in education from a theoretical standpoint, nor can we
validate ex post facto the same principles for political action. The
most obvious implication is the lack of direction and the absence of a
political program. One possible consequence of this is "a false radicalism which engages in constant but ultimately meaningless trans-
gression of all defended viewpoints" (Hulme 1986, 6). This political
activism highlights David Harvey's concern that we may end up with
philosophical and social thought, which is characterized by ephemer-
ality, collage, fragmentation, and dispersion (Harvey 1989).

Political activism based on "false radicalism" doesn't challenge
the fragmented politics of divergent special and regional interest
groups. This situation, added to the secular, internecine struggles of
progressive groups, the structural and historical action of the capitalist state, and actions from the Right, undermines the communities
of learning and political action, hindering the ability of progressive
groups to challenge differential access to resources (influence, power,
and wealth), of elites and dominant classes in education. This "transgressive" activism may challenge the narratives of neo-conservative
and neo-liberal projects in education, which is not a minor accom-
plishment considering the power of the "common sense" narrative of
the Right, but it offers few if any guidelines for practical politics. The
problem is compounded when social subjects are considered to be
politically decentered (Torres 1996[c]; Morrow and Torres 1995).

The notion of the decentering of social subjects implies an
uncoupling of the close link between objective social interests and
subjective expressions (e.g., class consciousness) assumed by much

modernist social theory. The resulting contradictory loyalties of individuals increasingly undermines a central organizing principle of struggle. One oft-noted consequence of this relative uncoupling of social position and political action is that the "new" social movements are more concerned with cultural (and ethical-political) demands than distributional ones. Decentered individuals are not supposed to have "class consciousness" in classical terms, yet they strive to achieve "self-actualization" in Anthony Giddens' social psychological analysis (Giddens 1991; Morrow and Torres 1995).

Postmodernism argues that nation-states are now being dimmed in the context of a growing interdependent world, and in the context of more local struggles. Yet, as Immanuel Wallerstein argues, the history of the (capitalist) world system has been a historical trend towards cultural heterogeneity rather than cultural homogenization. Thus, the fragmentation of the nation in the world system is happening at the same time that there is a tendency towards cultural differentiation or cultural complexity, that is, globalization (Wallerstein 1991[b], 96). Globalization and regionalization seem to be dual processes occurring simultaneously. This fact has not been overlooked by certain strands of postmodernism, providing an avenue to understand the simultaneous rise of ethnicity and nationalisms with globalization, not necessarily as contradictory but related phenomena.

In this increasingly more complexly organized multicultural and multilingual world system, the bases of traditional forms of political community have been eroded. There is an emerging theory and practice of distrust in democracy. Hence, the previous models of democratic checks and balances, separation of powers, and the notion of democratic accountability no longer work, not even at the level of formal rather than substantive democracy. Distrust in democracy and democratic theory as part of a modernist discourse cannot be associated to all postmodernist strands per se. However, it poses problems for the changing patterns of power in education, and raises concerns about the narrowing of the meaning of democracy. The redefinition of the meaning of democracy needs to be extricated from the forming patterns of social regulation because: "Not only have the interests represented been narrowed; participation exists within a restricted range of problems and possibilities" (Popkewitz 1991, 215).

Any redefinition of the notion of democracy situates the school at the center of the modernist-Enlightenment project, again. Postmodernism would argue, however, that the ethical, substantive and procedural elements of democratic theory should be re-examined considering postmodern culture. The challenge for educators, parents, students and policymakers is to think critically about the failures of the past and about the myriad of exclusionary practices that still pervade the process of schooling—hence bringing to the forefront issues of power and domination, class, race, and gender. The validity of the notion of instrumental rationality guiding school reform should also be examined because it gives attention to administration, procedures, and efficiency as *the* prime criteria for change and progress, and because it assumes that there is a common framework structuring the experience of *all* people (Popkewitz 1987, 335–354; Torres 1996[b]; Popkewitz, in this book).

Thus, a central problem with postmodernist perspectives is that by ignoring the critical contributions of critical modernism, they fall into the trap of depoliticizing the process of human empowerment and liberation. Henry A. Giroux poses the problem bluntly: "The flight from foundationalism is at the same time often a flight from politics" (Giroux 1988, 61). Giroux continues: "Various brands of postmodernism, poststructuralism, and neo-pragmatism have declared war on all the categories of transcendence, certainty, and foundationalism. First principles are now seen as mere relics of history. The unified subject, long the bulwark of both liberal and radical hopes for the future, is now scattered amid the valorizing of decentering processes. Moreover, the attack on foundationalism has resulted in a one-sided methodological infatuation with deconstructing not simply particular truths, but the every notion of truth itself as an epistemological category." (Giroux 1988, 61)

In criticizing postmodernism, Jürgen Habermas's ethical rationalism provides the basis of a powerful counterattack against the flight of postmodern philosophy from ethics and politics, and constitute, to be sure, a central referent for emerging perspectives in sociology of education (Morrow and Torres, in press).

The Risks and the Challenges Ahead

Risks

Theory is a mode of discourse which goes beyond mapping (Paulston, 1996). Theory also goes beyond description, even beyond "thick description" and "history from below" discourses as proposed by advocates of educational ethnographies. Theory also goes beyond what advocates of the history of the subordinate social sectors would suggest, and certainly beyond the type of theory advocated by hypo-thetical-deductive approaches. R. Morrow and D. D. Brown have shown that "the narratives of scientific methodology are character-ized by stories obsessed with questions about empirical evidence, proof and validity" (Morrow and Brown 1994, 40).

Many of the new perspectives in sociology of education try to tell us a story; a story full of colorful characters, with a narrative thread which should be unveiled with as much detail as possible. In telling this story, the new perspectives try to advance a set of theories which, through the synthetic and analytical moments of empirical research, can be useful to illustrate the institutional educational processes involved in the story. In so doing, through iterations and critical analysis, the recent production of these emerging perspec-tives helps to offer a sequence of dynamic photographies; a magnifier to show the interrelatedness of interactive dimensions, and multi-faceted or multifarious nature of educational phenomena. While not discarding the need for multivariate analysis, new perspectives in sociology of education are more cautious—even skeptical at times— of empirical data as defined in the traditional paradigms.

Traditional positivist forms of explanation are suspected by crit-ics of making a linkage between theory and data which is too sim-plistic. Positivistic analysis is also suspected of containing a naive set of assumptions about the evolving nature of reality, and of reflecting indeed limited objectivity in the data that was supposed to represent, as a proxy, even the most tenuous contours of social real-ity. The question then is how to improve upon traditional empirical research involving the "descriptive and analytical (formal) lan-guages through which social phenomena are interpreted and ex-plained" (Morrow and Brown 1994, 41).

These criticisms notwithstanding, there is also a serious risk to cast aside the need to obtain data, any data in the traditional formal language, and to rely almost exclusively on empirical research of impressionistic accounts, detailed descriptions which do not tran-scend the facts as presented in the evolving narratives of the infor-mants, or stories that although socially constructed cannot replace the need for further structural analysis and criticism. Some data, even with all its limitations, is better than no data at all. That is the reason that a number of researchers, working with new perspectives in sociology of education, are worried about much of the postmod-ernist speculations. Many postmodernists analysis constitute simply a rehashing of evolving theoretical discourses, with sophisticate and yet, sometimes, extremely simplistic and logically contradictory set of observations, or even patronizing political suggestions. These risks bring us to the challenges ahead for the new perspectives in sociology of education.

Challenges

These emerging perspectives in sociology of education, almost by definition, have made notions of social justice, the promotion of goals of diversity, multiculturalism, and detracking (as an attempt to avoid school resegregation) central landmarks of their normative work (Wells and Oakes in this book). In addition, they have resorted to cultural studies in education that attempt to deal with areas virtually ignored by traditional researchers (Giroux in this book). Likewise, they have emphasized the importance and resilience of social movements as progressive responses to the bureaucratic behavior of the capitalist state (Apple and Oliver in this book). In striving to achieve these practical and political agendas, the emerging perspectives in sociology of education have seen the need to integrate theories in the scholarship of class, race, and gender as a cornerstone of their contributions to the debates. An important contribution is the discussion of critical marginality as a linchpin of the scholarship of class, race, and gender (Solórzano and Villalpando in this book), and the importance of critical race theories to assess the processes of resegregation of minority students, particularly blacks in the United States (Ladson-Billings in this book). It also will contribute to the study of the dynamics of self-selection, and the structural underpinnings of the process of college choice in the United States and its implications for working class, minority students, and women (McDonough, in this book).

For these emerging perspectives, education continues to play a major role in the socialization of the citizenship, in promoting a democratic culture (Mitchell, in this book), in promoting a public sphere, and creating public intellectuals who could challenge the status quo and through their labor could offer to society, as their mirror, the criticism of its structural and procedural problems. These public intellectuals will draw from the growing scholarship of class, race, and gender, and from the difficult—even agonic process—of trying to tell a story that integrates as many elements that constitute social identities as possible, without relinquishing the power of reason to the politics of identity as the sole criteria for praxis.

In this context, a number of critical themes deserve consideration by these new emerging perspectives. Most try to defend the notion of public education, in a properly deconstructed mode, as a precondition to solidify the social democratic pact. Several criticisms from the Right and from some currents of the Left need to be considered:

(a) Is it true that schools do not actually prepare students for a highly volatile and rapidly changing labor market? In short, can we assume that there is virtually little or no contribution of schools to workers' training?

(b) Is it true that the shared aims of citizenship education—"critical thinking" and better teaching—are in conflict with the presumed economic roles of education? In other terms, as Stanley Aronowitz suggests in several works—contrary to both radical and technocratic critiques of schooling—schools have never successfully prepared workers for specific occupations, except at the graduate level; at best, schooling is a "socializing" instrument insofar as students learn discipline and respect for authority. And, even in this respect, schooling has generally failed to socialize working-class kids whose rebellion against authority is, argue Stanley Aronowitz and William DiFazio (1994), among the most ubiquitous features of our time;

(c) Is it true that socializing children to respect authority, which defined the role of schools in the industrializing era, worked for some but not for others? Schools as socializers never worked for many children (take as an example the large number of pupils who attended religious or parochial schools and never practice their religion with the fervor and dedication expected). At a different level, the question is whether training in discipline and following orders is dysfunctional when post-industrial work requires people to act independently of constituted authority; and

(d) Finally, is the process of work that long has been considered by Liberal-Pluralists and Marxists as the defining human activity which defines the character of human nature, losing its ethical authority? If this is the case, this contributes to the crisis of an educational system that has defined itself in relation to the labor requirement of the social order. These arguments need to be addressed head on, and discussed critically from the emerging perspectives in sociology of education. Let us advance three critical standpoints.

First, at the level of the empirical argumentation, it is unclear that the picture that several right-wing and some left-wing critics of public education paint of the all-embracing crisis of schooling is entirely adequate. Our own research, and the research of the contributors of this book, has convinced us that there is plenty of knowledge acquisition and creation going on in the schools; that schools are segmented with excellent schools side by side with poor scholastic schools; that while resistance to cultural knowledge may prevail in several school settings this does not carry people a long way in dealing with the complexity of capitalist society and the evolving processes of discrimination, oppression, and domination. This knowledge production takes place in a convoluted mixture where students' and teachers' resistance, emancipatory practices, bureaucratic behavior, and ideological normatives all intersect in different ways, at different times, and for different purposes. It is unclear, then, whether the picture that these standard criticisms present to us aptly and accurately describes what goes on in schools and classrooms in America and elsewhere for that matter (Wells and Oakes in this book).

Second, if there are empirical questions about knowledge acquisition, citizenship training, and human capital formation in schools, then at least what can be said about the arguments is that they rest on a set of generalizations that can be, in a democratic conversation about schooling, questioned as perhaps too catastrophic at times, and even, we are afraid, as apolitical (Torres 1996[c]).

Third, at a political and practical level, it is clear to us that people, struggling to defend public education from the attacks of traditionalists, the New Right, fundamentalist education, voucher advocates, anti-multiculturalist forces, and so forth will find the critical arguments advanced above less than persuasive, and somewhat biased toward accepting the position of the Right, which claims that public education cannot be redeemed and should be done with. There is plenty of room for social reform, social transformation, and the implementation of innovative models of teaching and learning as described in recent contributions to the reform of public education (Apple and Beane 1995; Rose 1995; Wells and Oakes, in this book). This is not a debate waged in academic circles, but part of the national debate about schools. As discussed by Peter Applebome in *The New York Times*, "a vocal core of scholars and educational revisionists has created a stir by arguing that there has been no broad decline in American education and that the notion that schools are failing miserably has as much to do with politics as reality" (*The New York Times*, Wednesday, 13 December 1995).

What these new emerging perspectives all seem to tell us is that the dream of a public education system of good quality, one which constitutes a precondition for a reasonably well-trained labor force and politically competent citizenry in late capitalist societies, is not dead. But defending ardently public education does not mean that we are content with its present shape, form, and orientation. Yet, its demise in the hands of abrupt privatization and cultural strife will not contribute to democracy. Public education is ready to be reinvented in light of the promise of a democratic covenant, and certainly as an antidote, one of the many needed, against the deleterious trends of savage capitalist social relations. Indeed, what the new scholarship of class, race, and gender also tells us is that oppression, domination, and discrimination in schools and societies have not disappeared or gone away. If anything, oppression, discrimination, and domination have increased and appear now as a Meduza of many "cabezas." What this scholarship for social empowerment also tells us is that there is still enough democratic energy and utopian optimism to figure out that, in the long haul, fighting for a system of public education of good quality is a good fight for the good life of children and, by implication, for all of society.

Mike Rose, in the closing pages of his much-acclaimed *Possible Lives*, has captured the spirit of the fighting political hope of the new emerging perspectives in sociology of education. It deserves to be quoted at length, as a fitting conclusion of this introduction.

My work in the classroom has mostly been with people whom our schools, public and private, have failed: working-class and immigrant students, students from nonmainstream linguistic and cultural backgrounds who didn't fit a curriculum or timetable or definition of achievement and were thereby categorized in some way as different or deficient. There are, as we have seen along this journey, long-standing social and cultural reasons for this failure of our schools, tangled, disturbing histories of discrimination, skewed perception, and protection of privilege.

And yet there were these rooms. Vital, varied, they were providing a powerful education for the children in them, many of whom were members of the very groups defined as inferior in times past and, not infrequently, in our ungenerous present. What I began to see—and it took the accumulation of diverse classrooms to help me see it—was that these classrooms, in addition to whatever else we may understand about them, represented a dynamic, at times compromised and contested, strain in American educational history: a faith in the capacity of a people, a drive toward equality and opportunity, a belief in the intimate link between mass education and a free society. These rooms were embodiments of the democratic ideal. To be sure, this democratic impulse has been undercut and violated virtually since its first articulation. Thomas Jefferson's proposal to the Virginia legislature for three years of free public schooling, for example, excluded the commonwealth's significant

number of enslaved Black children. But it has been advanced, realized in daily classroom life by a long history of educators working
both within the mainstream and outside it, challenging it through
workingmen's organizations, women's groups, Black schools, appro-
priating the ideal, often against political and economic resistance,
to their own emancipatory ends.

The teachers I visited were working within that tradition. They
provided example after different example of people doing public
intellectual work in institutional settings, using the power of the
institution to realize democratic goals for the children in their
charge, and finessing, negotiating, subverting institutional power
when it blocked the realization of those goals. At a time of profound
disillusionment with public institutional life, these people were, in
their distinct ways, creating the conditions for children to develop
lives of possibility.

My hope is that these classrooms will help us imagine—and, in
imaging, struggle to achieve—what schools in the public domain,
and perhaps a range of public institutions, can be (Rose 1995,
412–413).

Notes

1. The notion of *Aufhebung*, the centerpiece of Hegelian and Marxist
dialectics, implies three different moments linked in a complementary way:
in the first place "to suppress" (*wegraumen*), in the second place, to retain
(*aufbewahren*), and in the third place "to sublate" (*hinaufnehmen*).

References

Apple, Michael W. and James A. Beane, eds. 1995. *Democratic Schools*.
Alexandria, VA: Association for Supervision and Curriculum Development.

Applebome, P. *Have Schools Failed?: Revisionists Use Army of Statistics to
Argue No. New York Times*, 13 December 1995, sec. B16.

Aronowitz, Stanley and William DiFazio. 1994. *The Jobless Future: Sci-tech
and the Dogma of Work*. Minneapolis: University of Minnesota Press.

Bowles, Samuel and Herbert Gintis. 1986. *Democracy and Capitalism*. New
York: Basic Books.

Bredo, Eric and Walter Feinberg, eds. 1982. *Knowledge and Values in Social
and Educational Research*. Philadelphia: Temple University Press.

Cooper, Robert, Estella Williams, Susan Yonezawa, Jeannie Oakes. "What does Race, Gender, Age and Reputation Got to do with It? Methodological Questions in Case Study Research on Schooling." Paper prepared for the Annual Meeting of the American Educational Research Association, New Orleans, April 1994.

Giddens, Anthony. 1994. *Modernity and Self-Identity: Self and Society in the Late Modern Age*. Stanford, CA: Stanford University Press.

Giroux, Henry A. 1988. *Schooling and the Struggle for Public Life: Critical Pedagogy in the Modern Age*. Minneapolis: University of Minneapolis Press.

Gitlin, Andrew, ed. *Power and Method: Political Activism and Educational Research*. New York: Routledge and Kegan Paul.

Harvey, David. 1989. *The Condition of Postmodernity*. Oxford, England: Martin Robertson.

Hulme, Peter. 1986. *Colonial Encounters. Europe and the Native Caribbean, 1492-1797*. London and New York: Methuen.

Liebman, Martin and Rolland Paulston. 1994. "Social Cartography: A New Methodology for Comparative Studies." *Compare* 24, no. 3: 233-245.

Morrow, Raymond A. and Carlos Alberto Torres. 1995. *Social Theory and Education. A Critique of Theories of Social and Cultural Reproduction*. Albany: State University of New York Press.

———. *Critical Social Theory and Education: Freire, Habermas and the Dialogical Subject*. New York: Teachers College Press, Columbia University, in press.

Morrow, Raymond and David D. Brown. 1994. *Critical Theory and Methodology*. Thousand Oaks, London and New Delhi: Sage.

Paulston, R., ed. *Social Cartography*. New York: Garland. In press.

Paulston, R. G. and M. Liebman. 1994. "An Invitation to Postmodern Social Cartography." *Comparative Education Review* 38, no. 2: 215-232.

Popkewitz, Thomas S. 1987. "Knowledge and Interest in Curriculum Studies." In *Critical Studies in Teacher Education. Its Folklore, Theory and Practice*. Edited by Thomas S. Popkewitz, 335-354. London, New York, and Philadelphia: The Falmer Press.

———. 1991. *A Political Sociology of Educational Reform: Power/Knowlege in Teaching, Teachers Education, and Research*. New York: Teachers College Press.

Rose, Michael. *Possible Lives*. 1995. Boston and New York: Houghton Mifflin Company.

Samoff, Joel. "More, Less, None? Human Resource Development: Responses to Economic Constraint." Paper prepared for the Interagency Task Force on Austerity, Adjustment, and Human Resources of the International Labor Office and the United Nations Educational, Scientific and Cultural Organization, May 1990.

Silos, Maureen. 1995. "Economics Education and the Politics of Knowledge in the Caribbean." Ph.D. diss. proposal. Los Angeles: University of California.

Torres, Carlos Alberto. 1996[a]. "Social Cartography, Comparative Education, and Critical Modernism: Afterthought." In *Social Cartography* by R. Paulston, 417–433. New York: Garland.

———. 1996[b]. "Adult Education and Instrumental Rationality: A Critique," *International Journal of Educational Development*, 16, no. 2: 195–206.

———. 1996[c]. "State and Education Revisited: Why Educational Researchers Should Think Politically About Education?" *Review of Research in Education* 21: 255–331.

Wallerstein, Immanuel. 1991[a]. *Unthinking Social Science: The Limits of Nineteenth Century Paradigms*. Cambridge: Polity Press.

———. 1991[b]. "The National and the Universal: Can There be Such a Thing as World Culture?" In *Culture, Globalization and the World-System*. Edited by Anthony D. King. Binghamton: State University of New York at Binghamton.

Wexler, Philip. 1987. *Social Analysis of Education: After the New Sociology*. New York and London: Routledge and Kegan Paul.

2

Education and the Reproduction of Class, Gender, and Race: Responding to the Postmodern Challenge*

❏

Raymond A. Morrow and Carlos Alberto Torres

Introduction

Whatever happened to theories of social and cultural reproduction in educational theory? Some British sociologists have recently found it necessary to "revivify" the notion of "cultural reproduction" as a "particularly fertile area for social theory," despite its *not* being currently "a fashionable concept."[1] For some time, we have similarly argued for revitalizing the concept in the sociology of education, a process inhibited by lingering misunderstandings and lack of awareness of more recent developments in this area of investigation, as well as by "postmodernist" attacks on all attempts to generalize about social reality.[2]

Certain half-truths about theories of cultural reproduction have become commonplace and contributed to their falling on hard times in educational theorizing. First, given their frequent use of strong forms of functionalist explanation, they are rather hastily dismissed as hopelessly "theological," along with Parsonian structural functionalism. Second, emphasis on the contributions of the "hidden curriculum" to the reproduction of a capitalist social order is taken to imply that education is "nothing but" ideology and thus incapable of contributing to progressive change or communicating things of universal

---

*Published in *Educational Theory*, reprinted with permission.

value. Third, reproduction theories are still widely associated with class-based reductionist analyses (which are "totalizing metanarratives," to use postmodernist terminology) typified by the assumption of a strict correspondence between schooling and the functional imperatives defined by the relations of production. Though these are all valid charges against forms of cultural reproduction theories that have been influential at some point in the past (most notably, structuralist Marxism), they fail to hit their mark with respect to the more subtle formulations that have come to inform contemporary critical sociologies of education.

Despite the various criticisms and qualifications of the original "correspondence principle" for economically based models, the general notion of social and cultural reproduction has remained—despite appearances—a central assumption of critical mental revisions to the model, involving both the incorporation of concepts of agency and resistance, along with the diversification of the causal nexus of power to include non-class forms of exclusion and domination. As well, the meta-theoretical status of such theorizing has shifted from that of a totalizing (functionalist) structuralism to that of a more fallibilistic, historically specific structural method.[3]

Does it make sense to continue to describe such approaches with the concept of "reproduction" at all? As one recent defender of the notion of cultural reproduction has charged, the concept was "seemingly high-jacked" (at least in Britain) by "the orthodoxy of studies in the theory of ideology and neo-Marxisms," thus distracting attention from the dynamic and positive dimensions revealed in other sources of this tradition.[4] This situation is said to require "an attempt to liberate the concept back into the wider arena of sociological debate," a process initiated in the work of Pierre Bourdieu.[5] As we will argue, such a rehabilitation has been long under way in both social theory and educational sociology in the guise of what we will term "practice-based," or "parallelist models of cultural reproduction."

Two broad shifts—one internal and another external—can be identified which have contributed to a reorientation of debates in these domains. The first shift, visible by the end of the 1970s, involved primarily immanent forms of self-criticism and was initially associated with theories of social and cultural reproduction in relation to theories of social inequality and stratification and to theories of the state. The outcome was a move away from the *correspondence principle,* in other words, the assumption of a strong structural link (isomorphism) between economic and educational structures. Subsequent developments in theories of educational reproduction, however, have also expanded the points of reference of the forms of social relations reproduced which are the target of social criticism, especially to gender and race as autonomous principles of structuration and domination.[6] The second shift (often interrelated with the first) involved a broader intellectual phenomenon associated with the notion of postmodernism (and the related, further radicalization of the methodological problematic of *poststructuralism*): a calling into question of aspects of all modernist conceptions of social theory, knowledge, and cultural change, not simply those associated with classical functionalism.[7] The consequence has been an external critique which provides a fundamental challenge to the modernist impulses (namely, enlightenment critique) behind the overall project of theoretical representation shared by all forms of reproduction theory, whether associated with the conflict of functionalist traditions, or whether voiced in the name of class, race, or gender.

Our argument builds on three related claims with respect to these theoretical transformations. First, though the actual term "reproduction" has often tended to slip out of sight, we suggest that the basic problematic of social and cultural reproduction remains a central preoccupation of critical theories of the relationship between schooling and society under the heading of "parallelist" models. These may still be considered models of cultural reproduction to the extent that they employ structuralist methodolgical strategies, though in manner they are highly sensitive to history, agency, and social practice.

Second, we argue that the resulting "parallelist" conceptions of social and cultural reproduction, despite many continuing theoretical difficulties, have effectively encouraged the exploration of the independent effects of class, gender, race, and other forms of domination in the context of schooling.

Third, such parallelist models are held to have nevertheless failed to address adequately three fundamental issues: that each of these forms of domination has a significantly different systematic character with crucial consequences for their conceptualization as forms of domination; that the analysis of their interplay has been somewhat obscured by the language of "relative autonomy" left over from structuralist Marxism; and that because the explanatory objectives of parallelist reproduction theory are necessarily more modest and historically contingent than those pursued by classic, structuralist reproduction theory, this model must avoid the postmodernist tendency to endlessly fragment and pluralize conflicts and differences, as if there were no systematic links among them.

In this essay, we will necessarily assume—and at points, defend—the continuing pertinence and analytical value of a radically revised critical modernist stance in social theory.[8] Whether or not this position is graced with the label "postmodernist" critical theory (in the manner of Henry A. Giroux and Stanley Aronowitz) is less important than the substantive issues at stake. Suitably revised, we argue, the concept of totality—including a perspective allowing for an analysis of interactions, interplay, and relationships between class, gender, and race in educational settings—facilitates a reconstructed model of social and cultural reproduction. This model is at the same time open-ended, takes modernity as an object of critical inquiry rather than as a premise, takes seriously the postmodernist critique both at the level of epistemology and the level of culture, and yet considers the political implications of theory and research in the context of a project of social, gender, and ethnic (including racial) emancipation. Politics is not taken here purely in its instrumental or pragmatic sense, but is also considered as a horizon that opens up possibilities for human action, and as a contested symbolic, material, and factual terrain intrinsically linked to public policy formation and individual identity and action.[9]

The Interplay of Class, Gender, and Race

Critiques of Class Reductionism: Parallelist Models

The importance of structuralist Marxism, and the related notion of a correspondence principle between economic and cultural life, was that it facilitated the shift from the economistic base/superstructure model to that of social reproduction as a way of understanding Marx's method and theory of society. To be sure, this theme was already apparent in a somewhat different form in early Frankfurt critical theory and in Antonio Gramsci's cultural Marxism, but Louis Althusser's structuralist Marxism provided the catalyst for a fundamental transformation of theories of education (and culture).[10] Of more immediate concern here are the poststructuralist (but not necessarily postmodernist) theories of educational reproduction that attempt to avoid the hyperfunctionalism and class reductionism still evident in the structuralist correspondence principle and related theories of social class.

Of *less* immediate concern here are the complex, multiple influences that have contributed to the rethinking of class and its relation to educational reproduction: neo-Weberian theory and mopho-genic systems theory,[11] contemporary Frankfurt critical theory,[12] French sociological structuralism,[13] British (neo-Gramscian) cultural studies,[14] and contributions voicing more directly the experiences and perspectives of women,[15] racial minorities, and others whose domination could not be subsumed within traditional class categories.[16] Our task is thus not to trace this intellectual history, but to point out the overall, cumulative consequences of these developments: a shift neither toward open models of social and cultural reproduction nor the primacy of particular determining factors (structural mechanisms) can be assumed in advance.

A first consequence of the critiques of early reproduction theory was the emergence of theories of *resistance* that could account for the possibilities of change. This required a theory of social action that endowed subjects with at least potential for transformative action, a theme closely related to "new social movements" theory.[17] Though enjoying particular prominence in critical pedagogy, this theme was part of an original rethinking of popular culture, structure, and agency in critical social theory. Within critical social theory, the key step has been reconceptualizing society in terms of distinction between analysis at the level of "systems integration' as opposed to "social integration," a strategy shared by both Jürgen Habermas and Anthony Giddens.[18] Classic social reproduction theory of the type proposed by Althusser operated exclusively at the level of systematic analysis, hence reducing agents to passive, interrelated "subjects." In contrast, purely interpretive, hermeneutic, and humanistic sociologies have focused on the social action of individuals and groups (social integration), at the expense of an analysis of systematic contradictions. The methodological consequences of linking systematic and social action analysis in critical theories have been twofold: (*a*) attention to the agency-structure dialectic in analyzing processes of social and cultural reproduction; and (*b*) a turn to historically specific (though often explicitly comparative) and ethnographic investigations capable of integrating generalizing and case study analysis something quite distinct from the neo-Foucauldian opposition of the universal and local *as if* local *or* regional analysis could dispense with generalizing social theory (though not in the sense of finding ahistorical, invariant laws).[19]

A second consequence of these developments has been that empirical studies based on theories of reproduction increasingly focus on the contingent aspects of *state* action. Theories of educational reproduction, which seek to escape the circularity of functionalist methodology, must focus on the state as the context within which social groups actively struggle to reproduce or transform existing relations between society and education.[20]

A third consequence has been a pluralization of the bases of potential domination as to invoke an infinite plurality of sources of conflict.[21] On the other hand, however, there has been an emerging focus on the interplay of three sources of domination: class, gender, and race. One could also add other dimensions of reproduction such as age, urban/rural distinctions, nonracial ethnicity, or minority religious affiliations, but these are not categories that have typically lent themselves to system-threatening social movement mobilization oriented toward inclusion and the redressing of inequities.[22] Nevertheless, in specific historical contexts these other forms exclusion may move to center stage.

What is at stake here is the issue of broadening the theory of class as part of a more general *theory of domination* that recognizes the diversity of social interests, yet persists in attempting to analyze theoretically and empirically the systematic relations among them. Classic approaches to class and reproduction theory depend upon a utilitarian conception of economic self-interest based on the primacy class structure within a problematic theory of history. For example, Erik Olin Wright, perhaps the leading North American proponent of a revised neo-Marxist theory of social class, puts it as follows:

> If class structure is understood as a terrain of social relations that determine objective material interests of actors and class struggle is understood as the form of social practice which attempts to realize these interests then class consciousness can be understood as the subjective processes that shape intentional choices with respect to those interests and struggles.[23]

But, as Stewart R. Clegg notes, given that these interests are conceived as "objective," how is it that the misrecognition of them occurs routinely? Notions of ideology and hegemony are invoked to explain the process of ideological incorporation into the dominant ideology. But this also begs the question of why it is the working class that is the focus of attention, rather than other interested collectivities. The issue here goes back to the problematic status of universalistic, objective interests definable by theoretical experts. Much of the postmodernist stress on the absolute character of diversity and difference stems from an abandonment of hope for any such Archimedean principle of theoretical unification.

As we will argue, this issue cannot be resolved theoretically in a deterministic synthesis, but it does suggest a dialogue between empirically informed and historically specific theoretical formulations, and the practices of actors in defining their collective aspirations in a more or less democratic public sphere. To the degree that the latter are absent or partial, theory necessarily makes claims relating to the notion of false—or at least, falsifying—consciousness, but this does not justify claims to theoretical absolutism.

The Case of Education

Not surprisingly, the interplay between class, race, and gender, and its contribution to social reproduction has emerged only recently as integrated research endeavor in the sociology of education. It is not surprising, therefore, that a special issue of the *Sociology of Education* on women, race, and educational experiences included five articles written by assistant professors.[24] Previously and particularly in the United States, there was a tendency for issues of class, race, and gender to be pursued as more or less independent topics without adequate concern with their interrelationships. This has been shown by Carl Grant and Christine Sleeter in their survey of the education literature from *1973–1983*.[25] As they note however, the theoretical problems of such research had been pointed out by the early 1980s in British cultural studies, as well as by Michael Apple, Stanley Aronowitz, Henry A.Giroux, and others in North America in the context of education. As Aronowitz and Giroux aptly noted:

> Oppositional behaviors are produced amidst contradictory discourses and values. The logic that informs a given act of resistance may, on the one hand, be linked to interests that are class-, gender- or race-specific. On the other hand, it may express the repressive moments inscribed in such behavior by the dominant culture rather than a message of protest against their existence. . . . The failure to include women and racial minorities in such studies has resulted in a rather uncritical theoretical tendency to romanticize modes of resistance even when they contain reactionary racial and gender views. The irony here is that a large amount of neo-Marxist work on resistance, although allegedly committed to emancipatory concerns, ends up contributing to the reproduction of sexist and racist attitudes and practices?[26]

Similarly, responding to the critics of Geoff Whitty's *Sociology and School Knowledge,* Michael Apple situated himself in relation to the neo-Marxist tradition, but does so in a manner that shows his awareness of the difficulties of classical Marxism in the treatment of class, race, and gender.[27] This position, often termed "nonsynchronous parallelist," requires a significant break with Marxist class theory.[28]

A paradigm case in point here is the criticism leveled against traditional Marxist interpretations by feminist authors. Many of their arguments have been devastating to orthodox assertions . . . so much so that many people on the Left believe that any attempt at understanding our social formation that does not combine *in an unreductive way* analyses of class and gender together is only half a theory at best. . . . The same, of course, needs to be said of race as well. The rejection of major aspects of the received orthodox Marxist tradition and the emerging sensitivity to the truly constitutive nature of gender and race demonstrate not a weakness but the continued growth and vitality of a tradition of critical analysis that is attempting to deal honestly and openly with the complexity of life under present conditions of domination and exploitation.[29]

As Cameron McCarthy and Apple point out, this parallelist approach (a notion comparable to but more inclusive than the concept of "dualist" used in feminist theory) is now broadly shared by critical researchers:

> Though subject to debate, it has become one of the more generally accepted positions in the critical community. It holds that at least *three* dynamics are essential in understanding schools and other institutions. These dynamics are race, gender, and class. None are reducible to the others. Class is not necessarily primary. The parallelist position has also led to a reevaluation of economically reductive explanations as well. The economy is exceptionally powerful; this is capitalism after all. But rather than economy explaining all, critically oriented researchers have argued that there are three spheres of social life—economic, political and cultural. These too are in continual interaction. These are, in essence, arenas in which class, race, and gender dynamics operate. Unlike base-superstructure models, it is also assumed that action or none can sometimes have an effect on actions in the another. The result is a theory of *overdetermination*, in which the processes and outcomes of teaching and learning and of school in general are produced by the constant interactions among three dynamics in three spheres.[30]

Apple's reference to British debates is not accidental, given his recognition of the significance of the interrogations of orthodox Marxist assumptions in British cultural studies, especially those of

Stuart Hall with regard to race, E. P. Thompson with respect to class consciousness as lived-experience, and Angela McRobbie, Michéle Barrett and others in feminist research.[31] Without making a strong priority claim, it can be argued that the earlier and broader reception of class-based reproduction theory in Britain led to an earlier debate on the limits of class reductionism, a process that can be broadly associated with the maturation of the cultural studies tradition and the continuing centrality of models of cultural reproduction, despite postmodernist influences and the tendency to privilege discourse analytic methods.[32]

But our particular concern is with tracing some of the key issues posed by critiques of conventional reproduction theory on the part of socialist feminist theorists and theorists of race. In particular, we wish to explore some of the continuing *difficulties* with parallelist models, a question that can be initially approached through issues posed in feminist theory. As we will see, the central problem of parallelist models is an excessive openness that tends to obscure the internal systematic connections between these three otherwise quite distinct and autonomous modes of domination.

Gender and Cultural Reproduction

In feminist theory this debate is reflected in the succession of traditional class, classic social reproduction, and dualist models. Feminist theory has provided the context in which the limits of class analysis and structuralist theories of social reproduction based on ultimate economic determination have been illustrated in convincing empirical and theoretical ways. In his instructive synthesis, R. W. Connell argues that social theory has approached the subject of *extrinsic theories of gender* in three chronological approaches from "class first" to "*social* reproduction" theory to "dual systems."[33] The first position argues that capitalism is the root cause of all inequalities and class struggle is primary. In the social reproduction model, a more powerful analysis developed—particularly in Britain under the influence of structural Marxism—in which "the family, sexuality or gender relations at large were the site of *reproduction* of 'relations of production.'"[34] Above all, this theory suggests a systemic connection between the subordination of women and economic exploitation in capitalism. The problem with this approach is that it must at the outset postulate an invariant structure, thus denying the historical character of social relations. However, argues Connell, a social structure should be seen as "constantly *constituted* rather than constantly *reproduced.*"

Social reproduction, therefore, is an object of strategy. When it occurs, as it often does, it is an achievement by a particular alliance of social forces over others. It cannot be made a postulate or presupposition of social theory. And the concept cannot take the explanatory weight that reproduction theories of gender place on it.[35]

Connell's second criticism is that reproduction does not easily make a connection between the needs of capitalism and what is specific about gender:

> It is clear enough that if capitalism is to continue, its dominant groups must succeed with some kind of reproduction strategy. But it is not at all obvious that doing this must produce sexual hierarchy and oppression. Much the same might be argued and sometimes is about racial and ethnic hierarchies or about hierarchies of age.[36]

For example, there is nothing inherent in capitalism to exclude women from the rank and file or from the upper levels of management. There are, to be sure, contingent factors that do so, for example, the "old boys club" as an expression of remnants of premodern patriarchy or the patriarchal organization of early capitalism in relation to family life, but this is not necessary for capitalism as such to thrive as a system. This, of course, leads to the dual system notion cautiously defended by Connell. Though the dependent housewife in a bourgeois nuclear family was characteristic of the reproduction of labor in a particular phase of capitalist development, this does not preclude the possibility of quite different forms for organizing such systemic imperatives in the future.

The third approach of dual systems theory is associated with socialist feminism more generally.[37] Dual systems theory's basic idea is that capitalism and patriarchy are distinct and equally comprehensive systems of social relations which meet and interact. This is comparable to the debate, on the democratic socialist left, that capitalism and democracy intersect at one point in time, but liberal democracy does not need to be tied to capitalism as a system of production of commodities through commodities—in other words, capitalism needs liberal democracy to thrive, but a multivocal definition of democracy can exist both in the context of a reformed capitalism, and outside this mode of production.[38]

Connell notes two difficulties in dual system theories that, we would add, are shared by all parallelist type models.[39] The first difficulty has to do with the ambiguity of the systematic properties of patriarchy; in other words, the sense in which it constitutes a *system* in the same sense as capitalism. It is not clear that the "systems" of patriarchy and capitalism are the same kind of thing: one may argue that patriarchy refers to a system of domination, perhaps similar to other systems of domination built on exploitation of particular features of groups, for example, their lack of legal power or recognition; while capitalism is built as a system of exploitation based on differential appropriation of social wealth through ownership of capital and labor power. Thus, Marx's theory of labor value comes into play as a different approach than pure domination through force (either physical or mental), through legal or theological norms, or through colonialism.

Second, it is not clear how to conceptualize the nature of the "interaction" between the two, and especially how this relates to either one explaining oppression or bringing about change. Dualist and parallelist theories are misleading to the extent that their resulting analytical distinctions imply analogous substantial distinctions. As Nancy Fraser argues in her critique of Habermas, dual systems theory

> is an approach that posits two distinct "systems" of human activity and, correspondingly, two distinct "systems" of oppression: capitalism and male dominance. But this is misleading. These are not, in fact, two distinct systems but, rather, two thoroughly interfused dimensions of a single social formation. In order to understand that social formation, a critical theory requires a single set of categories and concepts that integrate *internally* both gender and political economy (perhaps also race).[40]

Further, that internal relationship to capitalism is itself historically variable. As Fraser stresses, "male dominance is intrinsic rather than accidental to classical capitalism, for the institutional structure of this social formation is actualized by means of gendered roles. It follows that the forms of male dominance at issues here are not properly understood as lingering forms of premodern status inequality. They are, rather, intrinsically modern in Habermas's sense, since they are premised on the separation of waged labor and the state from child-rearing and the household."[41]

We would argue that the approaches suggested by both Connell and Fraser are very much within the tradition of what we find it useful to term "practice-oriented," or parallelist models of cultural reproduction grounded in explanatory strategies, comparative historical.

This point becomes especially clear in Connell's elaboration of a general theory of gender and power. First, it is an approach that is situated in terms of the European structuralist tradition, but one that couples structure with historicity and practice and has been "formalized theoretically" in the "dualist" accounts of Boutdieu and Giddens.[42] Second, he argues that as applied to gender relations the use of structuralist concepts has suffered from the assumption of some kind of single unifying structure."[43] That there might be some problem here is suggested by the remarkable proliferation of "ultimate causes" proposed for that single structure. Taking a cue from Juliet Mitchell's early work, he suggests that gender domination be viewed from the perspective of multiple and perhaps even contradictory structures, and proposes three fundamental (though interpenetrating) forms: (*a*) those to do with the division of labor, (*b*) those linked with power relations generally as authority, control, and coercive systems, and (*c*) those associated with *cathexis,* "with the patterning of object-choice, desire, and desirability, with the production of heterosexuality and homosexuality and the relationship between them."[44] Third, these processes are held nevertheless to be interrelated in determinate and determinable ways. Yet, as he concludes, this does not take the logical form assumed by classic structuralist reproduction theory:

> In none of this is there an ultimate determinant, a "generative nucleus" to use Henri Lefabvre's terms, from which the rest of the pattern of general relations springs. . . . There is, however, a unity in the field, an orderliness, which needs to be understood. . . . My argument, briefly, is that this unity is not the unity of a system, as functionalist analysis would imply. Nor is it the expressive unity that would be provided by the existence of a generative nucleus. It is a unity—always imperfect and under construction—of historical composition. I mean "composition" as in music: a tangible, active and often difficult process of bringing elements into connection with each other and thrashing out their relationships. . . . The product of the process is not a logical unity but an empirical unification. It happens on particular terms in particular circumstances.[45]

Race and Cultural Reproduction

To extend Connell and Fraser's type of questioning to the question of race, we are confronted with two fundamental questions regarding parallelist theories: the way in which the systematic character of *"racism"* differs from those of either capitalism *or* patriarchy; and further, the difficulties entailed in attempting to generalize about the interactions between race and class, or race and gender. With respect to the first question, the specific systematic character of racism is immediately illuminated by social closure theory; it does not have anything to do with physical differences of tangible significance (as in the case of gender) nor is it intrinsically linked to the exploitation of surplus value (as in the case of class) As in the case of gender, some version of a dualist (or parallelist) thesis appears most plausible as a way of initially disentangling racism from capitalism and class, as well as understanding its interrelation with other sources of domination.[46] As has often been noted, classical Marxism encounters difficulties in making race (along with gender) a central aspect of political economic explanations. More recently, however, it has been suggested that some neo-Marxist writers have managed to incorporate these questions with relative autonomy models which, as some commentators note, ironically, may undercut the specifically Marxist character of such analyses.[47]

Like patriarchy, racism is not unique to capitalism. Again, the parallelist thesis points to the crucial autonomy of racial categories independent of capitalist relations of production. The South African case is instructive here because a number of powerful capitalists have been supporting the abolition of apartheid as a system that has created a welfare state for whites only. Racism goes back to its precapitalist roots and has been associated with many different types of social formations, though closely associated with slavery and colonial expansion in its modern form.[48] There is racism in the theological debates in the Middle Ages of whether the "discovered" Indians in America have a soul or not, and whether Black slaves have a soul and deserve to be catechized.[49] Thus, as a historical process and product, racism, perhaps as much as sexism, originates in the depth psyche, although it becomes part of an overall process in which visible differences are hyperextended through socialization, reflecting entrenched social customs, prejudices, and common sense.[50]

In ways that parallel Connell and Fraser's discussion of gender, Robert Miles argues that racism is analytically distinct from capitalism and yet substantially and historically embedded in it. As a consequence, it is a necessarily contradictory phenomenon, rather than merely functional for capitalism as a mode of production or purely autonomous. He has suggested three instances to illustrate this thesis. First, "the reproduction and constitution of non- and pre-capitalist relations of production is a common dimension of the development of the capitalist mode of production." This is particularly important in the colonial state supported by an ideology of racism. Second, "the historical complimentarity between the specific economic forms of the capitalist relations of production . . . and the political form of the nation state has generated an ideology which attempts to make a sense of imagined community a basis for political stability." Third, "wherever the number of available persons is in excess of the available positions, some form of exclusionary practice grounded in a process of signification is necessary. Thus, within the capitalist mode of production, the ideology of sexism has justified the exclusion of large numbers of women from the labor market. . . . In similar manner, the racialization of a population establishes a hierarchy of suitability and the ideological basis for exclusionary practices.[51]

Nevertheless, racism also has a historically specific *internal affinity* with capitalist political economy. But again we encounter problems in moving from the analytical distinctions based on dualism or parallelism to the substantial historical realities of race, class, and gender. For example, race relations in Britain, as Miles has stressed, cannot be separated from the analysis of migrant labor, thus the necessity of *understanding* the internal relation between production relations, the state, and race, at least in this particular context. In this respect, the association of classical capitalism with racially tinged imperialism and nationalism also argues for an integral account. This historically specific conclusion about the *interdependence* of class and race does not necessarily contradict the more general parallelist proposition that in the abstract "capital" is racially (and gender) blind. Nevertheless, concludes Miles, this does not justify any kind of polarization between class and race, as if one could be understood independently of the other:

> The *"race"/class* dichotomy is a false construction. Alternatively, I suggest that the reproduction of class relations involves the determination of internal and external class boundaries by economic, political and ideological processes. One of the central political and ideological processes in contemporary capitalist societies is the process of racialization . . . but this cannot, in itself, over-ride the effects of the relations of production. Hence, the totality of "black" people in Britain cannot be adequately analyzed as a "race" outside or in opposition to class relations. Rather, the process by which they are racialized, and react to that racialization (both of which are po-

litical and ideological processes) always occurs in a particular historical and structural context, one in which the social relations of production provide the necessary and initial framework within which racism has its effects. The outcome may be the formation of racialized class fractions?[52]

A similar formulation by Michael Omi and Howard Winant in the United States frames these issues more explicitly in terms of concepts of social and cultural reproduction as they describe a process of "racial formation" in which the state plays a central role:

> The concept of racial formation should treat race . . . as a fundamental *organizing principle* of social relationships. . . . At the micro-level, race is a matter of individuality, of the formation of *identity*. The ways in which we understand ourselves and interact with others, the structuring of our practical activity—the work and family, and citizens and as thinkers (or "philosophers")—these are all shaped by racial meanings and racial awareness. At the macro-level, race is a matter of *collectivity*, or the formation of social structures: economic, political and cultural/ideological.[53]

This analysis of the interplay of the micro- and macro-levels must be complemented by our understanding of "the process of racial formation" as "an unstable and 'decentered' complex of social meanings constantly being transformed by political struggle."[54] They invoke Gramsci's notion of "unstable equilibria" to describe racial formation:

> The racial order is equilibrated by the state—encoded in law, organized through policy-making, and enforced by a repressive apparatus. But the equilibrium thus achieved is unstable, for the great variety of conflicting interests encapsulated in racial meanings and identities can be no more than pacified—at best—by the state?[55]

Therefore, any racial formation can be articulated (as can class and gender) in the context of the actions or inactions of the capitalist state. The importance of the role of the state in public education has been aptly discussed by Martin Carnoy and others?[56] Understanding the role of the state is a precondition of understanding schools as a site for the production of knowledge, skills, dexterities, morals, and behaviors; as a site for reproduction; and as a site for contestation or resistance.

Implications

What are some of the consequences that follow from the difficulties of parallelist models? We would like to touch upon three issues here. First, it should be stressed that the analytical approach of seeing gender and race as both abstractly autonomous and yet contingently internal to specific social formations does not yield abstract, determinist conclusions. Nor does it abandon the problem of causal connections to the metaphors of endless plays of difference. Rather, it calls for *local investigations* (which may involve case studies of regional or even national scope) that are formulated with questions posed in terms of comparative historical generalizations about the interplay of race, gender, class, and so on.

Second, the goal of "solidarity across differences" must be seen as that of variable difficulty. In important respects, it may be that biologically based gender differences, for example, the capacity for reproduction and the physiology of sexuality are more enduring and intractable than those of class, which reflect historically changeable relations of power and opportunity, and those of race, which are based on the added dimension of trivial phenotypical differences. In the case of black women, class, gender, and race combine in the constitution of individual subjectivities and social agents in a manner that has no parallel for white women or black men. It has been argued, for instance, that unlike white women, black working-class women "claim knowledge not only through gender, but through racial identity and relations."[57] However Wendy Luttrell's explorations of women's ways of knowing suggest that while class-based concepts pit working- and middle-class people against each other, and while racially based concepts pit whites against Blacks, it is "the invisible gender-based concept that pits collectivity against individuality and autonomy against dependence" and become the "basis for unequal power relations between working-class men and women."[58] A similar claim that students' gender self-definitions are more complex and less shared than those based on race or class has been made by Grant and Sleeter.[59] As they conclude, students in relatively integrated communities saw gender as a more divisive form of human difference than race and class.[60]

Third, the depth psychological basis of the processes of gender and race (the structure of *cathexis,* in Connell's terms) makes them more intractable and of a different order than those of class. Whatever the specific problems associated with Lacanian psychoanalysis and its reception, it has provided an impetus to understanding why racial and gender differences—like those of sexual orientation it-self—are different from others, especially those of class, which were the particular concern of liberal and socialist enlightenment alike. An important implication is that the nature of cultural criticism and its practical effects requires reexamination.[61]

A final comment regarding the interplay of race, class, and gender in education as cultural politics should be taken up. In debates about the problems of cultural reproduction, it has been argued that schools do not merely produce, distribute, and reproduce knowledge, cognitive or moral skills, and disciplinary molds. In so doing, they also constitute places for the formation of subjectivities, identities, and subcultures. Since knowledge and power shape the form and content of curriculums through ideological interests formed in class, race, and gender-specific terms, the notion of schools as a battle-ground is helpful to begin understanding the implications of these theoretical disputes for schools and non-formal education practices.

However, with the growing preoccupation with postmodern themes, by reducing the analysis of all educational activities to cultural politics, less attention is paid to the structural principles underlying the educational process.[62] The analytical and political implications of these omissions are potentially quite dangerous for political struggle, as teachers and educated practitioners, who are trying to make sense of their own daily work and that of their students, will recognize.

Yet, the impact of most postmodernist theorizing on educational theory would seem to have rather hastily collapsed these theoretical advances into what is dismissed as the obsolete methodology of "structuralism" and modernist universalizing of a type ostensibly rendered obsolete by poststructuralism. As a consequence, Jennifer Gore can without hesitation claim that her approach is:

> Consistent with major social theory debates over structural versus poststructural positions (those which find their grounding prior to the construction of discourses, for example, in the economy or in the category "women," and those which reject such universalized and decontextualized notions and enter debates and critiques in specific context). As is consistent with other poststructural critiques, I demonstrate the universalizing, dominating tendencies of critical and feminist pedagogy discourses as regimes of truth.[63]

A central problem of this type of formulation is that it runs the risk, on the one hand, of conflating two rather distinct theoretical discourses within critical pedagogy: that of a *model of cultural reproduction* which is grounded in an explanatory social science, as opposed to an *emancipatory pedagogical practice* which is grounded in a normative and practical discourse oriented toward transformative possibilities. To be sure, the original project of critical social theory envisions these two discourses as intertwined and mutually supportive, but their distinct epistemological and methodological status needs to be acknowledged. Indeed, this is the basis of the *internal dialogue* within critical theory, and a basis for the possibility that revisions in the social scientific model may falsify or at least require revisions in the practical-emancipatory discourse, just as the latter may pose new research questions for the former.

For the present discussion, we will accept the plausibility of Gore's focus on the instructional act as the context of a "regime of truth" involving the "micro" functioning of power relations, on the other hand—and this is a second risk of strong poststructuralist formulations—we have implicitly contested the view that postmodernist critiques of this type adequately address the problem of "universalizing principles" that have at times afflicted formulations of social and cultural reproduction. Even if the "social vision" of critical pedagogies is acknowledged as valuable by Gore, their repressive potential is held to be ultimately rooted in both a lack of self-reflexivity and "in the totalizing discourses of Neo-Marxism and the Critical Theory of the Frankfurt School."[64] But this latter point is misleading given the explicit *antifoundationalist* intentions of much recent critical social theory associated with critical pedagogy, and the forms practice-oriented models of cultural reproduction discussed here.

Such blanket (dare we say "essentializing"?) postmodernist critiques implicitly draw upon a formalized distinction—a binary opposition—between the "universal" and the "local" that is grounded in the older German debate confronting "nomothetic" and "ideographic" research, rather than the postempiricist realities of both critical social theory and a comparative historical sociology (or ethnography) concerned with the interdependence of theoretical generalization and particular case studies.[65] In this respect, we agree fully with the recent "materialist" feminist diagnosis of the problematic aspects of the postmodernist privileging of "local" and "regional" analysis:

> I think this rejection of systemic analysis needs to be re-evaluated now, particularly in light of the growing appeal of lucid post-modernism's regional analysis. . . . We need to advance a problematic in which the articulations of race, class, gender, and sexuality can be

understood in their historical specificity without abandoning analyses that situate them in terms of the social totalities that continue to regulate our lives. A global reading strategy can provide this without reenacting the totalizing strategies of a master narrative.[66]

From this perspective, historically oriented, open models of social and cultural reproduction remain an essential aspect of a critical modernist social science and cannot be readily subsumed under the notion of totalizing master narratives, partly because they originated as critiques of formalist, structural Marxism. As Nancy Fraser and Linda Nicholson conclude in their assessment of the implications of these issues for feminist theory:

> A first step to recognize, *contra* Lyotard, that postmodern critique need forswear neither large historical narratives nor analyses of societal macrostructures. This point is important for feminists, since sexism has a long history and is deeply and pervasively embedded in contemporary societies. However, if postmodern-feminist critique must remain "theoretical," not just nay kind of theory will do. Rather, theory here would be explicitly historical, attuned to the cultural specificity of different societies and periods and to that of different groups within societies and periods. . . . Moreover, postmodern-feminist theory would be nonuniversalist. When its focus became cross-cultural or transepochal, its mode of attention would be comparativist rather than universalist, attuned to changes and contrasts instead of to "covering laws."[67]

The preoccupation of this essay has been to show the continuing importance of the issues introduced by theories of social and cultural reproduction. In the reconstructed parallelist models entailing class, race, and gender, we find the bases for theoretically driven empirical research that can contribute to political practice and educational policy innovation. We hope it has become clear to the reader that in the background, as a shadow for our theoretical defense of a reconstructed and critical modernist theory, there are ongoing debates with respect to the implications of postmodernism for educational theory and research. We have tried to demonstrate that reconstructed theories of cultural reproduction remain central to the future of educational theory.

An integrated theory of class, race, and gender can only be as insightful as the concrete studies it produces, and the ways in which these work back into the theory itself. From this perspective a formalized, systematic theory is impossible, or at best, trivial. But we see a continuing need for historical, comparative, and even quantitative studies at the school level and also in non-formal education. These studies should understand that, while we may not be able to conceptualize entirely the multiple parallel determinations, or the interplay of class, race, and gender in education, we can at least try to support the struggle to overcome discrimination, oppression, and the deep structuring of subjectivities with classist, racist, and gender-biased overtones. This struggle has had a long history, and many anonymous heroes. This is not the time to romanticize the struggle, but neither is it a time to nurture historical amnesia.

Notes

1. Chris Jenks, "Introduction: The Analytic Bases of Cultural Reproduction Theory," in *Cultural Reproduction,* edited by Chris Jenks (New York: Routledge and Kegan Paul, 1993), p. 1.

2. For an exploratory formulation, see Raymond A. Morrow and Carlos Alberto Torres, "Social Theory, Social Reproduction, and Education's Everyday Life: A Framework for Analysis," a paper presented at the Canadian Western Association of Sociology and Anthropology Annual Meetings, University of Alberta, Edmonton, Canada, February 1988. This project has culminated in a book, Raymond A. Morrow and Carlos A. Torres, *Social Theory and Education: A Critique of Theories of Social and Cultural Reproduction* (Albany: State University of New York Press, 1995).

3. So, for example, Michael Apple points to the "need to interpret schooling as both a system of production and reproduction," in revising his earlier position in *Education and Power* (Boston: Routledge and Kegan Paul, 1982), p. 22. Stanley Aronowitz and Henry A. Giroux develop a typology of theories of reproduction: economic-reproductive (structuralist Marxism), cultural-reproductive (Bourdieu), and hegemonic-state models (Gramscian) and their relation to theories of resistance in *Education Under Siege* (South Hadley, MA: Berging and Garvey, 1985), 74ff. Giroux's more recent flirtation with postmodernism in his *Border Crossings* (New York: Routledge and Kegan Paul, 1992) does not involve abandoning this theme, though it could be argued that he fails to articulate adequately the "language of possibility" with the constraints of structure.

4. Jenks, "Introduction," p. 2.

5. Ibid., 6.

6. The impetus behind this first shift is reflected in three types of questioning: the meta-theoretical and theoretical response of poststructuralist (neo-Gramscian) cultural studies and critical theory to the reduc-

tionism and functionalism of structuralist Marxism' political and theoretical challenges on the part of women and racial minorities to voice their experience of domination; and theoretically driven empirical studies that began to fill the gender and race absences in theories of social and cultural reproduction. For the most part, however, these developments were carried out in the spirit of critical modernist conceptions of theory and research. See, for example, Daniel P. Liston, *Capitalist Schools: Explanation and Ethics in Radical Studies of Schooling* (New York: Routledge and Kegan Paul, 1988).

7. This second shift would demand an extended treatment well beyond the self-imposed limits of this essay. With respect to education, see, for example, Philip Wesler, *Social Analysis of Education: After the New Sociology* (London: Routledge and Kegan Paul, 1987); Patti Lather, *Getting Smart: Feminist Research and Pedagogy Within / In Postmodern* (New York: Routledge and Kegan Paul, 1991); and more generally, Pauline Marie Rosenau, *Post-Modernism and the Social Sciences* (Princeton, NJ: Princeton University Press, 1992). A further impetus for such reformulations derives from poststructuralist critiques, especially the work of Michel Foucault, which challenge Marxism and other essentializing forms of social analysis. The resulting strategies of interpretation have proved productive in rereading Frankfurt critical theory and Gramscian theory in particular, calling into question class reductionism from various perspectives. But it can be argued that this has contributed to a revitalization of critical theory rather than its obsolescence; see Raymond Morrow, "Critical Theory, Gramsci and Cultural Studies: From Structuralism to Poststructuralism," in *Critical Theory Now,* edited by Philip Wexler (New York: Falmer Press, 1991), p. 27–70.

8. While we agree that "all that is solid melts into air," we are still able find persuasive key works that defend a critical modernism, often including a constructive engagement with postmodernist social theory, including such otherwise diverse figures as Jürgen Habermas, Anthony Giddens, Pierre Bourdieu, and Fredric Jameson.

9. We agree with Mark Ginsburg when he states that: "Politics is concerned with the means of producing, reproducing, consuming, and accumulating material and symbolic resources." Mark Ginsburg, Sangeeta Kamat, Rahesware Raghu, and John Weaver, "Education and Politics: Interpretations, Involvement, and Implications," unpublished manuscript (University of Pittsburgh, 1993), p. 1. Politics therefore includes and interacts with all dimensions of human experience. Thus, the personal is also political, as feminist theory taught us long ago.

10. See Louis Althusser, *For Marx,* trans. Ben Brewster (London: NLF, 1977); Lous Althusser, *Lenin and Philosophy and Other Essays,* trans. Ben Brewster (New York: Monthly Review Press, 1971); Louis Althusser and Balibar Etienne, *Life le Capital* (Paris: Maspero, 1968); Harold Entwhistle, *Antonio Gramsci: Conservative Schooling for Radical Politics* (London:

Routledge and Kegan Paul, 1979); Antonio Gramsci, *Selections from the Priosn Notebooks*, ed. and trans. Quintin Hoare and Geoffrey Nowell Smith (New York: International Publishers, 1971); Stuart Hall, "Gramsci's Relevance to the Analysis of Racism and Ethinicty," *Communication Inquiry* 10 (1986): 5–27; and Walter L. Adamson, *Hegemony and Revolution: A Study of Antonio Gramsci's Political and Cultural Theory* (Berkeley: University of California Press, 1980).

11. One foundation for this mode of inquiry can be found in neo-Weberian conflict theories which are not ordinarily included in discussions of reproduction theory (for example, the ideas of Randall Collins), with the partial exception of the type of social closure theory found in Pierre Bourdieu (though he does not use the term). As Max Weber stressed, the original Marxist focus on class at the level of the relations of production could not adequately account for the contribution of various forms of domination evident at the level of market relations and the competition for scarce resources. More recent developments of this insight under the heading of *social closure theory* have attempted to reconcile this critique with an awareness of the crucial importance of the link between exclusionary processes and the specific form of production relations, as in Raymond Murphy, *Social Closure: The Theory of Monopolization and Exclusion* (Oxford: Oxford University Press, 1988). See also Margaret S. Archer, "Morphogenesis versus Structuralism: On Combining Structure and Action," *British Journal of Sociology* 33, no. 4 (1982): 455–83; and *Social Origins of Educational Systems* (London: Sage, 1984).

12. Robert E. Young, *A Critical Theory of Education: Habermas and Our Children's Future* (New York: Harvester Wheatsheaf, 1989).

13. Pierre Bourdieu and Jean-Claude Passeron, *Reproduction in Education, Society, and Culture*, trans. Richard Nice (Beverly Hills: Sage, 1977).

14. David Harris, *From Class Struggle to the Politics of Pleasure: The Effects of Gramscianism on Cultural Studies* (London: Routledge and Kegan Paul, 1992).

15. Carmen Luke and Jennifer Gore, eds., *Feminisms and Critical Pedagogy* (New York: Routledge and Kegan Paul, 1992); Patti Lather, "Deconstruction/Deconstructive Inquiry: The Politics of Knowing and Being Known," *Educational Theory* 41, no. 2 (1991): 152–71; and Lather, *Getting Smart*, p.

16. See generally, Robert Miles, *Racism* (London: Routledge and Kegan Paul, 1989) and with respect to the United States, Michael Omi and Howard Winant, *Racial Formation in the United States: From the 1960s to the 1980s* (New York: Routledge and Kegan Paul, 1986).

17. Ernest Laclau and Chantal Mouffe, *Hegemony and Socialist Strategy: Towards a Radical Democratic Politics*, trans. Winston Moore and Paul

Cammack (London: Verso, 1985); Ernesto Laclau, *New Reflections on the Revolution of Our Time* (London: Verso, 1990); Fernando Gutierrez Calderon and Mario R. dos Santos, *Los conflictos por la constitución de un nuevo orden* (Buenos Aires: Consejo Latinoamericano de Ciencias Sociales, CLASCO, 1987); Alan Touraine, *The Voice of the Eye, An Analysis of Social Movements* (New York: Cambridge University Press, 1981); and David Slater, ed., *New Social Movements and the State in Latin America* (Amsterdam: CEDLA, 1985).

18. See Anthony Giddens, *The Constitution of Society* (Berkeley: University of California Press, 1984), p. 139–44; and Jürgen Habermas, *Legitimation Crisis,* trans. Thomas McCarthy (Boston: Beacon, 1975).

19. For a formulation of this type of position in social theory, see Craig Calhoun, "Culture, History, and the Problem of Specificity in Social Theory," in *Postmodernism and Social Theory*, edited by Steven Seidman and David G. Wager (Cambridge: Basil Blackwell, 1992), p. 24–88.

20. Martin Carnoy, *The State and Political Theory* (Princeton, NJ: Princeton University Press, 1984); and Carlos Alberto Torres, *The Politics of Nonformal Education in Latin America* (New York: Praeger, 1990).

21. For two important variants of this critique in general social theory, see Ernesto Laclau and Chantel Mouffe, *Hegemony and Socialist Strategy;* and Jean L. Cohen and Andrew Rato, *Civil Society and Political Theory* (Cambridge: MIT Press, 1992). Some have concluded that the result has been at the price of abandoning "true" Marxism. See Ellen Meiksins Wood, *The Retreat from Class: A New "True" Socialism* (London: Verso, 1986); and Norman Geras, *Discourses of Extremity: Radical Ethics and Post-Marxist Extravagances* (New York: Verso, 1990).

22. See David Karen, "The Politics of Class, Race, and Gender: Access to Higher Education in the United States, 1960–1986," *American Journal of Education 99,* no. 2 (February 1991): 208–37, on the success of general and race-based, as opposed to class-based, mobilization for recruitment in colleges. See also Levy on the expanding role of fundamentalist education as a uniquely American phenomenon (it represents the fastest growing form of minority education) in *Private Education: Studies in Choice and Public Policy,* ed. Daniel C. Levy (New York: Oxford University Press, 1986).

23. Cited in Stewart R. Clegg, *Frameworks of Power* (Newbury Park: Sage, 1989), 112.

24. See the issue of *Sociology of Education 62,* no. 1 (1989). One may argue that this reflects a specific editorial policy to promote junior scholars, but it is more probable that it also reflects a shift of research focus that preoccupies a new generation of scholars.

25. Carl A. Grant and Christine E. Sleeter. "Race, Class and Gender in Education Research: An Argument for Integrative Analysis." *Review of*

Educational Research 56, no. 2 (1986): 195–211; see also their article, "Race, Class, and Gender and Abandoned Dreams," *Teachers College Record* 90, no. 1 (1988): 19–40.

26. Aronowitz and Giroux, *Education Under Siege*, 101–2; for the original formulation, see Henry A. Giroux, *Theory and Resistance in Education: A Pedagogy for the Opposition* (Amherst: Bergin and Garvey, 1983): p. 103, 105.

27. Geoff Whitty, *Sociology and School Knowledge: Curriculum Theory, Research and Politics* (London: Methuen, 1985). For an autobiographical account, see the interview with Raymond A. Morrow and Carlos Alberto Torres and first published as "Education, Power, and Personal Biography: An Interview with Michael Apple," *Phenomenology and Pedagogy* 8(1990): 273–90, and now reprinted in Michael W. Apple, *Official Knowledge* (New York: Routledge and Kegan Paul, 1993): 168–81. See also Carlos Alberto Torres. *Education, Power and Personal Biography: Dialogues with Critical Educators.* New York: Routledge, 1998.

28. Cameron McCarthy and Michael W. Apple, "Race, Class and Gender in American Educational Research. Toward a Nonsynchronous Parallelist Position," in *Class Race and Gender in American Education,* edited by Lois Weiss (Albany: State University of New York Press, 1988), p. 9–39.

29. Michael W. Apple, "Curriculum, Capitalism, and Democracy: A Response to Whitty's Critics," *British Journal of Sociology of Education* 7, no. 3 (1986): 320–21.

30. McCarthy and Apple, "Race, Class and Gender," p. 23.

31. See Stuart Hall, "Gramsci's Relevance to the Analysis of Racism and Ethnicity," *Communication Inquiry* 10 (1986): 5–27; Roberta Hamilton and Michéle Barrett, eds. *The Politics of Diversity: Feminism, Nationalism, Marxism* (Montreal: Book Center Inc., 1986). For useful surveys of these debates, see Patrick Brantlinger, *Crusoe's Footprints: Cultural Studies in Britain and America* (New York: Routledge and Kegan Paul, 1990); and Graeme Turner, *British Cultural Studies* (Boston: Unwin Hyman, 1990).

32. See Lawrence Grossberg, Cary Nelson, and Paul Trichler, eds., *Cultural Studies* (New York: Routledge and Kegan Paul, 1992).

33. Robert W. Connell, *Gender and Power: Society, the Person and Sexual Politics* (Stanford, CA: Stanford University Press, 1987), p. 47. As a consequence, early reproduction theories of education were considerably more open to the issues of gender and race, despite the primacy accorded to relations of production, as in Samuel Bowles and Herbert Gintis, *Schooling in Capitalist America: Educational Reform and the Contradictions of Economic Life* (New York: Basic Books/Harper, 1977); Michael W. Apple, *Ideology and Curriculum* (Boston: Routledge and Kegan Paul, 1979); and Michael W. Ap-

ple, ed., *Cultural and Economic Reproduction in Education: Essays on Class, Ideology and the State* (Boston: Routledge and Kegan Paul, 1982).

34. Connell, *Gender and Power,* 43.

35. Ibid., p. 44.

36. Ibid., p.

37. See Heide Hartmann's widely cited essay, "The Unhappy Marriage of Marxism and Feminism: Towards a More Progressive Union," in *Women and Revolution*, edited by Lydia Sargent (Boston: South End Press, 1981).

38. Samuel Bowles and Herbert Gintis, *Democracy and Capitalism: Property, Community, and the Contradictions of Modern Thought* (New York: Basic Books, 1986); and Adam Przeworski, *Capitalism and Social Democracy* (Cambridge, England: Cambridge University Press, 1985).

39. Connell, *Gender and Power,* p. 46.

40. Nancy Fraser, *Unruly Practices: Power, Discourse and Gender in Contemporary Social Theory* (Minneapolis: University of Minnesota Press, 1989), p. 139.

41. Ibid., p. 128.

42. Connell, *Gender and Power*, p. 94.

43. Ibid., p. 95.

44. Ibid., p. 97.

45. Ibid., p. 116.

46. See, for example, Cornel West, "Marxist Theory and the Specificity of Afro-American Oppression," in *Marxism and the Interpretation of Culture,* edited by Larry Grossberg and Cary Nelson (Urbana: University of Illinois Press, 1988), p. 17–29.

47. For various British perspectives on this issue and its implications for Marxism see especially the overview by John Solomos: "Varieties of Marxist Conceptions of 'Race,' Class and the State: A Critical Analysis," in *Theories of Race and Ethra'c Relations,* edited by John Rex and David Mason (Cambridge: Cambridge University Press, 1986), p. 84–109.

48. Eric R. Wolf, *Europe and the People Without History* (Berkeley: University of California Press, 1982).

49. Enrique Dussel recalls theologian Fernandez de Oviedo's question, 500 years ago: "Are the Amerindians human beings?" in Enrique Dussel, *Philosophy of Liberation*, translated by Aquilma Martinez and Christine Morkovsky (Maryknoll, New York: Orbis Books, 1985), p. 3. Frei Bartolome de las Casas, considered by many theologians of liberation as one of their

precursors in America, was arguing against Medieval Spanish theologians, about the qualities of human beings both Blacks and Indians alike, and their spiritual needs—yet, promoted Black slavery to liberate Indians.

50. Frantz Fanon, *The Wretched of the Earth,* trans. Constance Farington (New York: Grove Press, 1968).

51. Miles, *Racism,* p. 129–31.

52. Cited in Solomos, "Varieties of Marxist Conceptions," p. 100.

53. Omi and Winant, *Racial Formation,* p. 66.

54. Ibid., p. 68 (emphasis added).

55. Ibid., p. 78–79.

56. Martin Carnoy, "Education and the State: From Adam Smith to Perestroika," in *Emergent Issues in Education. Comparative Perspectives,* edited by Robert F. Amore, Philip G. Altbach, and Gall P. Kelly (New York: State University of New York Press, 1992), p. 143–62, Carnoy, *The State and Political Theory;* Martin Carnoy and Henry M. Levin, *Schooling and Work in the Democratic State* (Stanford: Stanford University Press, 1985), p, 1; Carlos Alberto Torres, "State and Education: Marxist Theones," in *International Encyclopedia of Education: Research and Studies* 8, (1985): 4793–4798; Torres, *The Politics of Nonformal Education in Latin America,* New York, Praeger; 1990. Martin Carnoy and Joel Samoff, *Education and Social Transition in the Third World* (Princeton: Princeton University Press, 1990).

57. Wendy Luttrell, "Working-Class Women's Ways of Knowing: Effects of Gender, Race, and Class," *Sociology of Education* 62, no. 1 (1989): 33–46.

58. Ibid., p. 41.

59. Grant and Sleeter, "Race, Class, and Gender and Abandoned Dreams," p. 19.

60. Ibid., p. 40.

61. As suggested provocatively by Mark Bracher in *Lacan, Discourse and Social Change: A Psychoanalytic Cultural Criticism* (Ithaca: Cornell University Press, 1993).

62. Morrow and Torres, *Social Theory and Education.*

63. Jennifer M. Gore, *The Struggle for Pedagogies: Critical and Feminist Discourses as Regimes of Truth* (New York: Routledge and Kegan Paul, 1993), xv.

64. Ibid., p. 114.

65. For an elaboration of the methodological implications of the inter-pretive-structural character of critical social theory, see Raymond A. Morrow and D. D. Brown, *Critical Theory and Methodology* (Newbury Park: Sage, forthcoming).

66. Rosemary Hennessy, *Materialist Feminism and the Politics of Discourse* (New York: Routledge and Kegan Paul, 1993), p. 26–36. But Hennessy's contorted effort to define a global "post-Althusserian social analytic" characterized as an anti-foundationalist, "postmodern Marxism" remains entangled in the Althusserian conception of mode of production, despite revising its claims in terms of "postmodern Marxist arguments for causality that also renounce any objective claims to scientific truth." This attempt to rescue Althusser is characteristic of those trained in the humanities cultural studies debates, as opposed to more sociologically grounded social theory where critical modernist forms of anti-foundationalism (for example, the work of Anthony Giddens and Jürgen Habermas) have remained central.

67. Nancy Fraser and Linds Nicholson, "Social Criticism and Philosophy: An Encounter Between Feminism and Postmodernism," in *Universal Abandon: The Politics of Postmodernism*, edited by Andrew Ross (Minneapolis: University of Minnesota Press, 1989), p. 24.

3

The Sociology of Knowledge and the Sociology of Education: Michel Foucault and Critical Traditions

❑

Thomas S. Popkewitz

Introduction

My concern in this chapter is with how Michel Foucault's methodologies for the study of power enable us to reexamine and revision the "foundations" of critical traditions inherited from nineteenth-century European forbearers. I see Foucault's work as both generative and illustrative of an intellectual tradition that provide certain breaks with the ordering principles of critical traditions dominating Western left thinking since the turn of the century. His concern with how the subject is constituted in power relations forms an important contribution to recent social theory concerned with the politics of "identity," as witnessed by the theoretical and historical work within the feminist movement. His consideration of change as ruptures and breaks, related to French philosophical and history schools, has thrown into sharp relief our conceptions of history and of the conventions of progress that underlie social and educational sciences. The pragmatism of Foucault's scholarship raises important questions about the relation of intellectual production to social practices, questions that are taken up as well within the work of Pierre Bourdieu, among others.

The attention given to Foucault is part of a larger sea-migration of critical traditions of social science since the post World War II period. By sea-migration, I mean the post-World War II mixing of European continental social theories that integrate historical and philosophical discourses with that of more pragmatic (and analytic) traditions in United States, Britain, and Australia.[1] If one reads educational literature in the United States since the 1970s, for example, different European writings provide important conceptual and methodological directions for the study of the politics of school curriculum. The translations and incorporation of European Marxists social philosophy, such as that of the Frankfurt School of critical theory from Germany, the Italian Marxist Antonio Gramsci, and more recently, French "postmodern" and feminist theories are important to the production of a "critical" space within the education. My raising the issue of "sea-migrations" early in this essay is to provide a reading of Foucault as occurring within intellectuals traditions that organize problems and methods of study.

My use of the term "critical" places the work of Foucault in a field concerned with the issues of power and domination in schooling. At one level, critical refers to a broad band of disciplined questioning of the ways in which power works through the discursive practices and performances of schooling. The various modes of critical inquiry are to understand, for example, how the marginization of people is constructed, the various forms in which power operates, and "of interrogating anew the evidence and the postulates, of shaking up habits, ways of acting and thinking, of dispelling commonplace beliefs, of taking a new measure of rules and institutions" (Foucault 1991, 11–12). Further, critical also entails a self-reflectivity about the implications of intellectual work as political projects.

Foucault's work, I believe, is important for entering into a conversation about a particular turn in critical thought during the past few decades. Whereas previous critical scholarship has associated knowledge as separate from and as part of the epiphenomena through which social material practices are formed, Foucault's work is illustrative of a move within critical traditions to focus on knowledge as a material element in social life. In particular, Foucault provides methodological strategies for interpreting how the constitution of the "self" and "individuality" are the effects of power; he joins that issue to a consideration of the social sciences as practices that deploy power. While I would want to relate the current moves in critical research to the sociology of knowledge conceptualized by Émile Durkheim and Karl Mannheim during the early years of this century, we also need to recognize a revitalization and revisioning of that work that responds to and is part of changing social and political conditions.

Foucault provides entrance to an intellectual tradition to emerge forcefully in the past decade to challenge the hegemony of Marxist theories about issues of power and the politics of social change. This challenge to Marxist theories, I am arguing, is not to displace them with another hegemony, but to recognize that there are certain changing conditions in the construction of power that are not adequately articulated through Marxist theories and, in some instances, obscured in previous critical traditions.[2] While I accept a need to be sensitive to structural relations, my concern is mainly with a view of power that is different from and, at certain points, complementary with that of the structuralism of Marxist theories.

The essay proceeds to provide a scaffolding of ideas whose resultant "logic" relates a number of cross-currents in social theory and history that vision and revision the critical projects of intellectuals. I first discuss historically the forming of critical traditions in the United States. I then proceed to Foucault's "decentering of the subject" in which he argues for understanding the relation of power and knowledge. In this discussion, I argue that Foucault maintains Enlightenment commitments to reason and rationality in the process of change; but alters the methodological approaches to the study of change and the politics of intellectual work. I further explore the shift in the study of power by considering power as that of sovereignty/repression and that of deployment/production. In the final sections, I consider the politics of intellectual work to challenge certain philosophical assumptions about the agent in considering social change.

Shifts in the Critical of Critical Research

If we look historically at critical traditions, they have been evident in Europe since at least the work of Marx in the nineteenth century, although they had a muted institutional development in the United States until the end of World War II. To understand this muted development, we can focus on the development of the social sciences into the DOG university, at the turn of the century. This institutionalization of social scientific knowledge was part of what current literature has called the "modernizing project" (see, e.g., Wagner 1994). During the late nineteenth and early twentieth centuries, changes were occurring that involved physical changes in labor, the development of the welfare state, and a social organization related to urbanization. At the same time, and significant in this discussion, modernization involved reconstructions of the principles through which individuals deemed personal competence, achievement, and a secularized notion of salvation in everyday life (see, e.g., Berger et al.

1973; Giddens 1990). The social sciences gave focus to "the social question"—how the rise of the intervention state could be interrelated with questions of individual freedom, personal self-discipline, and liberty.

The debate and struggles about how the knowledge of the nascent social science could relate to the management of freedom and the organization of social progress occurred within a particular liberal framework. That framework accepted the broad outline of progress that focused on the individual as the center of social progress. The state was to guide social betterment through the rationalization and administration of social institutions.

Within this project of modernization was little room for traditions that problematized social relations (Silva and Slaughter 1984; Noble 1991). Critical intellectual traditions, often focusing on relational issues of society, politics, and schooling, tended to be structured out of disciplinary debates.[3] The sociological work of teachers in the United States by Willard Wailer during the 1920s and 1930s was critical of existing mores but was not valued in the field until three decades later when conflict approaches were brought back into vogue.[4] In educational literature, we find that publications of The Society for the Psychological Study of Social Issues, the Psychological League of New York City, and the New America received little or no institutional support from the American Psychological Association during the depression years (Napoli 1981). The Kappan research series in 1936 published a Marxist interpretation of schools, but with an introduction to the pamphlet that looks similar to a warning on a cigarette package today—the reader should beware that the contents might cause some horrible disease. The educational pamphlets of the Labor Research Association tend to be lost to educational historians.[5] While there was debates about social class and race during the depression and early years of the war, and the conflict theories of the 1940s, they were forgotten, for the most part, in the social science and public discourse by the 1950s.[6]

The moral/political space in which social sciences emerged produce disciplinary systems that marginalized critical discourses until the late 1960s. At least four elements of the United States can be identified here.

First, there was a belief in an exceptionalism of the United States as a nation; with the notion of a nation tied to a religious sense of a "New World" and a manifest destiny of the country. During the Progressive Era, it was possible to be sympathetic to an ethics that sought social reform but difficult, for example, to argue for socialism, because the later challenged the belief in exceptionalism.

Second, empiricist discourses came to dominate the social sciences in a manner that valued instrumental concerns with directly useful knowledge. Knowledge which did not seem to offer practical help was itself devalued.

Third, critical traditions were marginalized because there were pervasive fears among various elites of social radicalism which was being imported from Europe. Beginning in the late 1920s, the United States had a pronounced anti-communism rhetoric, which continued into the 1950s as it became associated with McCarthyism. Little, if any of the social science during this period engaged in criticism of social institutions as part of a general critique of society. The pressures of anti-communism and the triumph of positivism occurred not only in social science, but also in the literature and art of the 1940s (see, e.g., Guilbaut 1983). Questions about political loyalty were coupled with a pervasive belief in social equilibrium, the latter providing a dominating assumption in the academy into the 1950s and 1960s.

A fourth element in the omission of conflict theories is related to an increasing professionalization in society. The Progressive Era (circa 1880–1920) inscribed the professionalization of knowledge as a central practice in the efforts to respond to the "social question" in the United States. The problem increasingly became how to plan and manage social institutions in order to provide a materially better and personally greater freedom. The professionalization of "the social question" produced certain ideological discourses about expertise, individuality, and value neutrality.[7] The ideology of expertise and neutral knowledge permeated the notions of aesthetics in the arts as well as the methods and theories of science and social science. By the 1950s, social policy was seen by many as no longer involved in questions of ideology; the famous 1950s essay by Daniel Bell about "The End of Ideology" epitomizes for many that partisan politics have disappeared in social questions.

Critical traditions were given legitimacy in university disciplines after the 1960s.[8] The conditions of conflict in the United States and in its foreign policy helped to challenge the belief in the United States as a "melting pot" and the destiny of the United States to spread its notions of democracy throughout the world. The radical caucuses in the United States social sciences during the Vietnam War and Civil Rights movement, for example, sought to challenge the compromises about theory that were made during the Progressive Era. Non-positivist and non-instrumental research programs were introduced to focus on social analysis. The translation of European critical literature were incorporated into and gave legitimacy to the U.S. social science and educational literature that focused on the cultural issues of power, such as those of Jürgen Habermas in Germany, Antonio Gramsci in Italy, and French Marxists writers. Jean Anyon (1980), for example, wrote about the structuring of class through the structuring of discourses in school classes; Henry A. Giroux (1983) spoke about the implications of the Frankfurt School to the development of a critical pedagogy and the teacher as a transformative intellectual.[9]

The legacies of marginalization, however, produced certain boundaries, as critical traditions sought to gain authority to speak for others outside the university. The notion of useful knowledge, for example, was so forceful and an anti-intellectualism so prevalent throughout the nineteenth and twentieth century that critical traditions after World War II accepted the idea of knowledge as having a practical use if only to claim the terrain occupied by empiricist traditions. Critical traditions, however, revisioned that practice as one that emerged from a critique of the present.

If we move to the contemporary field of critical educational traditions, it is well established and a productive part of the educational sciences. But at the same time, the epistemological principles of "critical" are being struggled over. If we think of critical educational research as a social room in which different groupings of people compete to be noticed, during the later part of the 1980s, "new kids" arrived to articulate and explore questions untouched or undeveloped in other critical traditions; these "kids" were later called "postmodern" and "poststructural," as well as, in some cases, as a revisioned Marxism that, as Stuart Hall (1986) called, "a Marxism without guaranteed." A new sea migration from France and Germany are positioned in these debates.[10] Foucault's writing is often an important flaming in the debates about the questions, methods, and politics of intellectual work.[11]

At the center of the debates is a discussion about the commitments to the Enlightenment. Each of the combatants, including postmodern theories, accept the Enlightenment's faith in reason and rationality (science) to seek a better society. The debates that have occurred among different factions in the critical traditions, from my vantage point, have not been the question of reason and rationality, but rather of the rules and standards of "reason" of the critique and who is to speak it. Certain postmodern writers, for example, suggest that certain strategies of the nineteenth and twentieth century, which define progress as an a prior philosophical assumption of theory, need to be rethought (Foucault 1984). These notions of progress may themselves be doctrines of "reason" that historically deploy power and need to be interrogated (Butler 1992). The problem of the Enlightenment is neither a doctrine nor a particular body of knowledge, but "an attitude, an ethos, a philosophical life in which the critique of what we are is at one time the historical analysis of the limits that are imposed on us and an experiment with the possibility of going beyond them" (Foucault 1984, 50).

We can explore changes in how these commitments are articulated through focusing on Peter Wagner's (1994) argument about modernity. Since the nineteenth century, he argues, there has been a reestablishment of control over social practices as older boundaries were eroded through processes of modernization. The modernization, however, was not only in the physical landscape in which one worked and lived as a social being. It also included the visioning/revisioning of the person through forms of individualization that segmented the person into discrete attributes and behaviors that could be supervised and observed to ensure progress. The social sciences, Wagner continues, were part of the process of modernization through proceeding to make intelligible, objectivist knowledge as the classificatory criteria through which individuals were to be disciplined and self-regulated, rather than through collective action of those being classified or the imposition of brute force. .

The issue of power in modernity, if we follow Wagner's more general argument, is significantly different from those of the nineteenth century. The deployments of power to order social and personal life have increased and made the distinctions between the public and the private no longer appropriate. The Welfare state insurance for unemployment, and classification systems that define people by age, occupations, martial status, and health status serve to revision individuality through "civilizing processes," to borrow from Norbert Elias (1978), that produce boundaries and permissible paths. While these efforts of modernity, Wagner continues, have sought to enlarge capabilities and competence, they also constructed systems that enclosed and interned as the inclusions also excluded (Wagner 1994).

The changing loci and strategies of power, which Wagner traces and Foucault's empirical studies underscore, I believe, require different intellectual practices to grasp and explore the processes of inclusion/exclusions in the politics of contemporary societies. The politics, I will argue throughout this chapter, is related to a version of the Nietzschean's notion of the "the will to power" in which the subject is disciplined through the rules of knowledge itself; thus, pointing to a changing project of politics in contemporary society. (Also see, e.g., Giroux 1992; McLaren 1994; Mahon 1992.) My consideration of Foucault, then, is to explore the politics of "identity" in contemporary society; how the discourses of social and educational sciences deploy power through knowledge; and how critical studies in education needs to be self-reflective about its epistemological structuring of its objects of inquiry.

The Philosophical Privileging of the Subject and its Decentering

Although marginal in terms of resources within the social sciences, the directions taken in previous U.S. critical sciences can be made sense of historically in relation to the dominance in the United States of empiricism, positivism, and exceptionalism. While critical traditions sought to identify the repressive mechanisms of society, certain rules of detachment and engagement were maintained that tied liberal and critical traditions. These relate to the epistemology of the philosophy of the consciousness which privilege the actor as the center of progressive change. In this section, I will explore how the tradition in which Foucault worked makes the notion of actor in social theory problematic through the attention to knowledge as a material effect of power. This shift in focus inscribes into theory an historical consideration of the social construction of knowledge and change.

The Philosophy of Consciousness

The assumptions of the philosophy of the consciousness are, at least, twofold. First, the epistemology of a social science privileged reason and rationality as giving direction to new, universal solutions for human emancipation. Second, change was premised on identifying the subjects who gave direction to change, either by locating the origins of repressive elements that prevented progress or to the groups that were to bring about a redemptive world.

Both critical and dominate liberal traditions in the social sciences were constructed within a particular doctrine related to nineteenth-century views of the Enlightenment. It was believed that systematic knowledge was the motor by which reason can direct social action and guarantee future betterment in society. In the dominant liberal literature of educational reform, the directions tended to be instrumentally organized. Change is thought of as logical and sequential, although is some recognition of the pragmatic qualities of social life (see, e.g., Fuller with Stiegelbauer 1991). The agents of redemption are the state educational researchers, who solve the riddles of school reform, and the change agents, who have become the teachers; they are "self" motivated professionals. The residues of the philosophy of consciousness can be found in educational theories about authentic and effective instruction and school restructuring: progress is identifying ideas and procedures through which teachers can act with the proper dispositions and sensitivities to goal-directed reforms.

Critical traditions, particularly those related to Marxism, also maintain commitments to progress through its philosophical assumptions about agents. With some hesitations and some dissent, redemption is guided by Marxist-Hegelian notions of a nineteenth-century hope about progress.[12] Ideas of "resistance," "voice," and empowerment in contemporary educational discourses inscribe this notion of progress. Intellectual work is to provide the universal norms and direction to social change—what I called "the obligatory last chapter" of critical research (Popkewitz 1991). The naming of the subject is important to the normative purposes of Marxist-Hegelian research. The principles of classification defines and makes visible the collective and unified subject that is to work towards autonomy and emancipation.[13]

The hope is inscribed in assumptions about contradictions and dialectics; that is, it is assumed that critical interrogations of social conditions will produce a new synthesis from the identified contradictions. The agents of redemptions in critical traditions are universalized notions of the workers, racially discriminated groups, and more recently, women.[14] One can read Paul Willis' (1977) classical study of working-class "lad" in this light. The strategies to overcome the repressive elements of society are embedded in the descriptions of contradictions that the researcher describes. The progress to be obtained is global and redemptive. While liberalism tends to place greater emphasis on individuals and the phenomenology of the subject in social change, critical traditions focus on the objectively constituted and constituting subject (see, e.g., Ben Hanhabib 1986).

The historical significance of the *philosophy of consciousness*, it is important to note here, was a recasting and constituting a particular doctrine to Enlightenment commitments. It was a radical nineteenth-century philosophical strategy which not only placed people directly into the knowledge about social change, but also challenged the reigning notions of theology and the chances of birth as the arbiters of progress. Moving across contemporary liberal and Marxist disciplinary projects at the turn of the century was a deep structuring of rules about progress in which the philosophical positioning of agents as an a priori condition of change.

But, as Robert Young (1990) argues, there is a confluence of the politics and institutions of the right and the politics and theoretical systems of the left in the incorporation of Hegelian dialectics. Marxism's reversing of the idealism of Georg Hegel, Young argues "remains explicit with, and even extends the system to which it is opposed" (1990, 3). The same universalizing narrative of an unfolding rational system of the world appears but as a negative form of the history from which Europeans imposed its nineteenth-century imperialism. The relation of the colonial systems and the dialectics are in its rules of knowledge, which presupposes a universal governing structure of self-realization in all historical processes. The construction of knowledge, Young argues, expropriates and incorporates the "Other" into a system that is totalizing and thus does not allow the "Other" legitimacy.

Decentering the Subject in Social Theory

The premises about progress and agents in the philosophy of consciousness is one of the major challenges posed in current debates about the social and education theory. The challenge is posed through the most suggestive and controversial element, that of the decentering of the subject. Across a wide band of studies in the humanities and social sciences, research has sought to make the constituted agent as the problem of research. If I schematically express the focus, it is the difference between studying blackness instead of Blacks; femininity instead of women, homosexuality instead of homosexuals, childhood as a linguistic concept instead of children.

The revisioning and visioning of research that accompanies the decentering of the subject is a way to understand the effects of power in modern society. The argument is that the a priori philosophical placement of actors in the narratives of social science obscures more than it reveals. If we look at Foucault and a feminist philosopher, Judith Butler (1993), for example, they raise questions about whether the maintaining of the historical subject who brings about change is, in fact, the effects of power. The strategies of naming actors in social practices is viewed as hiding the power relations in the rules of classification applied. The decentering of the subject problematizes our relation to present modes of reasoning through historically examining how self has come to be constituted as an autonomous "self."

The "decentering" of the philosophy of consciousness is given focus through making the knowledge as a central concern of social theory. If I draw on Foucault again, inquiry is to separate out "what contingencies have made us what we are, the possibilities of no longer being, doing, thinking, what we are, do, or think." It is to understand how the rules of reason that structure our practices for change and the classifications and distinctions among groups of people been constructed. Jana Sawicki (1988), for example, reviewing feminist research, argues that feminine forms of embodiment in dietary and fitness regimes, expert advise on how to walk, talk and dress, the ways in which hair is styled, as well as the wearing of make-up are "technologies that subjugate by developing competencies" and aesthetic tastes (Sawicki 1988, 174–175). The systems of ideas about the "self" are intertwined with performances and "skills" through which an individuality is constructed as "natural" and desirable for being a woman.[15]

As we approach educational research, the decentering of the subject projects embody a particular type of historical study of the present. It is considered with the systems of ideas and, as a result, "reasoning" about schooling has emerged. It centers attention to questions about what others have thought of as "natural" about schooling—how the teacher, learning, and childhood are constructed as subjects that are spoken about and acted on. Historically, there is an exploration of school practices and reforms to consider, for example:

> How do our systems of "reasoning" about teaching and children construct systems of differentiation and discrimination?

> What power relations are inscribed in the ways that we have historically come to think and act in the manner that we do?

> And,

> How are the ways in which we speak "truths" about teachers and children in schooling as the effects of power?

One way to think of contemporary school reforms is to understand its ways of defining "the educated subject." But the concept of an "educated subject" is neither a constant entity nor one which can be studied solely as a "philosophical" idea that is stable over time. It is a concept that has changed as the systems that regulate the person have shifted within changing social circumstances. Lynn Fendler (in press), for example, explores conceptions of the "educated subject" in ancient Greece, medieval, modern, and contemporary discourses of U.S. educational reform. Fendler's historical analysis, however, is not one of conventional historiography that charts changing events, ideas, and/or people. Her narrative identifies discursive breaks over time in the substance of what makes an educated person, the obligations and justifications of the person who is "educated," and the means and goals of that education. Further, she maps the changing relations of concepts of the "educated subject" to social and political conditions in which that "educated person" is constructed.

The analysis calls attention to radical shifts in contemporary school reform discourses in the forms of disciplining and governing of the "child." School didactics and teacher education reforms, for example, have focused on the child as constructing knowledge and as being a problem solver. When these foci of reform are examined from Fendler's analysis, we are able to identify new relations of knowledge and power. The new "educated subject" embodies new "technologies of the self," drawing on Foucault and feminist theories to consider how the child has become an object that is systematically classified, legislated, standardized, and normalized. The new technologies of pedagogy move institutional norms directly into the subjective space of the individual as the reforms seek to change the capabilities and dispositions of children. We can say that the effect of the reform discourses is to make political rationalities into the productive rationalities through which children are to think and act in the world. The desire, dispositions, and capabilities of the child in school, Fendler argues, is "mutually constitutive with society" rather than different. (Also see Baker, in press.)

Kenneth Hultqvist's (in press) study of changes that relate Swedish Welfare State policies and early childhood education also enable us to consider how reason is an effect of power and knowledge as a material practice. Hultqvist argues that the political rationalities of the Swedish State are inserted in the world as a practice. Using the preschool child as a vantage point, he explores how the school and similar social welfare activities contribute to producing children and young people as subjects of particular ways of living. Comparing the concept of "the child" in the Swedish welfare model of the 1930s, 1940s, and educational psychology and didactics in the 1970s, there appears a new "decentralized" child who is to be seen as self-motivated and self-governing. The discourse of the "decentralized" child is part of contemporary "decentralization" of the social welfare state and a wider reconstitution of governing practices that include pedagogy and social science in the 1990s. Hultqvist studies provide a broad historical understanding of how contemporary political rationalities and rhetoric such as that of "privatization" and "market" do not explain changes but are themselves part of long-term micro processes about how we think and "reason" about our "selfs."

Through such interrogation, the effects of power can be made visible and potentially disrupted. Research as critique "is not to make possible a metaphysics that has finally become a science; it is seeking to give new impetus, as far and wide as possible, to the undefined work of freedom" (Foucault 1980). He continues in another essay that

> One has to dispense with the constituent subject, to get rid of the subject itself, to arrive at an analysis which can account for the constitution of the subject within a historical framework. And this is what I would call genealogy, . . . that is, a form of history which can account for the constitution of knowledges, discourses, domains of objects etc., without having to make reference to a subject which is either transcendental in relation to the field of events or runs its empty sameness throughout the course of history (Foucault 1980, 117).

Systems of ideas are historical practices through which the objects of the world are constructed and become systems of action. (See Foucault 1988; also Dreyfus and Rabinow 1983, Noujam 1987; Rajchman 1985.)[16] By placing the subject into its historical constructions, we have the possibility to interpret and contest how power is deployed.

"The Linguistic Turn" and Knowledge as a Material Problem

Knowledge as a constitutive element in our material existence has been called "The Linguistic Turn" in social theory. Kathleen Canning (1994) argues, for example, that the "linguistic turn" is a scrutiny and reexamination of language as not only describing and interpreting the world but as constituting social practices and identity. The concept of *discourse* can be understood as emerging from this sense of language as constituting worlds and the "self." Discourse directs attention to how intent and purpose do not reside in individual's or groups but are functions of discersive rules. We can think of teachers, parents, administrators and policy makers, for example, as making decisions about school reform that embody particular discursive practices that order and divide the experiences of schooling. Concepts of learning, childhood, development—the commonplaces in schooling—are such discursive practices. There is an assumption that schools should promote learning and the development of the child. Such concepts function to differentiate and distinguish the world of schooling.

The ordering devises of action, however, are not only a creation of the individual who "thinks" about schools and children. The categories and dividing practices are historicially constructed. Thinking about the child who "learns" or "develops" are part of social imaginaries produced at the turn of the century to inscribe scientific thinking into the practices of schooling. While these imaginaries that have been continually revised, they function to link pedagogical ideas about social progress to the reason that orders children's growth, development and cognition (see, Popkewitz & Brennan, 1977). With this example of pedagogy as a discursive practice, we can recognize that purpose and intent are not necessarily the product of an individual but are produced through the prior rules of classification that demarcate and designate what is important to think about and act on to "make" productive and reasonable action. The "rules" do not appear as rules because of the naturalness and unquestionable parts in classrooms and school reforms.

We can think about the constitutive role of language if we think about sexuality. We realize that its meanings are intertwined with cultural systems: contending that the divisions of male vs. female are genital, chromosomal, or hormonal misses the point that these characteristics are discursively selected in a manner that links sexual boundaries to matters of reproduction, a strategy that historically has kept women in their "proper" place (Sampson 1993). The relation of systems of ideas to cultural systems and institutional patterns is often referred to as "discursive practices," a term that recognizes the interrelation of ideas, institutions, and technologies in the production of social life.

The significance of the "linguistic turn" is that it helps us recognize that when we "use" language, it may not be us speaking. Our speech is ordered through principles of classification that are socially formed through a myriad of past practices. When teachers talk about school as management, teaching as producing learning, or children who are "at-risk," these terms are not "merely" words of the teacher, but are part of historically constructed "ways of reasoning" that guide and classify how we are to "see," think, talk, and act as children and teachers. Learning, for example, is an invention of the 1920s, derived from behavioral psychology; it has provided a way for the teacher to administer the classroom. The use of the word does not stand alone: it is interred with a range of values, priorities, and dispositions concerning how one should see and act towards the world.

A different dimension of a the "linguistic turn" is found in the work of Jürgen Habermas (1971; 1981; 1987; Bernstein 1985), a member of the Frankfurt School of Critical Theory. Here, we can understand a relation between French critiques of reason and German or social philosophy. Habermas' writing on cognitive interests in knowledge and his later theory of communicative action embody a theory of language in a social theory of change. Habermas' theory, however, is formalistic, and ahistorical as he searches for the universal pragmatics of reason.[17] My focus on the linguistic turn is one that is not only historical and specific, but it also rejects the Hegelian view of progress, and focuses on the problem of power. Further, my argument throughout this chapter is that knowledge is political; it has normative implications, even though I will be seeking to revision how those normative implications are expressed.

A Social Epistemology as Social Theory

At this point, an homologies between Foucault's studies and the history of science and feminist scholarship concerned with the "politics of identity" can be identified (e.g., Butler 1992; 1993; Canning 1994; Scott 1991). This relation is exemplified in the Thomas Kuhn (1970) study of knowledge for understanding scientific change; although we use Kuhn advisedly here because of his idealistic conception of change. Kuhn studied in what is called an "epistemological tradition" of social science that is tied to French history and philosophy of science (see, e.g., Canguilheim 1976 1988; and Bachelard 1984) and brought to the study of social sciences through the work of Michel Foucault.[18] Epistemology is not, as in U.S. philosophy, a meta-discourse to find the ultimate rules of truth, but a effort to understand the conditions in which knowledge is produced. Thomas Kuhn, the French philosopher of science, and Michel Foucault shifted the focus of inquiry from the intentions of people to the changing principles through which knowledge itself is structured. Scientific change is located in the manner and the conditions in which concepts change. We can also identify the focus on epistemology in the Marxist theorist, Louis Althusser, a teacher of Foucault. Althusser worked from the tradition of the history of science prominent in French. It is interesting that Althusser's epistemological approach was criticized as not being Marxist (Young 1990). We can identify a similar epistemological move in postmodern feminism (see, e.g., Butler 1993). The (re)moving of the subject of women is to understand how, at different historical times, women are made into subjects through a weaving of different social practices and institutional patterns. Denise Riley (1988), for example, explored how the concept of "women" has moved over the past few hundred years from its placement in religious spaces as a "soul" dominated by the church to social spaces that revisioned women through their bodies and sexuality. Riley argues that there is no "essential" concept of woman but one that is historically formed in power relations. She locates how changing concepts construct the "subject" of women in changing patterns of power that normalize gender relations.

The strategy of inquiry, though, is not only one of knowledge but also it is part of a struggle to understand how power is deployed. In Riley's study of the concept of "women" we can focus on a social theory that inscribes history into its interpretations of change; that is, we can understand the interrelation of the changing concepts through which we reason about our "selfs" in social conditions that change over time.

At this point, I have placed Foucault into a field of thought that articulates a broad multidisciplinary conversation about the project of social science and history, elements to which I will return to throughout this essay. First, there is a strategy to focus on theory as an epistemological problem, that is, its provides a way of orientating and of problematizing the social conditions in which contemporary social life is constructed (see, e.g., Popkewitz 1991). It is to treat theory, as does Pierre Bourdieu, who is educated within the same intellectual milieu, as a "thinking tool"—"a *modus operandi* which practically guides and structures scientific practices . . ." (Bourdieu and Wacquant 1992, 161; also see Bourdieu 1984; 1989).[19] Second, the "decentering of the subject" and the linguistic turn is not to reject humanist, but the humanism which replaces how we view the subject as the center of reality. As I. Hacking (1986) has argued, "Foucault said that the Concept of Man is a fraud, not that you and I are nothing" (p. 39).

This notion of theory can be contrasted to two other views (Dean 1994, 3–4):

(1) A progressive theory which has a model of social progress through the teleology of reason, technology and found in positivism

of Comte and Marx, and certain interpretations of Weber's conception of rationalization.

(2) A critical theory proposes a dialectic in which present forms of reason and society are both negated and retained in a higher form. Instead of progress there are narratives of reconciliation of the subject with itself, with nature, with the form of its own reason. and,

(3) a theory that is a problematizing one to analyze the trajectory of the historical forms of truth and knowledge without the origin or end. The effect is to disturb narratives of progress and reconciliation, finding questions where others had located answers.

I will use the notion of "critical" in the discussion to maintain a common sense usage about social theory that is concerned with issues of power. However, my "sense" of "critical" will be of a problematizing theory that focuses on knowledge itself as the problem of inquiry. The strategy reverses the interests of the philosophy of consciousness by making the problem of study as that of the knowledge which inscribes agents. The decentering of the subject focuses on the categories, distinctions, and differentiations through which daily practices are organized and individuality constructed.[20] The social theory is also a theory of change through understanding how the "objects" of the world are historically constructed and changed over time. Such a strategy, I will argue later, is a political theory as well as a theory of knowledge, for the two are inseparable. The notions of social change and progress, however, are different from that of the philosophy of consciousness.

Sovereignty and the Deployment of Power

We can pursue further the implications of the linguistic turn to social theory by focusing more directly on the concept of power. We can think of epistemological theory as either reconceptualized or the dominant relationship of power to knowledge. Foucault, for example, reverses the traditional belief that knowledge is power and looks for power as embodied in the manner in which people effect knowledge to intervene in social affairs, not as something actors own.[21] Foucault's concept of power, I will argue, enables us to give attention to its productive dimensions, such as, how power works through individual actions to vision and revision our "selfs" as acting, thinking, and feeling individuals. This occurs when we consider the social and conceptual conditions through which we have come to reason about sexuality, criminality, medicine, and madness as the effects of power.

To explore Foucault's notion of power, I return for a moment to the philosophy of consciousness articulated in school studies of power. To be schematic here, the study of power is to identify its origin; that is, the actors who control and in whose benefit existing arrangements work. The centering of actors as the welders of power introduces a view of power as sovereignty. The notion of sovereignty gives attention to what groups are favored in decision-making and how the decisions distribute values to produce a context of domination and subordination—that of the rulers and the ruled. Most studies of school choice and privatization maintain this assumption of sovereignty. They ask either how do different marginalized groups "make use" of choice to gain access to education or profit from choice through better achievement. Power in this landscape is "something" that people can own, and that ownership can be redistributed among groups to challenge inequities; hence, the use of the term of "sovereignty."

The concept of *sovereignty* is found in much of the sociology of school knowledge. Power is a structural concept to explore the origins of domination and subjugation in society. Study is to identify the placeholders who prevent progress, how others resist that power, and how the relations of power among actors can be made more equal. For example, a sovereignty notion of power is embodied in current educational literature that "sees" social interests inscribed in reform reports and government policies that argue for a "back to basic" curriculum. The consequence of the reforms, it is argued, is to reproduce gender, racial, and class distinctions in society (Carlson 1992). Here, power is attached to actors who have the legitimacy to make decisions and allocate values within communities—a description that inscribes the commitments of the philosophy of consciousness. A central political problem of research is to identify (and alter) the unequal relations between the rulers and ruled. A central premise is that society entails certain groups, social interests and "forces" that historically formed and whose practices dominate and repress other groups.

The sovereignty notion of power produces certain strategies for understanding the politics of schooling. Class is a central concept for describing the production of social inequities, drawing its major insights from a Marxism to emerge in Europe and later in the United States. Scholarship in the last decade has related concepts of gender and race with that of class to describe the complex nexus in which sovereignty is exercised. Structural concepts of agency, resistance, and contestation have been used to posit ways in which the hegemony of the rulers are challenged and change can be sought (Weis and Fine 1993).

The sovereignty notion of power is paramount in the arguments about the "conservative restoration" in studies of U.S. educational reform from the 1980s. It is asserted that particular conservative groups of people insert their interests in schools through a variety of mechanisms; this includes the defining of cultural values and the organizing of the terrain in which the rules of political debate occurs (Shors 1986). The conservative restoration, it is argued, entails the exercise of power through teaching a particular moral/religious viewpoint about gender either through sex education or through advancing particular economic interests through science and technology curriculum.

It can be argued that the sovereignty notion of power is limited on a number of counts. Where the sovereign notion of power posits unified historical processes and structures, change entails "an amalgamation of institutional and discursive practices that function as a collective assemble of disparate parts on a single surface" (Crary 1990, 6). If one examines the "conservative restoration" thesis, for example, the changes reported in economy, culture, and politics begin well before the election of Ronald Reagan in the United States and entail a reorganization of knowledge and practices that occurred in an uneven pattern, within multiple institutions, and over a period that is longer than the "Reagan-Bush" era (see Kuttner 1991; Lekachman 1982; Popkewitz 1991; in press). What is reported as structural historical change in the "conservative restoration" is non-historical and non-relational.

Power as sovereignty often creates a dichotomous world in which there is the oppressor and oppressed, thus, producing a dualism whose effect is to define particular social groups as monolithic entities. The story often unfolds as one group dominates and the other carries social righteous but does not possess power. The dualism of oppressor/oppressed loses sight of the subtleties in which power operates in multiple arenas and social practices (see Popkewitz 1993). This is the difficulty that is confronted when consider race, class, and gender are considered as parallel concepts. The relation is asserted in educational research but the concepts of a parallelism are never theoretically integrated (see, e.g., Ladwig 1996). The concepts stand as separate categories not only to enable and conceptually integrate the multiple agendas that exist within social fractions and movements, but also to assemble the multiplicity of relations that exist within and among groups at any one time.[22]

At a different level, the sovereignty notion of power fails to recognize theoretically the significance of the productive elements of power which have no historically specific origin. While one can posit a generalized condition of capitalism as a background to the organization of power, this positing does not provide an adequate theoretical grounding for understanding how the capillaries of power works in modern societies. For one, there is no one "model" of capitalism; nor is its history as one of a single, unified development. At a different level, the historical contingencies and multiple boundaries in which race, class, and gender are constructed have no single origin or universal characteristics; they are constructed in relational fields that are fluid and multidimensional. Thus, while research and researchers can be sensitive to issues of race, class, and gender, the rules and standards of reasoning by which the subjects are "defined" are not essential categories of logic, but are historically constructed categories that embody and weave with social, technological, and institutional patterns.

Foucault suggests that there is a different but not necessarily incommensurate interpretation of power than that of sovereignty. That view concerns the productive quality of power. This notion of power concerns its effects as it circulates through institutional practices and the discourses of daily life. Foucault argues that power is embedded in the governing systems of order, appropriation, and exclusion by which subjectivities are constructed and social life is formed. Here, Foucault revises the Nietzchean notion of a "will to how" to consider how available systems of ideas discipline individuals as they act, see, think, and "see" themselves in the world. Strategically, the study of the deployments of power enables us to focus on the ways that individuals construct boundaries for themselves, define categories of good/bad, and envision possibilities. The concern of Marx with the productive characteristics of labor is thus inverted into the productive characteristics of knowledge itself (Dumm 1987). In some ways, we can consider the work of Foucault as expanding and providing a historical specificity to the observation of the early Frankfurt School. The early theorists focuses on the expanding rationalization and instrumental reasoning that underlies modernity.

The effects of power are to be found in the production of desire, and in dispositions and sensitivities of individuals (see also Noujain 1987; Rajchman 1985, for discussions of Foucault).[23] An example of this disciplining as productive can be given focus in the "commonsense" reading of labels on a food package to determine its "healthiness," or our earlier discussion of feminine attributes of combing hair as deployments of power. Embodied in these acts are disciplining technologies through which individuals construct boundaries and vision possibilities. The reading of food labels that count calories and the "fats" in food are not only cognitive acts, but they also tie into a disciplining of the body that relate images of the body to the disciplining of our body and our desires—what is defined as healthy is not only "health" but moral standards about what the body should look like and desire. Our attention to the productive elements of power moves from the controlling actors to the systems of ideas that normalize and construct the objects from which our worlds are acted upon. It is the effects of power that postmodern and feminist writings have focused on, with Foucault's work an important generative element of these explorations. For example, Gayatri Spivak (1992) discusses the problem of translation as a political practice that entails multiple deployments of power. Focusing on the translations of women's texts from the Third World into English, Spivak argues that the specific actor who writes these text cannot be designated by her subject position of gender or class. She explores how the discursive practices normalize and produce identities through a pervasive orientalism that obliterates Third World specificity and denies cultural citizenship. For Spivak, the concern is not to find the origin of repressive practices through a structural analysis that identifies the repressive mechanisms of class or gender: her concern is how sense is made to produce identities that are complex inscriptions of power relations. We can use the notion of the effects of power as a way to reconceptualize the problem of socialization in teaching and teacher education. Most research on teaching and teacher education assume the "subject" of children and teacher as stable categories—questions are asked about how teachers and students learn about the social relations and, at points, resist those arrangements. The notion of socialization can also ask about how the discursive practices of teaching construct what it means to be a teacher who administers children. For example, in a study of the socialization of teachers in the alternative professional program, *Teach For America*, the focus was on how the systems of reasons in the schooling "made" thinking, and acting "teachers" within particular social relations and historically defined power relations (Popkewitz, forthcoming).

The program was to recruit and train teachers to work with children of color and poverty in different parts of the United States. The problem of the socialization was treated as focusing on the systems of ideas through which rules of "reasoning" are applied to construct school competence, achievement, and salvation. The images and vi-

sions that classify the child of color and of poverty in schooling, I argue, normalizes certain sociopolitical distinctions in the practices of
teaching and learning. What is significant in the disciplining patterns of teacher education is that they are not only of the particular
reform effort, but also the rules of "reasoning" were of schooling and
the reform efforts to make schooling more "relevant" and accessible
for those groups positioned as different and "non-normal."

We can think about the writings which consider power as sovereignty or deployment as each maintaining general political commitments for social change, but with different assumptions in the loci of
study and the political of intervention. (For distinctions within postmodern literature concerning its political and nonpolitical loci, see
Rosenau 1992.) We can also recognize that neither interpretive
stance is totalizing but complementary; the former considers larger
historical structures through which daily life is constructed; the latter focuses on the micro-politics in which subjectivities are constructed. In the latter, we can attend more closely to how power
circulates through and is productive in daily life; providing a strategy for disrupting that knowledge/power relation through making it
visible and potentially resistible.

Regional Study Instead of Context:
Individuality in Discursive Spaces

One radical implication of the productive concept of power is its
focus on the specific, local, or regional sites of deployment. Attention
is given to the discursive field in which the subject is to be known.
We can think of the systems of ideas in schooling, for example, as the
construction of a discursive site from which the child is made into an
object of (self) scrutiny and observation. The systems of ideas normalize the way in which children are to be "seen," talked about, and
acted upon. Further, the categorizing of the child as an adolescent,
a learner, a personality with or without "self-esteem," a sibling, an
Hispanic, a psychological-clinical medical "problem" of growth are
classifications that transcend the particular institution of schooling
by means of the categories applied.[24] The conceptions of childhood
"travel" across the institutions of health, schools, social welfare
among others.[25] The discursive site of the "child" normalize competence, achievement, and well-being from which the individual can be
observed and acted upon.

The idea as region or discursive field focuses on how historically
constructed systems of ideas weave in the production of subjectivi-

ties. The histories that Foucault writes, for example, are histories of
how the person is made into a subject through particular rules and
standards in particular institutional patterns but which are not reducible to those patterns. His studies of the prison and the criminal,
the asylum and the insane, the clinical medical gaze, and bodily desires in the history of sexuality are examples of the constructions of
discursive fields. Each field is an assemblage that spans multiple institutions. The individuality seems to transcend particular events
and the social moorings of place, such as the child as a learner who
has no geographical location except through the categories that classify cognition, affect, and motivation.

The notion of discursive field enables us to focus on the actors
of the modern school, for example, as objects whose construction
form a region—the teacher, the child, the student, behaviorally dis-
abled child, and the school curriculum. What are constituted as
teaching, learning, and school assessment, for example, are not
merely "there" or negotiated by those who work in schools. With
learning concepts and information about science, social studies and
mathematics are problem-solving methods to direct how students
reason about the world at-large and the "self" in that world. The discourses of pedagogy, following Luke's (1990) studies of classrooms,
"operate not as an abstract set of ideas to be transposed into, inside
of, or within mind/consciousness, but as a material series of
processes that inscribe attributes of subjectivity into the social body
(1990, 5). Models of literacy in schooling display "particular postures
(correct way of maintaining one's body when reading), silences, ges-
tures and signs of Ôbeing in' the lesson that encode particular ways
of acting, seeing, talking, and feeling of the student" (1990, 18).

Curriculum becomes, from this viewpoint, part of a discursive
field through which the subjects of schooling are constructed as individuals to self-regulate, discipline, and reflect upon themselves as
members of a community/society (see, e.g., Lundgren 1983; Hamilton 1989).[26] For example, if we focus on the systems of ideas that
merged into the modern curriculum during the Progressive Era at
the turn of the century, the curriculum changes were a part of a vi-
sioning/revisioning of social commitment, and of individual service
and faith (Popkewitz 1987; 1991).[27] The ideas revisioned a pastoral
image of the person in relation to a modern, scientific notion of the
"rational" citizen.[28] The discourses of the child placed faith in the rational individual as the locus of change (see, e.g., Meyer 1986).[29]

The epistemological ordering of knowledge in the diverse theories
of John Dewey, G. Stanley Hall, and David Snedden can be under-

stood as attempts to bring professional, scientific knowledge into the school to regulate teachers' administration of children's thinking and social competence. The new psychologies of problem solving, measurement, and child development, for example, embodied distinctions and differentiations that regulated not only the information organized in school, but also the discursive systems of pedagogy inscribed what was to be personal competence and achievement.

We can think of the educational studies, then, as a social mapping of the epistemological practices and social conditions as they inscribe boundaries about what is to be authorized as reason/nonreason with respect to the objects of schooling. The mapping of discursive changes are interrelated to understanding how the principles of ordering are (re-)organized and (re-)visioned. The regional focus of competing discursive practices of educational reform enables an understanding of how particular rules and standards of truth cross institutional patterns and are not reducible to those patterns. The notion of region is a strategy which does not privilege a notion of chronological time, and philosophically the subject as a priori condition for considering social change and human agency, such as found in the philosophy of consciousness.

We can consider the significance of the regional focus on discursive fields if we return to the earlier discussion of Wagner (1994). He argued that the issue of power in modernity becomes significantly different from those of the early nineteenth-century notions of sovereignty. Knowledge as the deployments of power have increased and made the distinctions between the public and the private no longer appropriate. The strategy to locate individuals in discursive spaces is a way to understand and make problematic the classificatory criteria through which individuals are to be disciplined and self-regulated.

Decentering Progress: From Evolution to a History of Breaks

To this point, I have argued that the work of Foucault is related to a number of cross-currents in social theory and history that vision and revision the critical projects of intellectuals. The argument provides a scaffolding of ideas through which to understand the different elements. The linguistic turn enabled us to focus on the problematic of knowledge as the effects of power. The decentering of subject, for example, was viewed as a strategy to consider how the subject in modern life was constructed as a site and effect of power. The move to a regional or local study of discursive sites was viewed as a way to understand how the particular mechanism and practices that circulate in the microphysics of power operate.

In the last two sections, I want to further the scaffolding in which a theory of power and change are positioned. First, I explore a theory of change which considers the history of epistemological breaks and discontinuities, focusing on changes in the forms of reasoning through which the agent is constructed. Second, I challenge the political strategies inscribed in the philosophy of consciousness which made the a priori identification of the subject as essential for considering political work of intellectuals. For Foucault, change is not in the evolutionary progression of events or in the conscious efforts of people to influence those events; change is in disrupting the forms of reasons through which power is deployed (see also, e.g., Toulmin 1972; 1988). To make the constitution of the individual as historically constructed is to reintroduce a humanism that can potentially enlarge the capacity of people to act.

If we return to the argument of Thomas Kuhn (1970) about revolutionary and normal sciences, for example, he considered a view of historical change that did not involve the intent and purpose of actors, even though individuals and particular practices were part of his narrative about science. "Revolutionary science" gave focus to different sets of rules and standards about truth—what is to be studied, why, and how—from that of normal science. Further, the distinctions between how truth is told in normal and revolutionary science, for example, are not cumulative, rather, they involve ruptures in belief and cognition that occur within particular historical conjunctures. For example, Bachelard has pointed to physics in the ten years from 1920 to 1930, from a scientific viewpoint as long as an era as the previous five hundred years. There was, in this period, a remaking of the sciences own history as relativity theory and microphysics were redefined by its reaction to the past. Science becomes a series of "nons": non-Cartesian, non-Euclidean, non-Newtonian, non-Baconian (Young 1990, 50).

But we must go further than Kuhn in thinking about conceptual changes. How people tell the truth about the world is part of and expressive of social transformations by which relationships with the world and our "selves" are established. Michel Foucault (1975), for example, locates the birth of modern medicine in visible changes and in what was expressed about disease. In the eighteenth century, Foucault argues, the special configurations of disease and localizing of illness in particular pathologies replaced a classification system that dominated medicine. The latter saw the primary problem of medicine as the "envelopments, subordinations, divisions, resemblances" rather than as disease that is localized in organs (1975, 5). The new way of "seeing" enabled a clinical medical gaze that saw particular tissues as related to pathologies of individual organs rather than as related to the functioning of the organism as a whole. The new configurations of a medical gaze occurred alongside of and were made possible through the development of the teaching hospital and other institutional places in which medicine was practiced.

The history of medical practices was not a chronological one of a progressive advancement, or of a serial progress; it was of a time, if we turn to the French historical school of the Annales, that "goes at a thousand different paces, swift and slow; it bears almost no relation to the day-to-day rhythm of a chronicle or of traditional history" (Braudel 1980, 10). We can turn, as well, to the later Wittgenstein (1966) who provided a way of understanding historical change as multiple rates developing across different institutions at different times that come together in what can be called a "historical conjunction." Wittgenstein likened historical change to a thread made up of many fibers. The strength of the thread does not reside in the fact that some fibers run its entire length but in the fact that many fibers overlap.

From this perspective, the set of relations that become schooling—in its forms of expression and performances—exists across different dimensions of time and space rather than as a continuous history. Mass schooling, for example, was a nineteenth-century invention that emerged from different movements within society which, at a certain level, worked autonomously from each other.[30] Overlapping with changes in classroom teaching were the creations of institutions for teacher education (normal schools), the rise of the modern universities, the formation of social sciences, and the emergence of a psychology discipline. These multiple arenas of social practice occurred at the conjuncture with the emergence of the modern U.S. welfare state, which assumed governing functions of the new institution of mass schooling. At the same time, systems of ideas appear about the "educativeness" of the person—the child, school administration, psychologies of the individual, and progress among others. Interpretations of mass schooling, therefore, need to account for the multiple intersections of knowledge constructed in these varied arenas. It is in the conjuncture of these nineteenth-century practices that currently favored words, such as "professionalism," "educational sciences," and "subject matter teaching" need to be placed, and their assumptions genealogically explored.

To that end, we understand a social change of change that inquires into the breaks and ruptures in discursive fields that construction individuals. Ingolfor Johansson (1991; 1993), for example, presents a study of educational reform in Iceland from one such example. From the 1960s, Icelandic educational reform has been a key link in the project towards modernization of schools. Modernization can be viewed as rationalizing the organization of schools and the college of education.

But that organization involved more than establishing organizational linkages and personnel hierarchies. Modernization entailed a reclassification of the knowledge through which schooling was apprehended. This reclassification and reordering were evident in the debates about the school curriculum. Underlying the curriculum reforms in biology and social studies, for example, were particular sets of beliefs from which the school subjects were formed. Inscribed in the "new" curriculum knowledge was formulated not only as dispositions about historical progress, scientific reasoning, child development, but also democratic concerns about how schooling produced a more just society. Johansson explored how these sentiments were inserted into the educational field to legitimatize a particular professionalization of progress and of educational expertise.

To pursue how a discursive field recursively constructed social relations and actors in education, Johansson studied "pre-reform discourses" that emerged in the early twentieth century when Iceland was still under Danish rule. The curriculum knowledge gave focus to an elite form of knowledge which was phrased as developing "excellence." It embodied a congregational pedagogy and storytelling, Christian studies, nationalism, and an objectivism which sought to define categories of the world as unambiguous and unchangeable.

The post-World War II reform movement in Iceland replaced the "pre-reform" discourses with professional discourses of reform. These professional discourses within the educational arena competed with the "pre-reform" discourses. Johansson explored how the discursive themes moved among different institutional sites: the teacher unions, the Icelandic College of Education, The Icelandic University, The Ministry of Education, and The State Institute for School Development and Evaluation. The particular constructions of educational reform were embedded in a network of strategies that organized what was looked at as "educational" and how that looking conceived of the "things" of the world. A new social studies curriculum, for example, drawing on U.S. discussions of the late 1960s, argued for a modern, progressive school and a professionally competent teacher.

We can think of Johansson's mapping of Iceland as a way to locate changing power relations in the field of education through breaks in the discursive field. While Johansson's map ties the shifts in discursive fields to changing relations among actors and institutions within Icelandic education, the actors are located through their epistemological positions in the construction of the discursive field. That is, there are various people who defended the prevailing epistemologies of school practices, but at other times, the same people spoke about the reform discourses. In this sense, we can understand the concept of power as sovereignty and as less relevant as power explored epistemologically and relationally. The study of the changing discursive practices gave focus to how power was effected.

Johansson's historical sociology of schooling provides a strategy to bring an historical sensitivity to the interpretations of social change. He enables us to understand how the objects with which we construct purpose and practices of schooling change over time and as practices that deploy power. We may, for example, use terms like "curriculum," "teacher" or "classrooms" as ways of thinking and organizing what occurs within schools, but these terms inscribe epistemological orderings that continually need historical scrutiny as to their determinations of personal and social competence.

Intellectual Work as Political: A Reconsideration

Why make the linguistic turn rather than maintain the assumptions of the philosophy of consciousness? One could argue that focusing on the intent and purposes of social actors provides an important social as well as scientific commitment. It places people and their social worlds in history and centers on their role in producing social change. To remove people from history, it is argued, is to make the world seem deterministic and outside of the possibility of intervention.

In fact, efforts to remove the actor have been viewed as reactionary within the dogma of the philosophy of consciousness.[31] Not to have a visible actor—groupings of people and individuals—in narratives of social affairs is made to seem as antihumanistic (and even anti-democratic). It is not uncommon to hear people react to stories about schools by asking, "Where are the people in the story?" The assumption is of a world in which salvation can be found through positing a prion the universal actors, who will bring the good works, and in which potential is not prevented through the schemas of theorists who "decenter" the subject (see, e.g., Beyer and Liston 1992). Further, since there is no rhetoric of emancipation, then it is assumed that such issues are not of interest.

While this argument about the centering of human purpose and actors seems a reasonable analytic argument at first glance, the sociological consequence of this intellectual stance has not always been empowering. The practical consequences of an unquestioned centering of a subject entail multiple issues of power that are hidden in the rhetorical constructions. Judith Butler (1992) argues, drawing on feminist and postcolonial literature, that the centering of the subject is a particular invention of Western philosophy. When the subject is taken uncritically as the locus of struggle for knowledge about enfranchisement and democracy, scholarship draws from the very models that have been oppressed through the regulation and production of subjects (see also, Young 1990). Such a strategy, she argues, is both a consolidation and concealment of those power relations. Where the agency of individuals or groups are made to seem as natural, there is a tendency to lose sight of how the agendas and categories, which define oppositions, are historically formed. The systems of relevancies are taken for granted.

Further, the decentering of the subject, I have argued, is not to prevent the subject from acting, nor to give up the Enlightenment project. The strategy of decentering the subject is itself a product of the very self-reflectivity produced through the Enlightenment. The decentering of the subject has its own sense of irony: there is an acceptance of the need to construct knowledge that can enable people to act intentionally. The subject is made into a dimension of the questionable and of "insistent contest and resignification" (Butler 1992, 7), not as a foundation of research that is taken as the unquestionable. Constructing histories about how our subjectivities are formed (making the agendas and categories of the subject problematic) can provide a potential space for alternative acts and alternative intentions which are not articulated through the available common senses.

This insertion of the subject, therefore, occurs in at a different location than that argued in the philosophy of consciousness, but it is no less an acceptance of the need of and the challenge for a more viable and just possibility. The humanism is reinserted into social analysis by positing the givenness of the subject as historically constructed so people can break the rules of reason that subjugate.

The political project of many feminists inscribes this shift in intellectual work. An important strategy in constructing different social relations and social spaces for women is to challenge the hegemonies of "reason" that are inscribed in the gendered identities. The "politics of identity" studied in feminist scholarship can be viewed as an integral dimension of the political project itself. It is to historicize gender constructions in order to dislocate the inscribed identities of women and thus open up other possibilities.

The life and work of Foucault is another example of the insertion of the agent and the politics of the intellectual. His work, I think, entails a radical politics in intellectual work as it relates to social movements, but without the hortatory claims that privilege the position of the intellectual in an oracle. Foucault recognized that a particular contribution of intellectual work is undermining how power operates to discipline and regulate. His intellectual production intersects with but is also in a different social space than his activist work in prisons, asylums, and so on. Michel Foucault's practices, as well as those of Pierre Bourdieu not only involves political commitment and engagement but also recognizes the precarious qualities of being critical intellectuals engaging in social movements. They caution us not to reduce practices in one social space to the other, but to understand the historical complexities of their intersections.

Where researcher viewing research as a theory of political action, the position is an effect of power that extends the pastoral power of early church cosmologies. The rules of research as action conflate theory and practice in a manner that blurs fundamental distinctions by placing theoretical and practical knowledge, knowledge, and action into a single continuum that overlaps all constituents with each other (Callewaert, in press). This continuum, Staff Callewaert suggests, makes the researcher's knowledge become that which is normal about teacher's knowledge, a scenario in which "the scientist would have us believe that the practical knowledge that is at work in the actor's mind is scientific theory."

The "decentering" of the subject, to summarize to this point, embodies political commitments to question injustice and domination, but the strategies of intellectual work are different from the Left scholarship of the 1970s and 1980s. In one sense, the strategies of engagement respond to the failures of the older strategies of the Left that certain intellectuals felt in the aftermath of the 1968 rebellions in the United States and Europe as well as the colonial struggles outside of Europe. At the same time, it is also important to recognize the changing terrain of political struggles that relate to the politics of identity, such as in postmodern feminist and postcolonial writings, which tie the scholarship of "The linguistic turn" to political movements. The disruption of how we "tell the truth" about ourselves and others is viewed as a practical strategy for constructing options as to the rules through which power is deployed and themselves made visible.[32]

I return briefly to the argument of the philosophy of consciousness. In that argument the actor makes history; and, it is believed, to have no visible agent is to introduce a determinist world that has no possibility of change. My argument is to problematize that argument; for example, to focus not on actors but on our forms of reasoning and principles of ordering. Such a strategy is to destabilize the reigning forms of "reasoning." A seeming paradox is thus introduced as we revision the philosophical issues of agency and actors as a priori conditions of analysis and social action. In the social theory discussed here, the actor is present, but not as the agent in the narrative of inquiry, but by destablizing the conditions which confine and intern consciousness and its principles of order. Making the forms of reasoning and rules for "telling the truth" potentially contingent, historical, and susceptible to critique, is a practice to dislodge the ordering principles, thereby creating a greater range of possibility for the subject to act.[33]

At this point, I turn to an historical argument about science. Stephen Toulmin (1990), in examining the history of science, argues that we having been living under the specter of certainty since the late seventeenth century, even though the first work in science involved norms of skepticism. He suggests that possibly it is time that we give skepticism a try since certainty has not worked. To put this in a different way, there is a continual rhetorical stance in U.S. critiques of "the linguistic turn" that if one does not make explicit the normative commitments and the subject in the knowledge of social science, no one will act and the world will be incapacitated. This argument is to me an act of tremendous hubris as well as an odd historical argument. I can point to no instance of people being incapacitated to act because of intellectual knowledge; the problem is typically people act in ways that intellectuals do not approve of. Nor have social movements been disbanded when the identification of actors are intellectually blurred. The dualism of a problemating knowledge verses social reconstructions has no historical validity. People do continually act; they have no option but to act in their daily and collective lives. Perhaps, to return to Foucault and Toulmin, a problematizing theory may be one way to consider the politics of knowledge, the politics of intellectual work, and the politics of change.

Notes

1. I borrow the phrase "sea-migration" from the social-intellectual historian, H. Hughes, *The Sea Change: The Migration of Social Thought, 1930–1965*. (New York: Harper and Row, 1975); Charles Tally, "Future History," in *Interpreting the Past, Understanding the Present*, edited by S. Kendrick et al. 9–19 (New York: St. Martin's Press, 1990); L. Hunt, ed., *The New Cultural History* (Berkeley: University of California Press, 1989).

2. It might seem as thought I am asking to have my cake and to eat it as well here. But intellectual problems do not always fall into neat baskets; there are times when I need to ask structural questions as well as questions about power and knowledge. This is an ambiguity that I am willing to live with.

3. See Davis (1941), (1948); Langford (1936); also see Dahlberg (1985) for a discussion of the relation of this literature to theories of pedagogy.

4. Willard Waller, *Sociology of Teaching*, (New York, J. Wiley, 1932).

5. These educational pamphlets (Davis, 1941; 1948) and *The Kappan* monograph of Marxist research (Langford 1936) were brought to my attention in an office of a Swedish colleague, Daniel Kallós.

6. This is also appropriate in describing curriculum history. While scientific reasoning did dominate curriculum traditions, there were approaches that were critical of existing institutional arrangements. These have not been discussed until recently. Thriving in the early years of the century, they became selectively removed from the horizon of the study of schooling by the end of World War II. Few today are aware of the creation of Socialist Sunday Schools at the turn of the century (Teitelbaum 1987); the pedagogical programs of John Childs or Theodore Brameld, the critical interpretation of America's participation in World War I found in the successful 1930s textbooks written by Earle Rugg (Kliebard and Wagner 1987).

7. The shift in discourse also effected curriculum, see Kerry Freedman, 1987.

8. We need to consider the shift in the social space of intellectual work not only as that of intellectual work. In the 1970s, conflict in society shattered the belief in harmony necessary to follow World War II. The social conflict outside and inside the university as well as the more readily accessible European scholarship influenced directions taken into the 1970s. Also, the Left challenges occurred during one of the most expansive worldwide economic periods as well as the expansion of universities in which new academic positions were created. The increase of the social space in the U.S. universities, for example, permitted hiring of faculty in areas of expertise not represented within faculty.

9. One can compare the movement to incorporate European scholarship to explain the cultural conditions of inequities and injustice with the important book by Samuel Bowles and Herbert Gintis. Nineteen percent is drawn mostly from economic analyses; its references strongly omit European thought.

10. The French influence are usually references, but there is also a tradition within German historigraphy. See Reinhart Koselleck, *Futures Past*, trans. K. Tribe (Cambridge, MA: MIT Press, 1991).

11. Pauline Rosenau (1992) makes such a distinction in considering different movements within a field of scholarship that she calls "postmodern."

12. While progress itself is an idea that is at least found in Greek cosmologies, I pose it as a nineteenth-century view because of its tie to ideas of reason and rationalism; and with a hope and redemption that is secularized and related to state intervention practices (see, e.g., Nisbet, Almond et al. 1982; Manuel and Manuel 1979; Nisbet 1980; Popkewitz and Pitman,1986).

13. While these critical traditions are rounded on a philosophical anthropology, the work of the Frankfurt School, particularly Jürgen Habermas, has given greater emphasis to language theory. I will discuss this in the following section (see, e.g., Bernstein 1985).

14. I use the word "universalized"' to indicate the viewing of the different groups as undifferentiated and homogeneous. It is not to argue against being sensitive to such categories, but to understand them as having shifting and multiple boundaries, for they are constructed in historical "contexts."

15. These practices, we should realize, are not totalizing and without ambiguities and resistances, as Jana Sawicki "Feminism and the Power of Foucaldian Discourse," in *After Foucault: Humanistic Knowledge, Postmodern Challenges*, edited by J. Arac (New Brunswick, NJ: Rutgers University, 1988).

16. These theoretical concerns can be found in feminist theory, although focused upon a particular social arena. See Nicholson 1986 and Chris Weedon, *Feminist Practice and Poststructural Theory* (London: Basil Blackwell, 1987); M. Barrett and A. Phillips, *Destabling Theory* (Stanford, CA: Stanford University Press, 1992).

17. One can also understand the Frankfurt School as a reaction to fascism; while French social thought was a more general critique but at the same time responding to its colonial wars in the postwar period (Young 1990).

18. In a study of educational reform, the approach is called a "social epistemological" (Popkewitz 1991). The focus was on how the objects consti-

tuted as the knowledge of schooling are historically formed through power relations that structure coherence in the vagaries of everyday life. The emphasis is on the relational and social embeddedness of knowledge.

19. This can be contrasted to theory, in its more positivist sense, which is to tell you not only what to do but also how to find universal laws. Nor is theory a set of logical formulations that one applies to the practical problems of social life; it is, rather, a more pragmatic interplay as the epistemological categories of inquiry are in a constant interplay with the problems and phenomena of daily life. This is discussed extensively in Pierre Bourdieu 1993; Bourdieu and Wacquant 1992; and Bourdieu et al. (1991).

20. Michel Foucault's concern with how the modern subject is supervised and disciplined through social science discourses, and feminist theories and about how gender relations construct our perceptions, dispositions, and awarenesses are examples of the linguistic turn.

21. Also see James Marshall, "Foucault and Education," *Australian Journal of Education* 33 (2): 99–113 (1989) on the distinction of power.

22. For attempts to construct a historical and social analysis that integrates these categories, see Thomas Dumm, 1993; Nancy Fraser, "Sex, Lies, and the Public Sphere," *Critical Inquiry* 18: 295–612, 1992; Nancy Fraser and Linda Gordon, 1994.

23. These theoretical concerns can be found in feminist theory, although focused upon a particular social arena. See Linda Nicholson 1986, and Chris Weedon, *Feminist Practice*, p. 1987.

24. I am using the notion of region and field interchangeably here. They provide metaphors that signal complex sets of relations through which the objects of the world are known. The notion of region and field also provide a way to consider the location of various discursive systems that interact and change over time.

25. In the work of Michel Foucault and Pierre Bourdieu there are continual references to the notion of region as a site of power.

26. I use the words "community" and "society" as distinctions that are of historical significance. The former involves time/space relations that were local; the later involves more abstract conceptions of self as a citizen of a nation, as a worker, or as an ethnic group within some larger sets of relations. As these abstract notions of society are made part of one's definition of self, it changes the meaning and relationships in which communities are defined.

27. I think that it is important than many European countries do not have the word "curriculum." It is a word that emerged within particular state traditions in which the patterns of governing involve strong relations between official governmental agencies and professional associations of a civil society, such as Britain and the United States.

28. For histories of the curriculum, see, for example, Herbert Kliebard, *Struggle for the American Curriculum*, (New York: Routledge and Kegan Paul); H. Klibard, (1992); B. Franklin, *Building the American Community* (London: Falmer Press, 1986); D. Hamilton; *Towards a Theory of Schooling* (London: Falmer Press, 1989); and I. Goodson, ed., International Perspectives in Curriculum History (London: Croom Helm).

29. It is important to note that most of the discourses about schooling and curriculum were pragmatic, although there was a difference between the instrumental pragmatism of behaviorist psychology and the writings of John Dewey.

30. I explore this history in Thomas Popkewitz, 1991.

31. One needs to read current literature, feminist scholarship, as well as critiques of postmodernism in education to realize how political a question this privileging the subject is.

32. It is an interesting side note to our discussion that Michel Foucault's work has been influential in institutional reforms in multiple countries. This occurred without posturing an epistemology of progress in his scholarship that privileged the intellectual through arguments about some universal notion of the intellectual bringing progress through the a prior positioning of the "subject."

33. While I cannot explore this following in this essay, it is important to understand "The Linguistic Turn" in relation to the revitalization of pragmatism in social theory at the current time. The relation of pragmatism to critical educational research has been argued by C. Cherryholmes, *Power and Criticism* (New York: Teachers College Press, 1988). He maintains that there are certain "contingent foundations" towards normative goals when seeking change, but that these goals are always contingently organized as people work towards findings solutions to their pressing problems. Political strategies are worked out through problem-solving techniques that echo John Dewey's view that problems are not solved but merely give way to other ones; denaturalizing any immanent notion of progress. This pragmatism is found in the writing of the sociology of Pierre Bourdieu, and the historical philosophy of Michel Foucault, and the feminist philosophy of Denise Riley.

References

Almond, Gabriel, Marvin Chodorow, and Roy Pearce, eds. 1982. *Progress and its Discontents*. Berkeley: University of California Press.

Almond, Gabriel & Verba, Sidney (1963). *The Civic Culture: Political attitudes and democracy in five nations*. Princeton, NJ: Princeton.

Anyon, Jean. 1980. "Social Class and the Hidden Curriculum of Work." *Journal of Education* 62: 67–92.

Bachelard, Gaston (1984). *The New Scientific Spirit*. Boston: Beacon Press. (A. Goldhammer, Trans.).

Baker, Bernadette. (In press). Childhood-as-rescue in the emergence and spread of the U.S. public school. In T. Popkewitz & M. Brennan (Eds.), *Foucault's challenge, discourse, knowledge and power in education*. New York: Teachers College Press.

Barrett, Michael, and Anne Phillips, 1992. *Destabilizing Theory: Contemporary Feminist Debates*. Stanford, CA: Stanford University Press. In Press.

Benhabib, Seyla. 1986. *Critque, Norm, and Utopia; A Study of the foundations of Critical Theory*. New York: Colombia University Press.

Berger, Peter, Brigitte Berger, and Hansfried Kellner. 1973. *The Homeless Mind: Modernization and Consciousness*. New York: Vintage Press.

Bernstein, Richard J., ed. 1985. *Habermas and Modernity*. Cambridge, MA: MIT Press.

Beyer, Landon and Liston, Daniel (1992). "Discourse or moral action? A critique of postmodernism." *Educational Theory*, 42, 371–393.

Bourdieu, Pierre (1984). *Distinction: A Social Critique of the Judgment of Taste*. Cambridge: Harvard University Press.

——— (1989). Social space and symbolic power. *Sociological Theory*, 7, 14–25.

——— (1993). *Sociology in question*. London: Sage. (R. Nice, trans.)

Bourdieu, Pierre, and Lok Wacquant. 1992. *An Invitation to Reflexive Sociology*. Chicago: University of Chicago Press.

Bourdieu, P., Jean-Claude Chamboredon, and Jean-Claude Passeron. 1991. *The Craft of Sociology: Epistemological Preliminaries*. Trans. Richard Nice. New York: Walter de Gruyter.

Bowles, Samuel & Gintis, Herbert (1976). *Schooling in Capitalist America*. New York: Basic Books.

Braudel, Fernand. 1980. *On History*. Trans. S. Matthews. Chicago: The University of Chicago Press.

Butler, J. 1992. "Contingent Foundations: Feminism and the Question of "Postmodernism." In *Feminists Theorize the Political*. Edited by Judith Butler and Joan Scott, 3–21. New York: Routledge and Kegan Paul.

Callewaert, Staff (In press). Critical theory and educational discourse. In T. Popkewitz (Ed.), *Critical Theory in Educational Discourse*. Durban, S.A.: Heinemann.

Canguilhem, Georges. 1976. *On the Normal and the Pathological*. London, England: D. Reidel Publishing Co. (C. Fawcett, Trans.; Introduction by Michel Foucault)

————. 1988. *Ideology and Rationality in the History of the Life Sciences*. Cambridge, Massachusetts: MIT Press. (A. Goldhammer, Trans.)

Canning, Kathleen. 1994. "Feminist History after the Linguistic Turn: Historicizing Discourse and Experience." *Signs: Journal of Women in Culture and Society* 19: 368–404.

Carlson, Dennis. 1992. *Teachers and Crisis; Urban School Reform and Teachers' Work Culture*. New York: Routledge.

Cherryholmes, Cleo. 1988. *Power and Criticism: Poststructural Investigations in Education*. New York: Teachers College Press.

Crary, Jonathan. 1990. *Techniques of the Observer: On Vision and Modernity in the Nineteenth Century*. Cambridge, MA: MIT Press.

Dean, Mitchell. 1994. *Critical and Effective Histories; Foucault's Methods and Historical Sociology*. New York: Routledge and Kegan Paul.

Dreyfus, Hubert, and Paul Rabinow. 1983. *Michel Foucault: Beyond Structuralism and Hermeneutics*. Chicago: University of Chicago Press.

Dumm, Thomas. 1987. *Democracy and Punishment: Disciplinary Origins of the United States*. Madison: University of Wisconsin Press.

———— 1993. The new enclosures: Racism in the normalized community. In R. Gooding-Williams (Ed.), *Reading Rodney King: Reading Urban Uprising* (pp. 178–195). New York: Routledge.

Elias, Norbert. 1978. *The history of manners: The civilizing process* (Vol. 1). New York: Pantheon. (E. Jephcott, translator)

Englund, T. 1991. *Rethinking Curriculum History—Towards a Theoretical Reorientation*. Paper presented at the annual meeting of the American Educational Research Association: Symposium on Curriculum History. Chicago, April 1991.

Fendler, Lynn. 1966. What is it Impossible to Think? A Geneology of the Educated Subject. In T. Popkewitz & M. Brennan (Eds.), *Foucault's challenge, discourse, knowledge and power in education*. New York: Teachers College Press.

Foucault, Michel (1975). *The birth of the clinic; an archeology at medical perception*. New York: Vintage. (A. Smith, trans.)

———. 1979. "Governmentality." *Ideology and Consciousness* 6: 5–22.

———. 1980. *Power-Knowledge: Selected Interviews and Other Writings, 1972–1977*. Ed. and Tran. Colin Gordon. New York: Pantheon Books.

———. 1984. "What is enlightenment?," in *The Foucault Reader*. Edited by P. Rabinow, 32–50. New York: Pantheon.

———. 1988. "The Political Technology of Individuals." In *Technologies of the Self*. Edited by L. Martin, H. Gutman, and P. Huttan, 145–162. Amherst, MA: University of Massachusetts Press.

Franklin, Barry M. 1986. *Building the American Community: The School Curriculum and the Search for Social Control*. London: Falmer Press.

———. 1994. *From "Backwardness" to "At-Risk"; Childhood Learning Difficulties and the Contradictions of School Reform*. Albany, NY: The State University of New York Press.

Fraser, Nancy. 1989. *Unruly Practices: Power, Discourse, and Gender in Contemporary Social Theory*. Minneapolis: The University of Minnesota Press.

———. 1992. "Sex, Lies, and the Public Sphere: Some Reflections on the Confirmations of Clarence Thomas." *Critical Inquiry* 18: 295–612.

Fraser, Nancy & Gordon, Linda (1994). "A genealogy of dependency: Tracing a keyword of two U.S. Welfare States." *Signs: Journal of Women in Culture and Society, 19*, 309–367.

Fuller, M. with S. Stiegelbauer. 1991. *The New Meaning of Educational Change*. New York: Teachers College Press.

Freedman, Kerry (1987). Art education as social production: Culture, society and politics in the formation of the curriculum. In T. Popkewitz (Ed.), *The Formation of School Subjects: The Struggle for creating an American Institution* (pp. 63–84). London: Falmer.

Giddens, Anthony. 1990. *The Consequences of Modernity*. Stanford, CA: Stanford University Press.

Giroux, Henry A. 1983. *Theory and Resistance in Education: A Pedagogy for the Opposition*. South Hadley, MA: Bergin and Garvey.

———. 1992. *Border Crossings: Cultural Workers and the Politics of Education*. New York: Routlege and Kegan Paul.

Goodson, Ivor, ed. 1987. *International Perspectives in Curriculum History*. London: Croom Helm.

Guilbaut, Serge (1983). *How New York stole the idea of modern art: Abstract expressionism, Freedom and the Cold War*. Chicago: University of Chicago. (A. Goldhammer, trans.)

Habermas, Jürgen. 1971. *Knowledge and Human Interest*. Trans. J. Shapiro. Boston: Beacon Press.

————. 1981. *The Theory of Communicative Action; Reason and the Rationaliation of Society*. Trans. T. McCarthy. Vol. 1. Boston: Beacon Press.

————. 1987. *The Theory of Communicative Action. Lifeworld and System: A Critique of Functionalist Reason*. Trans. T. McCarthy. Vol. 2. Boston: Beacon Press.

Hacking, Ian. 1986. "The Archeology of Foucault." In *Foucault; A Critical Reader*. Edited by D. Hoy, 27–40. Cambridge, MA: Basil Blackwell.

Hall, Stuart (1986). "The problem of ideology-Marxism without guarantees." *Journal of Communication Inquiry, 10*, 28–43.

Hamilton, D. 1989. *Towards a Theory of Schooling*. London: The Falmer Press.

Hughes, H. 1975. *The Sea Change: The Migration of Social Thought 1930–1965*. New York: Harper and Row.

Hultqvist, Kenneth (In press). A history of the present on children's welfare in Sweden. In T. Popkewitz & M. Brennan (Eds.), *Foucault's challenge, discourse, knowledge and power in Education*. New York: Teachers College Press.

Hunt, Lynn, ed. 1989. *The New Cultural History*. Berkeley. University of California Press.

Johannesson, Ingolfur (1991). *The formation of educational reform as a social field in Iceland and the social strategies of educationalist, 1966–1991*. Unpublished Ph.D. Dissertation, University of Wisconsin-Madison.

————. 1993. "Principles of Legitimation in Educational Discourse in Iceland and the Production of Progress." *Journal of Educational Policy* 8: 339–351.

Kliebard, Herbert M. 1987. *Struggle for the American Curriculum*. New York: Routledge and Kegan Paul.

Kliebard, Herbert & Wegner, Greg (1987). Harold Rugg and the Reconstruction of the Social Studies Curriculum: The Treatment of the "Great War" in his Textbook Series. In T. Popkewitz (Ed.), *The Formation of School Subjects: The Struggle for Creating an American Institution* (pp. 268–288). London: Falmer Press.

Koselleck, Reinhart 1991. *Futures Past: On the Semantics of Historical Time.* Trans. K. Tribe. Cambridge, MA: The MIT Press.

Kuhn, Thomas (1970). *The Structure of Scientific Revolutions* (2nd ed.). Chicago: University of Chicago Press.

Kuttner, Robert. 1991. *The End of Laissez-faire: National Purpose and the Global Economy after the Cold War.* New York: Alfred A. Knopf.

Ladwig, James (1996). *Academic distinctions: Theory and methodology in the sociology of school knowledge.* New York: Routledge. 1996.

Lather, Patricia Ann. 1986. "Research as Praxis." *Harvard Educational Review* 56: 257–275.

Lekachman, Robert (1982). *Greed is not enough, Reaganomics.* New York: Pantheon Books. 1982.

Luke, Allan. 1990. *The Body Literate: Discursive Inscription in Early Literacy Training.* Paper given at the 12th World Congress of Sociology, July 8–13 1990, Madrid, Spain.

Lundgren, Ulf P. 1983. *Between Hope and Happening: Text and Contexts in Curriculum.* Geelong, Australia: Deakin University Press.

Mahon, M. 1992. *Foucault's Nietzschean Genealogy: Truth, Power, and the Subject.* Albany: State University of New York Press.

Manuel, Frank E., and Fritzie P. Manuel. 1979. *Utopian Thought in the Western World.* Cambridge, MA: Harvard University Press.

Marshall, James O. 1989. "Foucault and Education." *Australian Journal of Education* 33, no. 2: 99–113.

McLaren, Peter. 1994. *Life in Schools: An Introduction to Critical Pedagogy in the Foundations of Education.* New York: Longman Publishers.

Meyer, J. 1986. "The Politics of Educational Crisis in the United States." In *Educational Politics in Crisis.* Edited by William Cummings et al. New York: Praeger.

Napoli, Donald S.. 1981. *Architects of Adjustment: The History of the Psychological Profession in the United States.* Port Washington, NY: Kennikat Press.

Nicholson, Linda. 1986. *Gender and History, The Limits of Social Theory in the Age of the Family.* New York: Columbia University Press.

Nisbet, R. 1980. *History of the Idea of Progress.* New York: Basic Books.

Noble, David (Ed.). (1991). *The Classroom Arsenal.* London: The Falmer Press.

Noujain, E. 1987. History as Genealogy: An Exploration of Foucault's Approach. In *Contemporary French Philosophy*. Edited by A. Griffiths, 157–174. New York: Cambridge University Press.

Novick, Peter. 1988. *That Noble Dream: The "Objectivity Question" and the American Historical Profession*. New York: Cambridge University Press.

Öhrn, E. 1993. "Gender, Influence, and Resistance in School." *British Journal of Sociology of Education* 14, no. 2: 147–158.

Pignatelli, F. 1993. "What Can I Do? Foucault on Freedom and the Question of Teacher Agency." *Educational Theory* 43(4): 411–432.

Popkewitz, Thomas (1987). *The Formation of School Subjects: The Struggle for Creating an American Institution*. London: Falmer Press.

———. (1991). *A Political Sociology of Educational Reform: Power/Knowlege in Teaching, Teacher Education, and Research*. New York: Teachers College Press.

———. (1993). "Professionalization in teaching and teacher education: Some notes on its history, ideology and potential." *Teaching and Teacher Education,* 10, 1–14.

———. (in press). *The spatial politics of educational knowledge, constituting the urban and rural teacher*. New York: Teachers College Press.

———. *The School Politics of Educational Knowlege: Constituting the Urban and Rural Teacher*. New York: Teachers College Press. In press.

Popkewitz, Thomas and Brennan, eds. 1996. *Foucault's Challenge, Discourse, Knowledge and Power in Education*. New York: Teachers College Press.

———. *The Denial of Change in the Process of Change: Systems of Ideas and the Construction of National Evaluations*. Oslo, Norway: The Norwegian Royal Ministry of Church, Education, and Research. In press.

Popkewitz, T., and A. Pitman. 1986. "The Idea of Progress and the Legitimation of State Agendas. American Foucault: Proposals for School Reform." *Curriculum and Teaching* 1(1–2): 11–24.

Popkewitz, T., A. Pitman, and A. Barry. 1986. Educational Reform and its Millermial Quality: The 1980s. *The Journal of Curriculum Studies* 18: 267–284.

Popkewitz, T., B. Robert Tabachnik, Kenneth Zeichner. 1979. "Dulling the Senses: Researching Teacher Education." *Journal of Teacher Education*. Vol. 30, no. 5 p. 52–60.

Rajchman, John. 1985. *Michel Foucault: The Freedom of Philosophy*. New York: Columbia University Press.

Riley, Denise (1988). *Am I That Name: Reminism and the Category of "Women" in History*. Minneapolis: University of Minnesota Press.

Roseneu, Pauline. 1992. *Post-Modernism and the Social Sciences, Insights, Inroads, and Intrusions*. Princeton, NJ. The University of Princeton Press.

Sampson, Edward. 1993. Identity Politics; Challenges to Psychology's Understanding. *American Psychologist* 48: 1219–1230.

Sawicki, Jayna. 1988. "Feminism and the Power of Foucaldian Discourse." In *After Foucault: Humanistic Knowledge, Postmodern Challenges*. Edited by J. Arac, 161–178. New Brunswick, NJ: Rutgers University.

Scott, Joan (1991). *The evidence of experience*. Critical Inquiry, *17*, 773–797.

Shor, Ira (1986). *Culture Wars: School and Society in the Conservative Restoration 1969–1984*. Boston: Routledge and Kegan Paul.

Silva, Edward and Slaughter, Sheila (1984). *Serving Power: The Making of the Academic Socil Science Expert*. Westport, CT: Greenwood Press.

Spivak, Gayatin. 1992. "The Politics of Translation." In *Destabilizing Theory: Contemporary Feminist Debates*. Edited by M. Barrett and A. Phillips, 177–200. Stanford: Stanford University Press.

Tally, Charles. 1990. "Future History." In *Interpreting the Past, Understanding the Present*. Edited by S. Kendrick, P. Straw, and D. McCrone, 9–19. New York: St. Martin's Press.

Teitelbaum, Kenneth (1987). Outside the Selective Tradition: Socialist curriculum for Children in the United States, 1900–1920. In T. Popkewitz (Ed.), *The Formation of School Subjects: The Struggle for Creating an American Institution* (pp. 238–267). London: Falmer Press.

Toulmin, Stephen (1972). *Human understanding: The collective uses and evolution of concepts*. Princeton, NJ: Princeton University Press.

———. (1988). The recovery of practical philosophy. *American Scholar, 57*, 337–352.

———. (1990). *Cosmopolis, the Hidden Agenda of Modernity*. New York: The Free Press.

Wagner, Peter (1994). *The Sociology of Modernity*. New York: Routledge.

Waller, Willard (1965). *The Sociology of Teaching*. New York: J. Wiley.

Weedon, Chris. 1987. *Feminist Practice and Poststructural Theory*. London: Basil Blackwell.

Weis, Lois, and Michelle Fine, eds. 1993. *Beyond Silenced Voices: Class, Race, and Gender in United States Schools*. Albany: State University of New York Press.

Willis, Paul (1977). *Learning to Labour: How Working Class Kids Get Working Class Jobs*. Farnborough: Saxon House.

Wittgenstein, Ludwig (1966). *The philosophical investigations: A collection of critical essays* (2nd (Originally published in 1953) ed.). Notre Dame: University of Notre Dame Press. (G. Pitcher, ed).

Young, Robert (1990). *White mythologies: Writing, history and the West*. New York: Routledge.

4

Becoming Right: Education and the Formation of Conservative Movements

⬜

Michael W. Apple and Anita Oliver

Introduction

In *Social Analysis of Education*, Philip Wexler urged critical sociological work in education to devote much more of its attention to social movements.[1] These social movements provide crucial elements in determining the stability and instability of the practices and policies involved in curricula, teaching, evaluation, and beliefs about schooling, the state, and the economy in general. Struggles over schooling both participate in the formation of oppositional social and religious movements and are the subjects of these social and religious movements.[2]

Further, social movements give meaning to people's identities. In essence, they announce "I am (we are) here."[4] While some of these movements and identities may embody a politics with which many of our readers may disagree, there can be no doubt that they have become increasingly involved in struggles over what schools do and whose knowledge schools teach.

Throughout the United States, national organizations have been formed by conservatives to fight against what counts as "official knowledge" in schools. These organizations often reach out to local groups of "concerned citizens" and offer financial and legal assistance in their battles with school systems at state and local levels. Citizens for Excellence in Education, the Eagle Forum, the Western Center for Law and Religious Freedom, and Focus on the Family are among the most active. Mel and Norma Gabler, as well, have developed a system of opposition that aids parents and rightist groups throughout the country in their attempts to challenge educational policies and practices and to either change the content of books or have them removed from schools. The "Christian Right" has become an increasingly powerful movement in the United States, one that has had major effects on educational policy deliberations, curriculum, and teaching.[4]

Yet, it would be all too easy to read these organizations' imprint everywhere. Indeed, this would be a serious mistake not only empirically, but also conceptually and politically as well. While there is intentionality, too often we see rightist movements conspiratorially. In the process, we not only reduce the complexity that surrounds the politics of education, but we also take refuge in binary oppositions of good and bad. We, thereby, ignore the elements of possible insight in some (even right-wing) oppositional groups and ignore the places where decisions could have been made that would not have contributed to the growth of these movements.

A basic question undergirding this inquiry is this: How does the religious right grow? Our claim is that this can only be fully understood by focusing on the interactions, ones that often occur at a local level, between the state and the daily lives of ordinary people as they interact with institutions.

In no way do we wish to minimize the implications of the growth of rightist social movements. Indeed, the conservative restoration has had truly negative affects on the lives of millions of people in a number of countries.[5] Rather, we want to provide a more dynamic view of how and why such movements actually are found to be attractive. Too often, not only do current analyses assume what has to be explained, but they place all of the blame for the growth of rightist positions on the persons who "become Right." No one focuses on the larger sets of relations that might push people toward a more aggressive right-wing stance. Yet, this is exactly our point. People often "become Right" due to their interactions with unresponsive institutions. Thus, part of our argument is that there is a close connection between how the state is structured and acts and the formation of social movements and identities.

In what follows, we combine elements of neo-Gramscian and poststructural analyses. Our aim is partly to demonstrate how the former—with its focus on the state, on the formation of hegemonic blocs, on new social alliances and the generation of consent—and the latter—with its focus on the local, on the formation of subjectivity and identity and on the creation of subject positions—can creatively work together to illuminate crucial parts of the politics of education.[6] Behind this analysis is a particular position on what critical research should do.

In other publications, one of us has argued that, in all too much of the current critically and oppositionally oriented literature in education, "our words have taken on wings." Theoretical layer upon theoretical layer is added without coming to grips with the real and existing complexities of schooling. This is *not* an argument against theory. Rather, it takes the position that our eloquent abstractions are weakened in the extreme if they do not get formed in relationship to the supposed object of these abstractions—schooling and its economic, political, and cultural conditions of existence. Letting the daily life surrounding the politics of educational institutions rub against you is wholly salutary in this regard. In the absence of this, all too many "critical educational theorists" coin trendy neologisms but remain all too disconnected from the lives and struggles of real people in real institutions.[7] We hope to overcome that here.

"Accidental" Formations

As Geoff Whitty, Tony Edwards, and Sharon Gewirtz document in their analysis of the growth of conservative initiatives such as city technology colleges in England, rightist policies and their effects are not always the result of carefully planned initiatives.[8] They often have an accidental quality to them. This is not to deny intentionality. Rather, the historical specificities of local situations and the complexities of multiple power relations in each site mean that conservative policies are highly mediated and have unforeseen consequences. If this is the case for many instances of overt attempts at moving educational policy and practice in a conservative direction, it is even more true when we examine how rightist sentiments grow among local actors. Most analyses of "The Right" assume a number of things. They all too often assume a unitary ideological movement, seeing it as a relatively uncontradictory group rather than a complex assemblage of different tendencies many of which are in a tense and unstable relationship to each other. Many analyses also take "The Right" as a "fact," as a given. It already exists as a massive structuring force that is able to work its way into daily life and into our discourses in well planned ways. This takes for granted one of the most important questions that needs to be investigated. How does the Right get *formed*?

In previous work, it was argued that rightist policies are often compromises both between the Right and other groups and among the various tendencies within the conservative alliance. Thus, neo-liberal, neo-conservative, authoritarian populist fundamentalist religious groups, and a particular fraction of the new middle class all have found a place under the ideological umbrella provided by broad rightist tendencies. It was also shown how conservative discourses act in creative ways to disarticulate prior connections and rearticulate groups of people into this larger ideological movement by connecting to the real hopes, fears, and conditions of people's daily lives and by providing seemingly "sensible" explanations for the current troubles people are having.[9] Yet, this too gives the impression that the creative educational project that the Right is engaged in—to convince considerable numbers of people to join the broader alliance—works its way to the local level in smooth, rational steps. This may not be the case.

We want to argue that much more mundane experiences and events often underlie the rightist turn at a local level in many cases. While the Right *has* engaged in concerted efforts to move our discourse and practices in particular directions, its success in convincing people is dependent on those things that Whitty, Edwards, and Gewirtz have called "accidents." Of course, "accidents" are often patterned and are themselves the results of complex relations of power. But, the point is still a telling one. Acceptance of conservative tendencies is built in not always planned ways and may involve tensions and contradictory sentiments among the people who ultimately "become Right."

In illuminating this, we shall first describe the assemblage of cultural assumptions, fears, and tensions that underpin the cultural and religious right in the United States.[10] Second, we shall argue that the ways the bureaucratic state has developed is ideally suited to confirm these fears and tensions. Third, we shall then instantiate these arguments by focusing on a specific case in which a textbook controversy led to the formation of rightist sentiments in a local community. Finally, we want to suggest a number of important implications of this analysis for the politics of education and for attempts at countering the growth of ultra-rightist movements in education.

A World of Danger

There is a story told by a teacher about a discussion that arose in her elementary school classroom. A number of students were excitedly talking about some "dirty words" that had been scribbled on the side of a building during Halloween. Even after the teacher asked the children to get ready for their language arts lesson, most of them continued to talk about "those words." As often happens, the teacher sensed that this could not be totally ignored. She asked her students what *made* words "dirty." This provoked a long and productive discussion among these second graders about how certain words were used to hurt people and how "this wasn't very nice."

Throughout it all, one child had not said a thing, but was clearly deeply involved in listening. Finally, he raised his hand and said that he knew "the dirtiest word in the world." He was too embarrassed to say the word out loud (and also knew that it would be inappropriate to even utter it in school). The teacher asked him to come up later and whisper it in her ear. During recess, he came over to the teacher, put his head close to hers and quietly, secretly, said "the word." The teacher almost broke up with laughter. The dirty word, that word that could never be uttered, was "statistics." One of the boy's parents worked for a local radio station and every time the ratings came out, the parent would angrily state, "Those damn statistics!" What could be dirtier?

For large numbers of parents and conservative activists, other things are a lot "dirtier." Discussions of the body, of sexuality, of politics and personal values, and of any of the social issues surrounding these topics, are a danger zone. To deal with them in any way in school is not wise. But if they are going to be dealt with, these conservative activists demand that they must be handled in the context of traditional gender relations, the nuclear family, the "free market" economy, and according to sacred texts like the Bible.

Take sexuality education as a case in point. For cultural conservatives, sex education is one of the ultimate forms of "secular humanism" in schools. It is attacked by the New Right both as a major threat to parental control of schools and because of its teaching of "nontraditional" values. For the coalition of forces that make up the New Right, sex education can destroy the family and religious morality "by encouraging masturbation, premarital sex, lots of sex, sex without guilt, sex for fun, homosexual sex, sex."[11] These groups view it as education for, not about sex, which will create an obsession which can override "Christian morality" and threaten God-given gender roles.[12] These were important elements in the intense controversy over the Rainbow Curriculum in New York City, for example, and certainly contributed to the successful moves to oust the city's school superintendent from his position.

The vision of gender roles that stands behind these attacks is striking. Allen Hunter, one of the most perceptive commentators on the conservative agenda, argues that the New Right sees the family as an organic and divine unity that "resolves male egoism and female selflessness."[13] As he goes on to say:

> Since gender is divine and natural . . . there is [no] room for legitimate political conflict. . . . Within the family women and men—stability and dynamism—are harmoniously fused when undisturbed by modernism, liberalism, feminism, [and] humanism which not only threaten masculinity and femininity directly, but also [do so] through their effects on children and youth. . . . "Real women," i.e., women who know themselves to be wives and mothers, will not threaten the sanctity of the home by striving for self. When men or women challenge these gender roles they break with God and nature; when liberals, feminists, and secular humanists prevent them from fulfilling these roles they undermine the divine and natural supports upon which society rests.[14]

All of this is connected to their view that public schooling itself is a site of immense danger.[15] In the words of conservative activist Tim La Haye, "Modern public education is the most dangerous force in a child's life: religiously, sexually, economically, patriotically, and physically."[16] This is connected to the cultural conservative's sense of loss surrounding schooling and community.

> Until recently, as the New Right sees it, schools were extensions of home and traditional morality. Parents could entrust their children to public schools because they were locally controlled and reflected Biblical and parental values. However, taken over by alien, elitist forces schools now interpose themselves between parents and children. Many people experience fragmentation of the unity between family, church, and school as a loss of control of daily life, one's children, and America. Indeed, [the New Right] argues that parental control of education is Biblical, for "in God's plan, the primary responsibility for educating the young lies in the home and directly in the father."[17]

Here it is clearly possible to see why, say, sexuality education has become such a major issue for conservative movements. Its very existence, and especially its most progressive and honest moments, threatens crucial elements of the entire world view of these parents and activists.

Of course, issues of sexuality, gender, and the body are not the only focus of attention of cultural conservatives. These concerns are linked to a much larger array of questions about what counts as "legitimate" content in schools. And in this larger arena of concern about the entire corpus of school knowledge, conservative activists have had no small measure of success in pressuring textbook publishers and in altering aspects of state educational policy as well. This is critical, since the text still remains the dominant definition of the curriculum in schools not only in the United States but also in many other nations as well.[18]

For example, the power of these groups can be seen in the "self-censorship" in which publishers engage. Thus, for instance, a number of publishers of high school literature anthologies have chosen to include Martin Luther King's "I Have a Dream" speech, but only after all references to the intense racism of the United States have been removed?[19]

Another example is provided by the textbook law in Texas which mandates texts that stress patriotism, authority, and the discouragement of "deviance." Since most textbook publishers aim the content and organization of their texts at what will be approved in a small number of populous states that in essence approve and purchase their texts *statewide*, this gives Texas (and California) immense power in determining what will count as legitimate knowledge throughout the entire country.[20]

Quoting from the Texas legislation on textbooks, the author of a recent study of textbook controversy describes it in this way.

> Textbook content shall "promote citizenship and understanding of the essentials and benefits of the free enterprise system, emphasizing patriotism and respect for recognized authority, and promote respect for individual rights." Textbooks shall not "include selections or works which encourage or condone civil disobedience, social strife, or disregard of law," nor shall they "contain material which serves to undermine authority" or "which would cause embarrassing situations or interference in the learning atmosphere of the classroom." Finally, textbooks approved for use in Texas "shall not encourage lifestyles deviating from generally accepted standards of society." The Texas law's endorsement of free enterprise and traditional lifestyles and its prohibition of lawlessness and rebellion are regularly cited by textbook activists to support their efforts to remove material which, in their view, promotes socialism, immorality or disobedience.[21]

Clearly here, the "family" stands as the building block of society, "the foundation upon which all of culture is maintained." It provides civilization with its moral foundation. The family's strength and stability, in essence, determine the vitality and moral life of the larger society.[22] One of the ways it guarantees this is through its central place in instilling children with the proper moral values and traits of character that can withstand the "moral decay" seen all around us.

Yet, it is not only the family's place as a source of moral authority that is important here. The family, and the "traditional" gender roles within it, demands that "people act for the larger good" by taming the pursuit of self-interest that is so powerful in the (supposedly) male public world.[23] Rebecca Klatch notes that:

> Implicit in this image of the family is the social conservative conception of human nature. Humans are creatures of unlimited appetites and instincts. Left on their own, they would turn the world into a chaos of seething passions, overrun by narrow self-interest. Only the moral authority of the family or the church restrains human passions, transforming self-interest into the larger good. The ideal society is one in which individuals are integrated into a moral community, bound together by faith, by common moral values, and by obeying the dictates of the family, church, and God.[24]

In this way of constructing the world, *all* of the nation's problems are attributed to moral decay. The signs of decay are everywhere: "sexual promiscuity, pornography, legalized abortion, and the displacement of marriage, family, and motherhood."[25] Even widespread poverty is at base a moral problem, but not in the way progressives might see this as the results of social policies that have little ethical concern for their effects on the poor and working class. Rather, as George Gilder put it in a speech at the conservative activist Phyllis Schlafly's celebration of the ultimate defeat of the Equal Rights Amendment, "The crucial problems of the poor in America are not material. This is something [we] must understand. The poor in America are richer than the upper fifth of all people during most of America's history. They are some of the richest people in the world. The crucial problems of the poor are not material but spiritual."[26]

Given this definition of the problem, poverty, and other aspects of moral decay so visible in our major institutions such as schools can only be solved through moral renewal, prayer, repentance, and a clear recognition of the centrality of religious belief, morality, and "decency."[27]

We should not take lightly the view of schooling—and the perception of reality that lies behind this view—that such movements espouse. Perhaps this can be best seen in a letter circulated to conservative parents and activists by the Eagle Forum, one of the most active rightist groups associated with Phyllis Schlafly. The following letter, or similar ones, has been found throughout school systems in the United States. It takes the form of a formal notification about parents' rights to schools boards.

> Dear School Board President ————,
>
> I am the parent of ———————, who attends ———————
> School. Under U.S. legislation and court decisions, parents have the primary responsibility for their children's education, and pupils have certain rights which the schools may not deny. Parents have the right to assure that their children's beliefs and moral values are not undermined by the schools. Pupils have the right to have and to hold their values and moral standards without direct or indirect manipulation by the schools through curricula, textbooks, audio-visual materials, or supplementary assignments.
>
> Accordingly, I hereby request that my child be involved in NO school activities or materials listed below unless I have first reviewed all the relevant materials and have given my written consent for their use:
>
> • Psychological and psychiatric examinations, tests, or surveys that are designed to elicit information about attitudes, habits, traits, opinions, beliefs, or feelings of an individual or group;
>
> • Psychological and psychiatric treatment that is designed to affect behavioral, emotional, or attitudinal characteristics of an individual or group;
>
> • Values clarification, use of moral dilemmas, discussion of religious or moral standards, role-playing or open-ended discussions of situations involving moral issues, and survival games including life/death decisions exercises;
>
> • Death education, including abortion, euthanasia, suicide, use of violence, and discussions of death and dying;
>
> • Curricula pertaining to alcohol and drugs;
>
> • Instruction in nuclear war, nuclear policy, and nuclear classroom games;
>
> • Anti-nationalistic, one-world government or globalism curricula;

- Discussion and testing on inter-personal relationships; discussions of attitudes toward parents and parenting;

- Education in human sexuality, including premarital sex, extramarital sex, contraception, abortion, homosexuality, group sex and marriages, prostitution, incest, masturbation, bestiality, divorce, population control, and roles of males and females; sex behavior and attitudes of student and family;

- Pornography and any materials containing profanity and/or sexual explicitness;

- Guided fantasy techniques; hypnotic techniques; imagery and suggestology;

- Organic evolution, including the idea that man has developed from previous or lower types of living things;

- Discussions of witchcraft and the occult, the supernatural, and Eastern mysticism;

- Political affiliations and beliefs of student and family; personal religious beliefs and practices;

- Mental and psychological problems and self-incriminating behavior potentially embarrassing to the student or family;

- Critical appraisals of other individuals with whom the child has family relationships;

- Legally recognized privileged and analogous relationships, such as those of lawyers, physicians and ministers;

- Income, including the student's role in family activities and finances;

- Non-academic personality tests; questionnaires on personal and family life and attitudes;

- Autobiography assignments; log books, diaries, and personal journals;

- Contrived incidents for self-revelation; sensitivity training, group encounter sessions, talk-ins, magic circle techniques, self-evaluation and auto-criticism; strategies designed for self-disclosure (e.g., zig-zag);

- Sociograms; sociodrama; psychodrama; blindfold walks; isolation techniques.

The purpose of this letter is to preserve my child's rights under the Protection of Pupil Rights Amendment (the Hatch Amendment) to the General Education Provisions Act, and under its regulations as published in the Federal Register of Sept. 6, 1984, which became effective Nov. 12, 1984. These regulations provide a procedure for filing complaints first at the local level, and then with the U.S. Department of Education. If a voluntary remedy fails, federal funds can be withdrawn from those in violation of the law. I respectfully ask you to send me a substantive response to this letter attaching a copy of your policy statement on procedures for parental permission requirements, to notify all my child's teachers, and to keep a copy of this letter in my child's permanent file. Thank you for your cooperation.

Sincerely,

It is clear from this letter how much the state is distrusted. Here, schooling *is* a site of immense danger. The range of prohibitions covered documents, the sense of alarm these parents and activists feel, and why they would closely examine what their children are supposedly experiencing in schools. In the minds of conservatives, raising these objections is not censorship; it is protecting the entire range of things that are at the center of their being.

State Formation and Bureaucratic Control

It is in the conflict over this range of issues that new parts of the state are formed. We have often employed a reified vision of the state. The state is seen as a thing. It is simply there. Yet, at all levels, the state is *in formation*. Not only is "it" an arena in which different groups struggle to legitimate and institute their own senses of needs and needs discourses,[28] but it also is itself formed and changed in both its content and form by these struggles.

Throughout the United States at local levels, school districts have established mechanisms to regulate conflict over official knowledge. As we showed, rightist populist social movements, especially Christian fundamentalists, have raised fundamental (no pun intended) objections to an extensive array of curricula, pedagogy, and evaluative procedures. Thus, for example, textbooks in reading and literature have been challenged for their "secular humanism," their sponsorship of "socialism," occultism, their "overemphasis" on minority culture, and even their supposedly veiled espousal of vegetarianism.[29]

Focusing on textbook controversies is crucial in a number of ways. First, in the absence of an overt and official national curriculum in the United States, the standardized textbook that is partly regulated by and aimed at widespread state adoption provides much of the framework for a hidden national curriculum.[30] Second, even though many teachers use the textbook as a jumping off point rather than something one must always follow slavishly, it is the case that teachers in the United States do in fact use the text as the fundamental curriculum artifact in classrooms to a remarkable degree. Third, the absence of a codified national curriculum and the history of populist sentiment here means that many of the most powerful protests over what counts as official knowledge in schools have historically focused on the textbook itself. It provides an ideal fulcrum to pry loose the lid from the dynamics underlying the cultural politics of education and the social movements which form it and are formed by it.

Given the power of these groups, many school districts have offices and/or standardized procedures for dealing "efficiently and safely" with these repeated challenges. One of the effects of such procedures has often been that the institutions construct nearly all challenges to official knowledge in particular ways—as censorship, and as coming from organized new right groups. Thus, the educational apparatus of the state expands as a defensive mechanism to protect itself against such populist pressure. Yet, once this structure is established its "gaze" defines social criticism in ways it can both understand and deal with. This has crucial theoretical and political implications for how we see the role of the state in the politics of education. For it is in the growth of such bureaucratic procedures and the associated length of time that it takes to rule on challenges that the Right often finds fertile soil. In order to understand this, we need to say more about how we should see the state.

"The state may best be studied as a process of rule."[31] In Bruce Curtis's words, state formation involves "the centralization and concentration of relations of economic and political power and authority in society." State formation typically involves the appearance or the reorganization of monopolies over the means of violence, taxation, administration, and *over symbolic systems.*[32] In essence, state formation is about the creation, stabilization, and normalization of relations of power and authority?[33]

Education is not immune to this process. This is part of a much longer history in which the state, through its bureaucratic administration, seeks to keep the "interests of education" not only from the control of elites but also from the influence of populist impulses from below.[34] This is crucial to the story we are telling here.

Bureaucratic systems have substance. Émile Durkheim recognized a century ago that efficiency "is an ethical construct, one whose adoption involves a moral and political choice." The institutionalization

of efficiency as a dominant bureaucratic norm is not a neutral technical matter. It is, profoundly, an instance of cultural power relations.[35]

No bureaucracy can function well unless those who interact
with it "adopt specific attitudes, habits, beliefs, and orientations."
"Proper" attitudes toward authority, "appropriate" beliefs about the
legitimacy of expertise, willingness to follow all of the "necessary"
rules and procedures—these are crucial to the maintenance of
power,[36] even when such power is recognized as acceptable.

This process of freeing the interests of education from elite and
popular control was and is a crucial element in state formation.[37]
The state grows to protect itself and the self-proclaimed "democratic" interests it represents in response to such attempts at control. In
the instance of Christian fundamentalists, insurgent cultural forces
from below—the "censors"—have created a situation in which the
state expands its policing function over knowledge and establishes
new bureaucratic offices and procedures to channel dissent into "legitimate" channels.

Curtis puts it exactly correctly when he states that the "stan-
dardization and neutralization of judgments [has] tended to make
implicit, rather than explicit, the class-specific content of educational
governance."[38] Bureaucratic procedures that have been established to
promote "the public interest"—and which in some interpretations
may do so—are there to try to forge a consensus around and an acceptance of cultural legitimacy that may be rooted in strikingly antagonistic perceptions of the world.

Yet, what happens when these "appropriate" and "proper" beliefs and responses fracture? What happens when the state loses its
hold on legitimate authority, when its clients—in interaction with it
over a period of time—come to refuse its monopoly over what counts
as legitimate symbolic authority?

To answer these questions, we now want to turn to how this dynamic works out in the real world by focusing on the conflict over a
textbook series in a local school district where the parties in con-
tention became immensely polarized and where populist pressure
from below increasingly turned actively conservative. In the process,
we shall show how the workings of the bureaucratic state paradoxically provide fertile ground for parents to "become Right."

Professionals and Censors

The site of this study, Citrus Valley, is a semi-rural community
of about 30,000 people now within commuting distance from several

larger western cities because of the growth of the interstate highway system. It is in the midst of a building boom that is predicted to almost double the population of the area. This is likely to change the atmosphere from that of a quiet, slow moving, rural community to one resembling a small, faster paced city. Much of its growing population will likely consist of commuters.[39]

The average household income in 1989 at the beginning of the controversy was estimated to be $23,500. Demographic data indicate that nearly twenty-five percent of the current population is between the ages of 65 and 79. The many "senior citizens," and the approximately fifty trailer parks, suggest that Citrus Valley is seen by many people as an attractive place to retire as well.

There are no large industries in Citrus Valley, but the city would certainly like some to move in. In fact, the largest single employer is the school district, with just under 600 employees of which half are teachers. In 1980, 72 percent of the adult residents over age 25 had a high school education or less. Approximately 10 percent had graduated from college. A significant portion of the residents with college degrees work for the school district. The population of Citrus Valley is 95 percent European American, with a slowly growing Latino population. It is primarily a working-class community, but one with a clearly growing and increasingly visible commuter middle class.

Even with the growth of commuting, a large portion of the townspeople are lifetime residents. One person described the community as "people, it's a real ethic here. People believe in traditional values. And they believe in responsibility and working as a community."

Certain things are evident in this brief demographic description. One is the changing nature of class relations in the community. People are moving out of the large metropolitan area newly within commuting distance of Citrus Valley. Fears of violence, a search for "better schools," lower housing prices, and other elements are producing a situation in which members of the new middle class are becoming increasingly visible in the town. This class fraction is noted for its sympathy for child-centered pedagogy and for what Basil Bernstein has called "loosely framed" and "loosely classified curriculum and teaching."[40] Thus, a tension between "country" and "city" and between class-related educational visions may lie beneath the surface.

Second, the changing nature of the community is occurring at a time of perceived fears of downward mobility and a very real economic crisis in the United States where many western states—and the one in which Citrus Valley is located in particular—are experiencing economic dislocation and its attendant apprehensions about the future. Needless to say, farm economies are certainly not immune to these fears and dislocations. For many individuals, this will have a profound impact on their sense of what schooling is for, on what should and should not be taught, and on who should control it. For many working-class women and men, economic anxieties and fears of cultural collapse are rightly difficult to separate.

In the middle of these transformations and the possible tensions that underlie the town's outward tranquillity and "tradition," the school district has decided to move to a new orientation in its language arts program. In this, it was following the guidelines and timetable laid out by the state's Department of Education for all school districts. The state guidelines strongly urged school districts to use a literature-based approach to teaching language arts and in fact Citrus Valley had already previously begun employing such an approach built on a core of books chosen by the teachers themselves. Both teachers and administrators were enthusiastic about what they perceived was the initial success of their literature/whole language emphasis. The logical step for them was to search for a textbook series that would complement the goals and practices already partly in place.

This particular state allocates funds for purchases of state adopted material—largely textbooks that have passed through the complicated political and educational screening process necessary for winning approval as a recommended text by the State Board. Seventy percent of these allocations must be spent on such recommended texts, while the majority of the remaining money may be used to purchase non-adopted supplementary material. School districts may use their own funds as well to buy unadopted material, but in a time of fiscal crisis this is considerably more difficult. Thus, money is available largely for commercially produced and standardized textbooks. The task is to find ones that come closest to the approach you believe in.

Yet, there are many such texts available. To make it more likely that a particular textbook would be chosen, inducements are often offered by publishers. The amount of "free" materials, for instance, given to school districts by a publisher is often considerable. This is common practice among publishers, since textbook publishing is a highly competitive enterprise.[41] In the case of Citrus Valley, the "gift" of such free material seemed to have an impact on the choice.

Citrus Valley began processing a new language arts textbook series in the 1988–89 school year. This was the year for changing

reading/language arts textbooks as school districts sought to accommodate revised state guidelines for introducing new series. The result of this process was the selection of the *Impressions* reading
series, published by Holt, Rinehart, and Winston. The series uses a
whole language, literature-based methodology—one grounded in a
loosely classified curriculum orientation—which this particular
state strives to implement in all schools.

When school began in the fall of 1989, there was no reason to
suspect that there would be any problems with *Impressions*, although it *had* been challenged in other districts in this state and in
other states as well. After all, the steps for piloting and implementing a new series had been carefully followed. The district introduced
the new series with confidence and enthusiasm. The memos circulated around the district after the selection of *Impressions* reflected
the pleasure after much effort of finally having made a choice that
seemed in tune with the district's goals. In June, after telling the
teachers that close to 150 boxes of the new books had arrived, one
district administrator made a prophetic statement. She wrote,
"Have a wonderful summer! We have an exciting next year in store
for us." Truer words had never been spoken.

Within the first two months of the school year, some parents and
teachers began to complain about the books. Parents became concerned about the content of the texts. Not only were the stories
"scary," but there were concerns about the values that were in them
and about mistakes in spelling and printing. The parents objected to
a number of the selections in the textbook that the publisher had
sent to the district. For example, one poem from a fifth grade book
was about pigs in a swamp near some houses. The pigs "live on dead
fish and rotting things, drowned pets, plastic and assorted excreta."
The poem ends with the pigs having consumed the flesh in the pond,
and now having a taste for flesh they look up towards the shore. The
district explained that the poem carried an environmental message.
For the parents, it was violent and fearful, a claim they made even
more strongly about some of the other material in the books for even
younger children.

Parents began talking to each other and slowly a more organized sense began to emerge as community members went to school
board meetings and had meetings in local churches. Ultimately, a
group of parents formed Concerned Citizens of Citrus Valley (CCCV)
in an effort to convince the school board to withdraw the series. The
board and the school administration acted in two paradoxical ways.
They treated the challenge as nearly an act of aggression. They, in

essence, "geared up for war." At the same time, they slowed the process of challenge down by channeling it through the bureaucratic procedures that had been developed—often for very good reasons in many districts so that teachers and administrators could be protected from outside attacks. In this way, "proper attitudes" and efficient procedures are wedded in the local state's response.

Nearly every parent who was interviewed who opposed the books stated that their original introduction to the content of the textbooks began when their child came home and was made upset by a particular selection in the texts. CCCV parents as they organized were unwilling to be identified with outside groups. They felt that their intelligence was being questioned when supporters of the books accused the CCCV of being controlled by "outside forces." According to them, when their children brought home stories that were disturbing, causing nightmares, or frightening them, the parents' first reaction was disbelief. Textbooks were "innocuous." Thus, they were more than a little surprised to read stories in their children's books that seemed inappropriate and were even more surprised and dismayed by what they felt was the Board's and the administration's "heavy handed" response.[42]

As the conflict grew, CCCV organized a recall campaign against a number of board members. The school system dug in its heels against "far right censors" and the community itself was badly split. For the board and the school administration, the CCCV was a symptom of a larger national censorious movement organized around a Far Right agenda. "Giving in" meant surrendering one's professional expertise to the forces of political reaction. For the CCCV, the issue increasingly became one of parental power and of a school board and school bureaucracy that refused to take citizens' complaints seriously and that was arrogant.

Crucial to understanding the situation here is the fact that the leadership of CCCV began to seek to form connections with the religious right only after confronting the district administration and the school board for a long period of time. In fact, the connections were never very strong between CCCV and any outside group. Late in the controversy, one person ultimately did become a liaison between rightist groups and that person is now firmly cemented within a national organization for "religious rights" and assists in rightist political campaigns. Yet, even here, prior to this controversy, this person was not only uninterested in such causes but also was opposed to them.

When the CCCV parents were repeatedly rejected by the local school leadership, they were drawn into the rhetoric and views of the

New Right. They felt, rightly or wrongly, that their concerns were minimized and trivialized by both the district administration and the school board from the beginning. Since they were largely dismissed by the holders of educational authority, then and only then did they begin looking outside the community for groups to dialogue with who held views similar to their own about the nature of the textbooks that had been implemented in the schools. Organizationally, CCCV parents remained on their own, but the New Right increasingly came to be seen as a more attractive set of beliefs and as an ideological ally.

Thus, even when the district made limited attempts, as it did, to convince the protestors of the educational benefits of the new pedagogy and curricula, these efforts were dismissed. One is not likely to subscribe to the views of authorities who disparage you. The schools' immediate response, then—to treat these parents as far-right ideologues who were simply interested in censoring books and teachers—helped create the conditions for the growth of the ideological movements they were so frightened of.

Let us examine this a bit more closely. It was the case that most members of the CCCV were what might best be called "traditionalists." They, indeed, were wary of change. They did like their community as it was (or at least as they perceived how it was). In their minds, they were opposed to the textbook series because of what they felt was its violence, its capacity to frighten children, and its negativity. By and large, the majority of the community seemed to lean in such a traditional direction. Yet, the CCCV parents saw themselves as trying to find a middle ground between the Right and what they considered the "liberal left." Most of them were quite surprised to find themselves identified as part of the Right. Rather, their self-perception was as "hard working citizens" who wanted to maintain positions that allowed them to conduct their lives as they had been doing in the past. Time and again, they restated the position that they were just "ordinary people" who wanted the best for their children.

The parents who originally organized to oppose the textbooks were made up of people from a variety of religious and political persuasions. There were Catholic, Jewish, "mainstream" Protestant, evangelical and fundamentalist Protestant, Mormon, and non-church and agnostic members. Also interesting is the fact that only a few church leaders became involved in the controversy in open support of the CCCV parents. There was little evidence that this was a "fundamentalist" religious issue organized initially either from the outside or by evangelical leaders eager to take on the schools as bastions of secular humanism. In fact, because of the religious diversity and a reluctance to be identified as New Right, many CCCV parents were quite hesitant to hold meetings in a church. However, given the paucity of buildings that were large enough to hold well attended public meetings, when a local pastor volunteered his church for CCCV use, with some caution, it was chosen as the meeting place.

There were other characteristics, however, that seemed to differentiate CCCV members from others in the community. While they were diverse religiously, in general, they did not hold public office and they did not feel that they were part of a network that was central to the community's power relations and daily lives. Many expressed feelings that they were on the fringes of local power. Nor were they economically homogeneous; the group included some local business people and professional, as well as working-class members.

At the first meeting of the CCCV about 25–30 people came. At the second meeting there were seventy-five. As the conflict intensified, seven hundred people packed into the local church that had been volunteered. The intensity is made evident in the fact that police were stationed at a school board meeting called to discuss the textbooks. Over two hundred and fifty concerned community members jammed into the meeting room. The tension was visceral.

In many ways, then, most CCCV parents were in the beginning what might best be called "ordinary middle of the road conservatives" without significant affiliations to rightist activist groups; they did not have a larger ideological or religious agenda that they wished to foist on others. Certainly, they did not see themselves as censorious ideologues who wished to transform the United States into a "Christian nation" and who mistrusted anything that was public.

To reduce the conflict to one of relatively ignorant parents or simpleminded religious fundamentalists, trying to use censorship to further the aims of a larger rightist movement, is both to misconstrue the ways ordinary actors organize around local struggles and to underestimate these people themselves. Such a position sees "dupes"—puppets—in instances such as this and radically simplifies the complexities of such situations. In many ways, such simplifying views reproduce in our own analyses the stereotypes that were embodied in the school administration's and the school board's response to the issues raised by the parents.

The rapidity with which the district responded in such enormous proportions, as if it was in essence preparing for war, seemed to be the catalyst which actually drove the parents in the direction of

rightist groups and caused CCCV parents to form a stronger oppositional position than they might have otherwise taken. As soon as the
CCCV parents challenged the district, the district immediately reduced the issue to one of "censorship." This very construction reduced the complexities to a form that was both familiar to the
"professional" discourse of school administrators and teachers and
enabled the district to respond in ways that did not leave open other
interpretations of the motivations and concerns of the parents.

At the beginning of this controversy, information was shared by
women talking to women in public places and in their homes. Moth-
ers told each other about the contents of the books when they picked
up their children after school, as they met for lunch, and while they
visited their friends. (As the controversy developed, however, more
men became involved and exerted more leadership, thereby signal-
ing once again the relationship between gender and the public
sphere.)[43] For some of the women who worked very hard in the
CCCV group, it was the discounting of their concerns that led to
even more persistence in getting answers to questions about the
textbooks, about the process involved in their selection, and in organizing activities against the books themselves. Their response to the
school's resistance and to the local state's definition of them as partly
irresponsible was to become even more determined in their efforts to
disseminate information about the books. Even though they were
not visibly angry and confrontational, and even though they became
increasingly strong in their opposition to the series, they were
pushed into resistance by not being taken seriously.

The women involved in CCCV had initial political intuitions,
but these were not fully formed in any oppositional sense. They included both social/cultural conservatives and laissez-faire conservatives with the former grounded in a belief in the importance of
religiosity, "the family," and "tradition" and the latter grounded in
ideas about "individual freedom," "American patriotism," and the
"free market," thereby documenting the diversity within even the
more moderate conservative positions held. Yet, the most common
themes of CCCV women were the sovereignty of the family and the
perceived attack on their rights as parents to control their children's
education. Added to this was their perception that *Impressions* did
not represent America accurately or sufficiently. However, these
women did not begin the controversy in previously defined conscious
positions of conservatism. Rather, they were startled at the beginning that there was a problem with the textbooks in their community. Through the months of the conflict, their stances became

formed and became more clear as a result of having to find a way of making sense out of the schools' response.

Thus, as the conflict deepened, one of the leaders of CCCV became increasingly influenced by Francis Schaeffer, a conservative theologian who supported the idea of absolute truth. As this parent searched for ways of understanding her growing distress, she found Schaeffer's ideas more and more attractive. For Schaeffer, there are "true truths." There are rights and wrongs, basic immutable values, that enable us to know with certainty that some things were absolutely right and other things are absolutely wrong. Without this, according to Schaeffer, there is no Christianity.[44]

This becomes much clearer if we again take another example of one person deeply involved in CCCV, a mother of a child in one of the schools that were using the textbook series. At the outset, she was not a deeply religious person. She rarely attended church and had no strong loyalties to any one organization and would have rejected the label of "New Right." Her advice to others involved with her at the beginning was to work with the district and not organize. As her views were directly confronted and challenged by the district and her position seemingly stereotyped, she began to look more closely at what she felt she had to do with her opposition to the books. Her views were repeatedly minimized and she was accused of being "right wing." As a result of this, not only did she become a part of the development of CCCV by parents, but at the end of the controversy became deeply involved with Christian women's groups on national political issues. What began as a concern over the content of books, ended with individuals like her becoming active members of right-wing national movements.

At the end of the conflict, the school district announced a "solution." It would continue to use *Impressions* and its core literature program. It would also allow (continue, actually) the practice of allowing parents to request up to two alternative assignments to these materials each semester. It then went further. The district implemented alternative classes for those parents who had become totally opposed to *Impressions*. Parents were asked to return a letter in which they were asked if they wanted their children to be in a special non-*Impressions* class. They were told that "This may result in a classroom or school site change for your child. In the event a site change is necessary, you will need to provide transportation."

While this response does show some flexibility on the part of the school system, it immediately created a difficult situation for parents who worked outside the home or who were unable to provide transportation for their children. Work schedules, a lack of two (or even one) cars, economic disadvantagement, and other elements created a situation in which parents often had no alternative but to keep their children in the *Impressions* classrooms. Thus are the seeds of further alienation sowed.

As the next school year began, the district reported that 82 percent of the parents had chosen to put their children in *Impressions* classes. Whether this is evidence of choice or of having no real alternatives due to the conditions we mentioned above is unclear. Yet, when nearly 20 percent of parents actively choose very different experiences than officially defined knowledge for their children, it is clear that the controversy continues to simmer not too far below the surface.

There were other changes in the openness of the school system concerning the processes by which official knowledge was chosen. For example, parents are now included in the early stages of textbook selection. The school district administrators and the school board are now much more aware of the complex politics surrounding parental concerns and the consequences of the "professional" decisions they make. Above all, however, there is a tense watchfulness on all sides and a polarization that is deeply cemented into the community. An active Right now exists in powerful ways.

Conclusion

We have been interested here not only in illuminating the complex process through which people become Right, though such analyses are crucial in understanding cultural politics in education, but we also have a theoretical agenda. Too often, traditions talk past each other in critical educational studies. Neo-Gramscian, postmodern, and poststructural theories are seen as opposites. We reject these divisions for a more integrative approach. We have taken tools from the neo-Gramscian tradition—an emphasis both on the power of the state and on the ideological currents within common sense and on the power of cultural movements from below, without ignoring the economic context of social action. We have complemented this with a focus on identity politics and the state's role in circulating subject positions which are then reappropriated by real people in the complex politics of the local level. Behind this is a claim that the study of social movements and the condition of their generation, in a time of increasingly aggressive attacks on the school and on the very idea of "the public" by rightist groups, is essential. Integrating these various perspectives to more fully comprehend this is an ambitious agenda. But the politics of education needs to be treated with the integrative seriousness its complexity deserves.

The implications of what we have described here are of great importance to any analysis of the formation of rightist movements and to the role of the school in identity formation. Many writers have talked about the school as a productive site. It is a site of the production of student identities and of the production of a politics of identity formation.[45] Yet, other identities are produced in interaction with state agencies such as schools. Oppositional identities centered around conservative cultural politics are formed as well. This is clear in the instance—one of many we expect—that we have investigated here.

The subject positions made available by the state were only those who were "responsible" parents who basically supported "professional decision making" or "irresponsible" right-wing censors. The construction of this binary opposition created a situation in which the only ways that parents and other community members could be heard was to occupy the spaces provided by the state. These were expanded and partly transformed, of course. But, the only way in which attention was paid to these concerned individuals was for them to become increasingly aggressive about their claims and increasingly organized around conservative, cultural, and religious themes. Social identities are formed in this way. Thus, moderately conservative and "moderate" community members are slowly transformed into something very different. The Right becomes the Right in a complex and dynamic set of interactions with the state. (How the local state is itself transformed by this is, of course, worthy of inquiry in this regard, but that will have to wait until another investigation.)

At the outset of this analysis, we drew on the arguments of Whitty, Edwards, and Gewirtz where they claimed that the Right grows through "accidents." It grows in halting, diffuse, and partly indeterminate ways that are located in an entire complex of economic, political, and cultural relations. We shall miss much of this dynamic complexity if we only focus on conservative movements from the outside of the situations in which they are built. We have suggested that a primary actor here is the bureaucratic state, which may have expanded its policing functions over knowledge for good reasons but which responds in ways that increase the potential for rightist movements to grow.

Thus, one thing became clear during this study. The linkages between parents who challenge textbooks and national "authoritarian populist" groups grow during a controversy and as a result of such a controversy, rather than being driven by outside groups. In the case we have related here, a striking change is evident. A number of CCCV parents have not only become part of a larger network of New Right activists, but are proud of making such connections, connections that would have seemed to them to be impossible before. Here we need to stress again that these are individuals who had no prior links with New Right organizations and who had no desire to have any connections with such conservative groups until well into the *Impressions* controversy. Equally important is the fact that these newly formed links are continuing to grow stronger as new conservative political identities—extensions of the subject positions originally offered by the local state—are taken on by these people.

Economic conservativism and populism become linked to religious fundamentalism in these local ways. "Concerned citizens," upset by what the schools have defined as official knowledge and who are (correctly) worried both about the downward economic mobility of their children and the values that they are being taught, put these two forms of conservatism together not through any natural process, but in a manner that places the aspects of the state at the center of the formation of social allegiances and social movements.

Our points are not meant to imply that everyone has "free agency," that people "freely choose" to become Right (or anything else) in a vacuum. Indeed, exactly the opposite is the case. The increasing dominance of conservative positions on the entire range of issues involving education, the economy, sexuality, welfare, "intelligence,"[46] and so on in the media and in public discussions means that people in cities such as Citrus Valley and elsewhere live in a world where rightist discourses constantly circulate. It is now increasingly hard not to hear such interpretations, even harder to hear positions opposed to them. However, there are multiple ways in which such discourses can be heard or read. Acceptance is but one of them.[47]

One is left here with many questions. But in our mind, among the most important is this. Could it have been *different*? If the schools had listened more carefully, had not positioned the parents as censorious right-wingers, would there have been a more progressive result? This is not "simply" a question about research. Given the Right's hegemonic project and the success of its ideological transformations, if schools are one of the crucial sites where these transformations occur, then interruptions of the bureaucratic gaze of the school and concrete struggles at a local level may be more important than we realize not only in the short term but also the long term as well.[48] In fact, it is just as crucial that schools focus their critical gaze on themselves and on how *they* may participate in creating the conditions in which ordinary citizens "become Right."

Fears about a declining economy or concerns about what is taught to one's children do not necessarily need to be sutured into an authoritarian populist attack on the state, nor do they necessarily have to be connected to the entire range of issues the Right stands for. Moderate and moderately traditional positions may not be ones all of our readers may believe in, but there is a world of difference between such positions and the aggressive campaign against all that is public and on the very idea of a truly public school that emanates from the far right. The widespread effects of such groups can only be limited if the larger number of the public who have populist concerns about schools are not pushed to the right.

There is evidence that a different response to the politics of official knowledge by schools can have very different results. Though this is discussed in much greater detail in *Democratic Schools*,[49] it is worthwhile noting the experiences of schools that deal with such possibly polarizing situations in more open ways. Thus, to take but one example—Fratney Street School in Milwaukee, a city that has suffered severely from the downturn in manufacturing jobs and from very real class and race antagonisms—faced a situation where political conflicts around class and racial dynamics could have provided quite fertile ground for the growth of rightist sentiments.

Situated in a "border area" in which its student population was one-third working-class European-American, one-third African-American, and one-third Latino/Latina, the issues of whose knowledge was represented in the texts, of what an appropriate pedagogy would be, and of whose voices within that tense and diverse makeup would be listened to could have been as explosive as those which surfaced in Citrus Valley. These issues could have been ripe for the development of similar movements as those found in the case we have analyzed here. Yet, they did not lead to such development and in fact led to the formation of cross class and race coalitions for more progressive curricula and teaching and widespread support for the school.

Partly, this was due to a group of teachers and administrators who—as a group—opened up the discussion of curricula and pedagogy to the multiple voices with a stake in the school, including parents, community activists, and students. There was constant attention paid to this, not as often happens in many school districts as a form of "public relations," which usually is largely a form of the "engineering of consent," but as an ongoing and genuine attempt to relate both the content of the curriculum and the decisions over it to the lives of the people involved. Partly, it was the result of the immense amount of work done by the educators involved there to publicly justify what they felt was best for students and why, in words and in a style that could not be interpreted as arrogant, elitist, or distant, and to listen sympathetically and carefully to the fears, concerns and hopes of the various voices in the community. And, finally, it was due to a decidedly non-hierarchical set of beliefs both about what happens within the school and between the school and the wider community(ies) of which it was a part.

None of this guarantees that the Right's restorational project will be transformed. Situations and their causes are indeed partly "accidental." Yet, the experiences at Fratney Street School and at other schools speaks to a very different articulation between the local state and its population, and it speaks to the very real possibility of interrupting a number of the conditions that lead to the growth of rightist social movements. There is work to be done.

Notes

A briefer version of this chapter appears in Michael W. Apple, *Cultural Politics and Education* (New York: Routledge and Kegan Paul, 1996).

1. Philip Wexler, *Social Analysis of Education* (New York: Routledge and Kegan Paul, 1987).

2. See Michael W. Apple, *"Power, Meaning, and Identity,"* British *Journal of Sociology of Education* 17(1996):125–144.

3. Kathleen Casey, "The New Narrative Research in Education," in *Review of Research in Education*, edited by Michael W. Apple, vol. 21 (Washington, DC: American Educational Research Association, 1996).

4. Joan Delfattore, *What Johnny Shouldn't Read* (New Haven: Yale University Press, 1992).

5. See Michael W. Apple, *Official Knowledge: Democratic Education in a Conservative Age* (New York: Routledge and Kegan Paul, 1993; Michael B. Katz, *The Undeserving Poor*, (New York: Pantheon, 1989); and Jonathan Kozol, *Savage Inequalities* (New York: Crown, 1991).

6. See Bruce Curtis, *True Government By Choice Men?* (Toronto: University of Toronto Press, 1992). For an insightful example of the integration of these often disparate programs of analysis.

7. Michael W. Apple, *Teachers and Texts* (New York: Routledge and Kegan Paul, 1988); and Apple, *Official Knowledge*, p.

8. Geoff Whitty, Tony Edwards, and Sharon Gewirtz, *Specialization and Choice in Urban Education* (New York: Routledge and Kegan Paul, 1993).

9. Apple, *Official Knowledge*; and Michael W. Apple, "The Politics of Official Knowledge: Does a National Curriculum Make Sense?" *Teachers College Record* 95 (1993):222–241.

10. These assumptions may not be totally the same in other nations, especially in the relative power of religious fundamentalism. Further, not all segments of the cultural and religious Right agree. For ease of presentation here, however, we will gloss over some of the differences within this movement for the moment.

11. Allen Hunter, *Children in the Service of Conservatism* (Madison: University of Wisconsin Institute for Legal Studies, 1988), p. 63.

12. Ibid.

13. Ibid., p. 15.

14. Ibid. It is important not to see such positions as "irrational." For many right-wing women, for example, such a belief is wholly sensible given the conditions in which they live. Joan Sherron DeHart gets it exactly right when she states that "We must recognize the screams of antifeminist women as the rational responses of people who live in a deeply gendered and profoundly precarious world—a world in which identity, social legitimacy, economic viability and moral order are deeply rooted in conventional gender categories." See Joan Sherron DeHart, "Gender on the Right: Behind the Existential Scream," *Gender and History* 3(1991):261.

15. Apple, *Official Knowledge*.

16. La Haye, quoted in Hunter, *Children in the Service of Conservatism*, p. 57.

17. Hunter, *Children in the Service of Conservatism*, p. 57.

18. See Michael W. Apple and Linda Christian-Smith, eds., *The Politics of the Textbook* (New York: Routledge and Kegan Paul, 1991).

19. Delfattore, *What Johnny Shouldn't Read*, p. 123.

20. See Apple, *Teachers and Texts*; Apple, *Official Knowledge*; and Apple and Christian-Smith, *The Politics of the Textbook*.

21. Delfattore, *What Johnny Shouldn't Read*, p. 139.

22. Rebecca Klatch, *Women of the New Right* (Philadelphia: Temple University Press, 1987), p. 23.

23. Ibid., p. 24.

24. Ibid., p. 24.

25. Ibid., p. 26.

26. Gilder, quoted in Klatch, *Women of the Right*, pp. 28–29.

27. Klatch, *Women of the New Right*, p. 29.

28. Nancy Fraser, *Unruly Practices* (Minneapolis: University of Minnesota Press, 1989).

29. See Delfattore, *What Johnny Can't Read*.

30. See Apple, *Official Knowledge*; and Apple and Christian-Smith, *The Politics of the Textbook*.

31. Curtis, *True Government By Choice Men?*, p. 9.

32. Ibid., p. 5 (emphasis added).

33. Ibid., p. 32. Curtis adds domination and exploitation to this list.

34. Ibid., p. 172.

35. Ibid., p. 175.

36. Ibid., p. 174.

37. Ibid., p. 192. See also Apple, *Official Knowledge*, pp. 64–92.

38. Curtis, *True Government By Choice Men?*, p. 197.

39. The material in this section is drawn from Anita Oliver, "The Politics of Textbook Controversy: Parents Challenge the Implementation of a Reading Series," (Ph.D. diss., University of Wisconsin, 1993).

40. We want to be cautious not to overstate our reading of the class dynamics of this situation. The new middle class is itself divided. Not all fractions of it support "invisible pedagogies" such as whole language approaches. Basil Bernstein hypothesizes that those members of the new middle class who work for the state are much more likely to support such loosely classified and loosely framed pedagogies than those who work in the private sector. This and particular professional ideologies, may partly account for the fact that most teachers, though not all, in Citrus Valley supported the whole language emphasis found in the state guidelines and in *Impressions*.

41. See Apple, *Teachers and Texts*, especially pp. 81–105.

42. About the same time that parents first complained about the books, some teachers also brought complaints, but of a very different nature. Teachers reported that some of the stories in the books did not match the table of contents in the student anthologies. Obviously, there was a distinct possibility that the wrong books had been shipped or that there were misprints. However, as the conflict intensified, the local teachers union became increasingly vocal in its support for the *Impressions* series and for the school district administration. Of all the groups involved in this study, teachers were the most reluctant to be interviewed. This is understandable given the tensions and fear in this situation.

43. Fraser, *Unruly Practices*, pp. 113–144; see also, Michael W. Apple, "Texts and Contexts: The State and Gender in Educational Policy," *Curriculum Inquiry* 24(1994): 349–359.

44. See Francis A. Schaeffer, *The Francis A. Schaeffer Trilogy* (Westchester, Illinois: Crossway Books, 1990).

45. See, for example, Philip Wexler, *Becoming Somebody* (New York: The Falmer Press, 1992).

46. See, for example, the widely discussed and hopelessly flawed volume by Richard Herrnstein and Charles Murray, *The Bell Curve* (New York: The Free Press, 1994). The sponsorship of this volume and its authors by conservative foundations, and these groups' ability to place the authors on highly visible media outlets, is worth noting. It would be important to investigate the role of such conservative groups in sponsoring and circulating, and thus helping to make publicly legitimate, positions that have been discredited scientifically many times before.

47. See Apple, *Official Knowledge*, pp. 61–62.

48. Examples of more democratic responses can be found in Michael W. Apple and James A. Beane, eds., *Democratic Schools* (Washington, DC: Association for Supervision and Curriculum Development, 1995).

49. Ibid.

5

Social Closure, Professional Domination, and the New Middle Strata: Rethinking Credentialist Theories of Education

❑

Raymond A. Morrow and Carlos Alberto Torres

Introduction: The Problematic

Sociological concepts must be continuously revised as the nature of social reality undergoes transformation. The dramatic beginning of C. Wright Mills' *White Collar* signaled the pivotal significance of a phenomenon that Max Weber had only glimpsed; that is, the way in which the so-called middle strata were in the process of redefining the class relations of advanced capitalism:

> The white-collar people slipped quietly into modern society. Whatever history they have had is a history without events; whatever common interests they have do not lead to unity; whatever future they have will not be of their own making. . . . Internally, they are split, fragmented; externally, they are dependent on larger forces (Mills 1951, ix)

Yet, they have since come to constitute the largest social grouping in advanced societies where the "working class" is no longer the majority. Not surprisingly, this phenomenon is also a key aspect of the crisis of historical materialism and has provoked wide-ranging revisions of neo-Marxist and critical theories of social inequality (Wright 1978; 1985; Giddens 1973; Cohen 1982). These issues have figured most prominently in the sociology of education, in the context of theories of status competition (the theory of cultural capital), and credentialization (Bourdieu et al. 1977; Collins 1979). Whereas structural Marxist theories of social reproduction stressed the close functional link (i.e., correspondence) between the school and the creation of a docile working class (Bowles and Gintis 1976), they were incapable of adequately addressing the peculiarities of middle class occupations and related educational institutions and curricula. Status competition and credentialist theories filled this gap, but their relationship to the more general problematic of cultural reproduction theory has not been adequately developed.

Somewhat oversimplified introductory accounts to the sociology of education tend to contrast "neo-Marxist" and "functionalist" theories of educational expansion and related interpretations of "what schools teach," that is, the hidden curriculum required for work in capitalist society and the explicit curriculum, which reproduces forms of consciousness that sustain capitalist culture, as opposed to the teaching of cognitive and citizenship skills (Hurn 1985, 77–108, 202–244). As David Hurn skeptically concludes, one's response to these issues turn upon initial ideological predilections and the fact that (with partial exception of Bourdieu) "very little empirical evidence is provided" and writers "base their case on the plausibility of their logic rather than on evidence that students, in fact, acquire this unidimensional consciousness" (Hurn 1985, 214–5). Even more cynically, status competition theorists such as Randall Collins and John Meyer are held to suggest "education functions as a kind of cultural currency that enables the holder to purchase certain kinds of adult status but that has little or no definable content" (Hurn 1985, 215).

Hurn's discussion is representative of the educational sociology literature with respect to a number of strategic confusions. First, non-Marxist theories of cultural reproduction such as that of Pierre Bourdieu's is not clearly distinguished. Second, affinities between status competition theory and Bourdieu's notion of cultural capital is glossed over. Third, the theory of class (i.e., stratification and inequality) on which respective theories of educational expansion are based are not made fully explicit. Finally, an excessively positivist notion of "evidence" obscures evaluation of the empirical arguments with respect to critiques of consciousness and ideology advanced by radical and critical theories.

One of our concerns here is to look more closely at the relationship between status competition theories in education (or what we will also call theories of credentialization, i.e., status competition for educational qualifications) and theories of cultural reproduction (a category somewhat broader than neo-Marxist if it is to include Bourdieu, and more focused than the notion of conflict theory). Our general argument will wager that theories of status competition applied to credentialization need to be rooted in: (a) a more general theory of social closure which in turn can be linked with an open-ended model of cultural reproduction; (b) a substantive critique of professional knowledge; and (c) a more adequate theory of the middle strata or classes.

The rise of middle strata is a process closely associated with the expansion of mass public education and forms of certification. As opposed to the forms of apprenticeship training and trades union organization characteristic of the working class, the model for the middle strata has been that of the so-called liberal professions (medicine, law, architecture, etc.), even though the bureaucratic context of most middle-class work does not allow full appropriation of the professional model (Larson 1977). What struck nonfunctionalist students of these processes was that education and certification had become itself a site of social struggle, one with profound implications for the reproduction and transformation of class relations.

Two of the most influential and important contemporary efforts to study the educational implications of these phenomena can be found in the work of Pierre Bourdieu (e.g. 1977) and his notion of "cultural capital" and Randall Collins' *The Credential Society* (1979). We will argue this these path breaking contributions to "credentialization theory" suffer from two major limitations: first, they do not provide a sociological framework for critically analyzing the knowledge claims of credentialed occupations, even though they do indirectly call them into doubt by stressing the political aspects of their social construction; second, they do not adequately address the question of the relationship between the new credentialed middle strata and the changing nature of the class system as a whole. Further, we will argue that social closure theory, especially in the form advanced by Raymond Murphy in his *Social Closure* (1988), provides a general framework within which these neglected issues can be effectively taken up. At the same time, Murphy's account needs to be linked up with and further developed in response to contemporary discussion in critical theory and the nature of class.

Our central thesis will be that despite the limitations of any theory of the "new middle class" as a major class actor with collective consciousness, the fusion of the principles of closure as credentialization and professional-technical knowledge as a potential form of ideology and domination has made educational systems the central institutional agency of a new form of social power and principle of class stratification, but one that cannot be understood except in relation to more traditional forms of power based on capital and access to the state. In other words, the social and cultural reproduction of society needs to be understood in terms of these new principles of "cultural capital" and "instrumental knowledge" (or power/knowledge) as forms of domination and control, even as they are not *only* that and cannot, beyond a certain point, compete with or replace more traditional forms of power.

Cultural Capital and Credentialism

In using the term credentialist educational theory we are referring primarily to the broadly convergent formulations of Pierre Bourdieu and Randall Collins, despite important differences in their overall sociological approaches. What they share, however, is analysis of status competition in education based on a critique of the technocratic assumption that given structures of education and professional training correspond to some rational economic and technical logic, as opposed to being shaped by the competition between groups to use educational qualification as a means of legitimating class positions. Further, unlike economic correspondence theories, they do not tie credentialization to the immediate economic imperatives of capital , as opposed to the competition between and among class actors. In short, credentialist theory challenges the uncritical functionalist (Parsonian) assumption that the evolution of the "knowledge complex" represents the progressive unfolding of instrumental reason (Parsons and Platt 1973).

Randall Collins

In the case of Collins, of course, his approach is explicitly defined as neo-Weberian. It is useful to begin with his work (even though Bourdieu's dates back earlier and influenced Collins at certain points), because it represents a relatively pure version of status competition theory. Collins begins with a critique of the limitations of Bourdieu's theory of cultural capital: "The specifics of Bourdieu's reproduction argument are quite plausible. But the model does not actually disprove a technocratic interpretation of education-based work skills or even a biological hereditist explanation of class advantages" (Collins 1979, 9). Further, "their larger mechanism explaining the macro-pattern of educational stratification and its historical development is obscure in Bourdieu's model" and implies functionalist argument, even if a critical one (1979:10).

Instead, Collins proposes an historical analysis which effectively demonstrates that "the enormous expansion of education since the mid-nineteenth century *has had no effects at all* in increasing social mobility" (Collins 1979, 182); that beyond the transition to mass literacy, the contribution of education to economic productivity is limited and that the education system is vastly overexpanded for other reasons (Collins 1979, 1–21); that the resulting "income revolution" has had quite diverse consequences, but not one that can be reduced to a white-collar/blue-collar opposition and has not produced a widespread increase in the equality of opportunity (Collins 1979, 183–90); and that the United States has entered an era of "sinecure politics," resulting from the ongoing crisis of the credentialist system with continuing credential inflation (Collins 1979, 191–204). This last aspect creates a particular problem for school reformers, even radical ones:

> None of them came to grips with the underlying issue: the fact that education is part of a system of cultural stratification and that the reason most students are in school is that they (or their parents on their behalf) want a decent job. This means that the reasons for going to school are extraneous to whatever goes on in the classroom (Collins 1979, 192).

Pierre Bourdieu

The sociology of education of Pierre Bourdieu (and his collaborators) is generally regarded, not without justification, as a species of cultural reproduction theory. What is distinctive about his approach, however, is that, unlike economic correspondence reproduction theories (Althusser; early Bowles and Gintis), the focus of analysis is upon the reproductive consequences of educational systems for the strategies of class actors, not the economic system as such. What is also missed, in stressing the structuralist (and functionalist) side of this argument, is that Bourdieu is primarily indebted to Max Weber for his theory of "cultural capital."[1] The result is that in Bourdieu's work an account of status competition is embedded in a more general theory of cultural reproduction that gives particular attention to the rising and declining elements of the middle strata.

Whereas Collins argument, given its objective of disconfirming technocratic and human capital theories, focused on the size of the

American education to demonstrate its irrelevance to work requirements, Bourdieu begins with the assumption that schooling is indeed not only relevant for job placement, but also for the "habitus" or status qualities it inculcates, rather than the technical skills required.

For Bourdieu, the middle positions of the social field are relatively uncertain and indeterminate, converting status struggles into a set of "mobile crossing points, or rather, a set of shifting cross-points where agents meet for a certain time as they are carried along by similar or opposite, rising or falling trajectories" (Bourdieu 1984, 345). The resulting forms of habitus tend to make a virtue of necessity through values and taste that facilitate coping with the pressures of competition. Different starting points within the petite bourgeoisie thus embody different collective histories and different strategies for attempting to gain control over future destinies in relation to the past and perceived ongoing changes. The "declining petite bourgeoisie" (e.g., people who are older and with limited education such as owners of small businesses and shopkeepers) are impelled toward a conservatism of taste that separates them from the bon vivant life-style of manual workers and opposes them to the "progressive" virtues of the rising, younger, and more educated groups. The "expectant bourgeoisie" is diverse in origin and shares an opportunism in taste, but one based on discipline and asceticism with an orientation to a future; it will "make sense" of their sacrifices (perhaps through their children). Finally, the "new petite bourgeoisie" are oriented toward new and emerging career opportunities with uncertain conditions of entry, that is, neither cultural nor social capital offering automatic success. Reacting against the existing petite bourgeoisie, this fluid category embraces vaguely aristocratic pretensions of taste combined with a liberation ethic oriented toward consumption with limited means. From Bourdieu's perspective, therefore, the link between education and outcome for middle groups has become increasingly uncertain and less and less secured through traditional forms of cultural capital. Implicitly, then, for Bourdieu, education has also become increasingly irrelevant for work requirements, though the emphasis shifts from Collins' emphasis on technical skills to the dramatic changes in the forms of habitus conducive to practical "success" given the emergent forms of economic competition.

Critical Commentary

The respective advantages and problems of Collins' and Bourdieu's work is thus evident. Collins effectively provides empirical support for a critique of the functionalist and technocratic proposition that the expansion and particular structure of the American educational system can be explained in terms of objective, rational criteria. But his effort to translate this into a more general account of social stratification suffers from an inadequate exaggerated account of the role of credentialed groups with the notion of a "credentialed society." Also, his reductive and cynical treatment of credentialed knowledge leaves little scope for constructive critique and policy alternatives.

Bourdieu, on the other hand, provides an analysis which, though biased by the peculiarities of French education and culture, illustrates in great empirical detail the various mechanisms and processes of cultural competition and their relation to class reproduction. In this respect, his analysis usefully complements Collins' historical analysis. As well, he provides considerable insight into the various strategies of components of what he calls the "petite bourgeoisie," thus going beyond Collins in acknowledging the continuing relation of such groups to the structure of labor and capital as axes of power and inequality, that is, part of a process of social and cultural reproduction. But his analysis does not adequately address or take into account current debates in stratification theory, largely ignores the contradictory aspects of reproductive processes (i.e., resistance), and does not go much beyond Collins with respect to a constructive critique of professional knowledge.

Social Closure Theory

Social closure theory provides—we would like to argue following Murphy—a more general framework for revising credentialist and status competition theories by developing a general theory of domination and resistance, as well as (potentially) more explicitly linking the theory of cultural reproduction with an analysis of the empirical mechanisms in which reproduction is maintained and/or transformed.[2] In particular, it helps deal with the latent functionalism and ahistorical character of much of Bourdieu's theorizing, as well as the absence of attention by Collins to non-credentialist bases of power and stratification in capitalist forms of society. Moreover, it is more explicitly open to the insights developed by critical theories of professional domination and related redefinitions of the class form of the middle strata and the class structure of advanced capitalism generally.

Frank Parkin: Neo-Weberian Closure Theory

Though rooted in certain Weberian insights, contemporary social closure theory has its origins in Frank Parkin's (1979) biting and acerbic critique of Marxist class theory in the name of a "bourgeois critique"[3] Parkin's theory begins with a distinction between two reciprocal modes of closure (exclusion and usurpation), which represent distinct strategies for gaining rewards and resources. Exclusionary closure involves the downward exercise of power by a dominant group able to close off opportunities to subordinate groups; ursurpationary closure is characterized instead by an upward exercise of power (usurpation practices), which are oriented to gaining advantages from the dominant group.

Raymond Murphy's Extension of Closure Theory

The approach of Parkin (and the related notions of "sinecures" and credentialization in Collins 1979) is criticized by Raymond Murphy, nevertheless for not considering the "deep structure" of closure (Bourdieu is more successful here), as opposed to its surface aspects. Hence, Parkin's voluntaristic and subjectivist theory of class is charged (as is that of E. P. Thompson) with overreacting to structuralist Marxism. Instead a rich set of concepts based on social closure theory are developed for recovering the distinction between "structural class situation and conscious collective action in order to refocus class analysis upon the dialectical interaction of the two" (1988, 128). In the process, Murphy develops what could be called a "structuralist" reading of Weber, which converges with that of a critical theory and avoids voluntarism and methodological individualism of much neo-Weberian theory. Collins' more limited theory of credentialism is also criticized for its narrow stress upon a "particular set of exclusion rules" (such as credentials), thus ignoring the "deep structure of closure." If Collins had done so, Murphy argues, it would have required him to have rewritten a book not about *The Credential Society*, but also one on *Credentials in Capitalist Society*, thus, taking into account, the derivative and secondary nature of exclusion through educational qualification, as opposed to the principal types stemming from property ownership.

Murphy's revision of social closure theory, however, provides conceptual resources for reintegrating the theory or professional domination and that of the class character of credentialled groups into a more general theory of credentialization and power which can be used to deal with some of the limitations of existing models of cultural reproduction.

Murphy's critique of existing closure theory is based on his effort to elaborate "the relationships between rules of closure and their structure" (1988, 65). The strategic importance of this is demonstrated by the way Parkin (along with Collins) fails to account for the "vastly different power and advantages accruing to credentials and to property and the unequal importance of the two as rules of exclusion under capitalism" (1988, 66–7). To deal with this problem, Murphy presents a threefold distinction between "principal," "derivative," and "contingent" forms of exclusion. Principal rules of exclusion are ultimately backed by the apparatus of the state (legal and ultimately coercive sanctions), and are rooted in the primary determinants of "access to, or exclusion from, power, resource, and opportunities in society" (1988, 70). Title to private property has served as the primary form of exclusion in capitalist societies as has the communist party in state socialist societies.

Derivative rules of exclusion are derived from but not the same as the primary ones. Typical here are the more traditional collectivist forms of derivative rules, such as racial, ethnic, religious or general criteria, as well as the individualistic forms more typical of credentialism. Derivative forms may be legally sanctioned, but more often and increasingly operate on an informal basis. The other forms of exclusion are contingent in that though not based on the principal form , their mode of use cannot be understood except in relation to the overall structure determined by it. Typical examples of this form are professional credentialization and elements of general exclusion which precede capitalism or the party apparatus. In reality, of course, derivative and contingent rules normally overlap: "A particular set of *rules* of exclusion can have both derivative and contingent *forms*. (1988, 72). Credentials thus may be characterized by a derivative aspect deriving from their origin as a type of private property, along with a contingent dimension origination in rules related to training requirements.

This framework is in turn applied to a classification of three types of overall societal structures of exclusion: (*a*) a more typical tandem model where derivative and contingent rules are tied to a principal one (e.g., Western capitalism; East Bloc state socialism); (*b*) a dual or paired structure characterized by two principle, complementary principal systems (e.g., property and race in South Africa; property and citizenship in the case of the poor of the Third World who are excluded from migration); and (*c*) two opposed sets of principal exclusion rules (e.g., the opposition between capitalist and state socialist societies at the world system level).

As Murphy argues, the creation of codes of credential exclusion is not arbitrary. Nor it adequate to focus on either status-cultural requirements (e.g., Collins) or technical-functional ones (e.g., Parkin) in isolation from each other or the larger structures of power:

> The success of any credentialled groups in carving out a monopoly depends on its success in propagating the claim that its credentials certify the presence of some skill (and that their absence indicates lack of that skill) and that the skill itself is necessary and of value. Such success is not a matter of intellectual rigors, but rather of ideological struggle, itself founded on the structure of power in society. *It is not just a question of the power of that particular credentialled group, but of the structure of power in society within which group can carve out its own position of power.* Whether particular skills are judged necessary, valuable, or even present, and hence the exchange value of the credentials . . . depends on that nature of the overall societal context and its power structure (1988, 182; emphasis added).

In developing this line of thinking, Murphy suggests several types of analysis: (*a*) the types of skills claimed, (*b*) the organization of credentialed groups, (*c*) their relationship to the principal form of societal exclusion, and (*d*) the role of credentials as individualist codes of exclusion.

(*a*) It is proposed that skills can be differentiated into three basic types: *cultural skills* related to the development and diffusion of knowledge and the manipulation of symbols (e.g., artists, pure scientists, intellectuals, teachers, etc.; *technical skills* which allow the application of knowledge in the sense of manipulating things (e.g., engineers); and *political skills*, which is linked to management of the exercise of control over people, that is, "the capacity to act to one's advantage in a filed of power relationships" (1988, 184). A credentialed group, to be sure, is typically based on all three with one dominating. Medicine, for example, is defined by a core of technical skills, but is coupled with political and cultural ones as well. Where Murphy stops short, nevertheless, is linking these skills as types of knowledge to the existing literature on professional domination, a point also evident in his analysis of the "rationalization" of closure (as we shall see in a minute).

(*b*) Further, credentialed groups vary along an atomist-corporatist dimension with respect to their organization. The holders of university degrees are atomized because they are not directly represented by an association promoting their interests; in contrast, medical doctors are at the corporatist end of the continuum given their legal monopoly over medical services and the evaluation of medical competence. Such corporations differ significantly from unions given the primary stress upon credential exclusion.

(c) In capitalist societies, the key aspect of the relationship to the primary form of exclusion is whether credentialed groups are located in the private sector (hence willingness and ability of clients to pay) or public sectors (based on needs as defined by the state). Nevertheless, both share an interest in avoiding competition, which requires different strategies in these two context.

(d) Finally, there has been a profound historical shift from collectivist to individualist codes of exclusion, resulting in what Murphy refers to as the "rationalization of exclusion, monopolization, and closure." (1988, 190). Earlier forms of exclusion were, to put in terms of pattern variables, ascriptive (e.g., class, religion, ethnicity, etc.), whereas now they are increasingly based on individual achievement criteria. Max Weber's theory of rationalization is outlined in terms of his stress up the following key elements of this process: formal vs. substantive rationality; intellectualization; depersonalization; and control (1988, 196–201). The key rationalized institutions are held to be bureaucratic organizations, the formal legal system, the capitalist market economy, and an "inner orientation" of personality structures (1988, 202–208). As Murphy concludes, ". . . there is an implicit end in this process of formal rationalization: that of control (over nature, economic competitors, ideological adversaries, political opponents, and military enemies)" (1988, 218). But the resulting form of change is hardly revolutionary: "a change towards the elimination of domination and closure, rather it consists of controlled change-modification of domination and closure in order to strengthen mastery and render it deeper, more comprehensive, more subtle, and more legitimate" (1988, 218–9). The individualization of closure criteria result in a "formal equality" but does not lead to substantive equality:

> The rationalization of closure involves the monopolization of the means, not only of production, but also of destruction, administration, and of knowledge, and the exclusion (or "separation" to use Weber's term) of those who directly use those means and of the population generally from their control. It involves centralized, hierarchical, bureaucratic control over those means, whether by private enterprise and the bourgeoisie under capitalism, or by the Communist Party and its dominant class under state socialism. Structurally both are systems of closure and domination (1988, 231).

These processes, to be sure, are not without contradictory aspects, especially the tension between formal and substantive rationality. With failure of performance and the inability to define and realize substantive ends, existing primary structures of domination can be surprising vulnerable (witness the East Bloc in Europe). This is linked to the usurpationary potential of the dominated: "The great untapped resources of human capital and intelligence in the remaining members of excluded groups generates a contradiction based on the logic of rationalization itself, on unequal resources in a contest where all are supposed to compete on an equal footing. This is a potential basis of usurpation using the logic of rationalization itself" (1988, 226).

An Agenda of Outstanding Issues

Professional Domination: Knowledge and Power

Though surprisingly Murphy makes no reference to their work or those directly influenced by them, his general line of argument with respect to the rationalization of closure should be quite familiar to those acquainted with the writings of Herbert Marcuse and Jürgen Habermas. The point here is not so much to fault Murphy's scholarship—which is concerned with deriving this reading of Weber from closure theory—but the remarkable convergence with critical theory's critique of instrumental rationalization (see Morrow, forthcoming).

Theories of credentialization indirectly call professional and expert knowledge into question by viewing it as a symbolic resource in struggles for social positions and the legitimating of rewards and working conditions. In this respect, such theories are the direct opposite of functionalist and human capital theories which uncritically exalt existing forms of professional competence and knowledge claims. Yet, as functionalists do point out, and can back up with some empirical evidence, education generally and professional training in particular is not about nothing, or just status competition: real skills are imparted with significant social and economic consequences (Freidson 1986). It is for this reason a more constructive alternative is required to complement status competition theories, that is, a critical sociology of knowledge and ideology capable of a more refined evaluation and analysis of professional domination.

Two elements appear to be necessary for such a more comprehensive conception. First, following Murphy and others (e.g., Martin and Szelenyi 1987), it is necessary to acknowledge that credentialed work includes both technical-functional and status characteristics, the significance of which is mediated by larger structures of power. Second, it is important to stress that the technical-functional dimension cannot be value-neutral precisely because its use is embedded in structures of power and domination. Though Murphy develops a framework in which this latter question can be incorporated (i.e., the distinction between primary and derivative forms of closure), this is not explicitly developed, except indirectly with the notion of the "rationalization of closure." But his stress is upon how such rationalization sustain inequality in new forms, without specifying more precisely how such domination operates.

In modern social theory, three key sources of opposition to the technocratic thinking underlying professional domination can be identified which should be included in a comprehensive theory of credentialization: the critique of instrumental reason developed in the Frankfurt School tradition (Illich 1971; 1973; Misgeld 1985; Rouse 1987; Morrow and Torres 1990); the analysis of the power/ knowledge complex developed by Michel Foucault (e.g., see Miller 1987); and the multiple sources and contexts of popular resistance which—even if misguided in various ways (e.g., medical quackery)— have taken the form of (anarchistic) challenges to professional monopolies of power and knowledge. Such contributions would have to be incorporated into a more adequate account of the consequences of social closure for the structure of domination.

Cultural Reproduction, Hegemony and the State

As Murphy himself suggests—but does not develop—in the context of a short commentary on Pierre Bourdieu and Jean-Claude Passeron's theory of educational reproduction, closure theory has the potential to specify in empirically precise ways "how the school system can be autonomous and yet at the same time contribute to the reproduction and legitimation of the existing social class structure of society" (Murphy 1988, 150). Implicitly, the resulting reconceptualization of the concept of relative autonomy could be extended to all other areas of cultural life, thus rescuing now languishing theories of cultural reproduction from the well-known limitations of functionalist reasoning (see Connell 1983, 140–161; Liston 1988). As well, the important shift from collectivistic to individualistic codes of exclusion, which are referred to as involving "class protection" *rather than* "class reproduction" (Murphy 1988,

166), is potentially confusing in that, as Murphy himself concludes, the result is merely an opening up, *not* really an abolition of class reproduction. From this perspective, however, it becomes easier to historicize the concept of reproduction in ways lacking in the existing literature (but see Müller et al. 1987).

Further, social closure theory is not adequately integrated with critical theories of the state of hegemony. Though the role of the state under state socialism (where the party functions as the principal source of exclusion) is considered in some detail, the capitalist state *as such* is given almost no attention (except marginally in the context of the legal sanctioning exclusionary processes). Yet, it is evident that neo-Gramscian analyses of hegemony and resistance (e.g., Aronwitz and Giroux 1985), as well as Jürgen Habermas (1975) and Claus Offe's (1984) legitimation crisis theory, could benefit from a confrontation with closure theory, which would benefit both.

The Question of the New Middle Classes

The more general observation which underlies all efforts to make sense of the remarkable expansion of the middle strata, which on most accounts constitute the largest groups in the stratification of advanced societies, is that the process of production has been transformed. Some speak rather uncritically of a "postindustrial" society (Bell 1976), a "knowledge society" (Holzner and Marx 1979), or an "information society" (Porat 1978). Clearly such conceptions serve an important ideological function in legitimating the aspirations of these middle strata, but the realities of power and control give little evidence of the political dominance of those groups.

The three leading theories of credentialization are more critical, to be sure, but also provide unsatisfactory and/or incomplete analyses of the class situation middle strata, which are the primary beneficiary of educational qualifications. A long-standing tradition of discussion has considered the question of whether the professional middle strata should then be considered as a social class and if so, in what sense. Without such an analysis, the theory of credentialization cannot be integrated into a more general account of stratification, power, and the state. There have been a wide variety of efforts in this context which is beyond our purposes to review here. Yet, we would question the more extreme formulations (e.g., Gouldner 1979; Ehrenreich & Ehrenreich 1978) which argue the thesis that credentialed groups have or can constitute themselves as a class in the strong classic sense.[4] On the other hand, it appears equally problematic to subsume credentialed occupations under the heading of "contradictory class locations" (Wright 1978; 1985) whose existence is completely subordinate to the primary determinants of property and the proletariat.[5] The most fruitful strategies appear to those which acknowledge the necessary synthesis of Marxian and Weberian perspectives (e.g., as initiated by Giddens 1973), acknowledge the usefulness of social closure theory (e.g., Disco 1987), and attempt to link the "service class" component based on professional-technical knowledge to comparative analysis of the current transformations of capitalism (e.g., Abercrombie and Urry 1983; Lash and Urry 1987). Only from the results of such investigations can the changing significance of credentialist processes be traced.

Conclusion

Towards Integration

As we have tried to show, social closure theory as expanded by Raymond Murphy provides a framework for rethinking the nature of credentialization as a form of status competition; such as revised social closure theory has three key advantages. First, it allows considering credentialization in relation to the power structures of property ownership, not as some kind of completely autonomous process. In identifying property ownership as a primary mode of exclusion, he is able—unlike Randall Collins and only vaguely Pierre Bourdieu—to locate processes of credentialization within a larger framework of structural power relations. Still, closure attention to the mediating role in this context of the reproduction of relations of hegemony requires further development. In short, it opens the way for a reconciliation of social closure theory with an open-ended model of cultural reproduction.

Second, it allows connecting closure processes with an analysis of the potential deformations of professional knowledge deriving from (a) the external power interests driven by ownership of capital; and (b) internal exclusionary struggles to head off competition. As well, by differentiating types of skill credentials and analyzing the organization and the "rationalization of closure," social closure theory in this form not only opens the way to a critical examination of the knowledge claims of credentialed groups, thus implicitly joining social closure theory, but also opens the way to a critical examination of the knowledge claims of credentialed groups, thus implicitly joining social closure theory with analyses of professional domination. Again, this is an area where social closure theory would benefit from incorporating insights from critiques of the power/knowledge complex and instrumental rationalization.

Third, it allows conceptualizing the class form of the middle strata in terms derived in part from its own internal logic, as opposed to the class forms represented by ownership of capital or simple labor power. Thus, social closure theory also provides a more satisfactory conception which allows for a subtle analysis of the peculiar class formation produced by credentialization, one which cannot be comprehended within either the orthodox or revisionist conceptions of class as simply a location in the mode of production: the middle strata neither constitute a unified class actor nor can be viewed as simply contradictory class locations which are inherently secondary relative to labor and capital without any reality as an independent source of class stratification and power. Their relative significance, however, must be analyzed historically and comparatively and cannot be read off from any general theory of class structure or modes of production.

Implications for Advanced Societies

Correspondence theories of education, rooted in structuralist Marxist theories of social and cultural reproduction postulated a strong functional link between the needs of capitalist economies and the educational system. The theories in question here approach the question of the social functions of education from a somewhat different perspective: their reproductive consequences for the social strata, who benefit from and control educational institutions, and only secondarily now these are in turn mediated by the overall process of economic reproduction. The advantage of Murphy's version of social closure theory is the possibility of incorporating status competition and credentialist theories within an open-ended model of cultural reproduction.

The most obvious implication of credentialist theory is a critique of technocratic and human capital theories of development, and the illusion that the expansion of education by itself will resolve problems of persisting social inequality. These conclusions, of course, converge with theories of educational reproduction in general.

The more specific contribution of a reinterpretation of credentialism via social closure theory lies in its capacity, when extended in the directions of critical theory (i.e., a critique of professional knowledge) and appropriate forms of class theory along the lines suggested by Murphy and Giddens, to provide a more differentiated account of exclusionary processes and how they might be regulated in an equitable fashion. That would require breaking up, or at least weakening, various professional monopolies, but does not necessarily imply the total denunciation of professional competence along Maoist of Illichian lines. What it would require, however, is the development of systems of social accountability, which could transform much professional training and the regulation of professional work. Despite its many obvious flaws, the collegial form of regulation within the university offers a useful model given the way in which different discipline are forced to cooperate in mutual evaluation of peers, thus precluding that any discipline be allowed exclusive rights to self-evaluation. Physicians are ultimately accountable only to other physicians whereas university physicists are accountable to chemists, engineers, and the university community as a whole.

Implications for Developing Societies

In the case of developing societies, a general theory of credentialization based on social closure and critical theory warns again any direct imitation of Western models of professions, despite the obvious importance of technical advancement. As well, the concept of the primary form of closure attunes analysis to the multiple ways in which domination may be secured, a point most decisive for any effort to abolish "capitalism." In this context, development of informal educational structure and paraprofessional occupational models regulated by social needs becomes imperative, though the key difficulty remains the primary forms of exclusion (including international relations of dependency) which may distort these processes.

Notes

1. This influence is clearly recognized, however, by Fritz Ringer who suggests Pierre Bourdieu "has given more searching attention to the symbolic contents of educational traditions, and to social categories and meanings more generally, than any other social theorist since Max Weber" (1987, 10).

2. Though the term "closure theory" is associated with the work of Frank Parkin, as Raymond Murphy points out: "The fact that Bourdieu does not use the word 'closure' should not blind us to the theoretical affinity between his analysis and closure theory, just as the absence of the word itself

from Collins's writings should not lead us to ignore the fact that his analysis is a form of closure theory" (1988, 40, fn. 7).

3. As Nicholas Abercrobie and John Urry charge, "It is not clear that the methods or effects of Frank Parkin's model are greatly different from some of those Marxists he so strongly criticises. . . . In sum, it has become increasingly difficult to decide what theory belongs in which camp. Analysis of the middle classes raises this problem particularly acutely. As "Weberians have become worried about the Boundary Problem, and 'Marxists' have recognised the importance of middle classes, the theoretical waters were bound to become muddy" (1983, 91). Nevertheless, as a more highly generalized theory, social closure analysis avoids the inescapable dogmatism of those still imbued with essentialist conceptions of class and a teleological theory of history as criticized in Jean Cohen, *Class and Civil Society* (Amherst, MA: University of Massachusetts Press, 1982); Laclau, Ernesto and Chantal Mouffe, *Hegemony and Socialist Strategy*, trans. Winston Moore and Paul Cammack (London: Verso, 1985); and Ernesto Laclau and Chantal Mouffe.

4. Critics have rejected such "new class" theory from a variety of perspectives (e.g., Aronwitz 1978; Cohen and Howard 1978; Eyerman, et al. 1987).

5. For an interesting attempt, however, to synthesize Erik Ohlin Wright and Pierre Bourdieu, see Bill Martin and Ivan Szelényi, "Beyond Cultural Capital," in *Intellectuals, Universities and the State in Western Societies*, edited by Ron Eyerman, Lennart G. Suesnsson and Thomas Söderquist (Berkley: University of California Press, 1987).

References

Abercrombie, Nicholas and John Urry. 1983. *Capital, Labour and the Middle Classes*. London: George Allen and Unwin.

Althusser, Louis. 1977. *For Marx*, trans. Ben Brewster. London: NLF.

Aronowitz, Stanley. 1978. In *Between Labor and Capital*. Edited by Pat Walker, 213–242. Montreal: Black Rose Books.

Aronowitz, Stanley and Henry A. Giroux. 1985. "The Professional-Managerial Class or Middle Strata" in *Education Under Siege: The Conservative, Liberal and Radical Debate Over Schooling*. South Hadley, MA: Bergin and Garvey.

Bell, Daniel. 1976. *The Coming of Post-Industrial Society: A Venture in Social Forecasting*. New York: Basic Books.

Bourdieu, Pierre. 1979. *La Distinction: critique social du jugement*. Paris: Minuit.

————. 1984. Distinction: *A Social Critique of the Judgement of Taste*. Cambridge, MA: Harvard University Press.

————. 1989. *La noblesse d'état: Grandes écoles et esprit de corps*. Paris: Minuit.

Bourdieu, Pierre, and Jean-Claude Passeron. 1977 [1970]. *Reproduction in Education, Society, and Culture*. Translated by Richard Nice. London and Beverly Hills: Sage.

Bowles, Samuel and Herbert Gintis. 1977. *Schooling in Capitalist America: Educational Reform and the Contradictions of Economic Life*. New York: Basic Books/Harper.

Cohen, Jean. 1982. *Class and Civil Society: The Limits of Marxian Critical Theory*. Amherst, MA: University of Massachusetts Press.

Collins, Randall. 1979. *The Credential Society: An Historical Sociology of Education and Stratification*. New York: Academic Press.

Connell, R. W. 1983. *Which Way is Up? Essays on Sex, Class and Culture*. Sydney, London, and Boston: George Allen and Unwin.

Disco, Cornelis. 1987. "Intellectuals in Advanced Capitalism: Capital, Closure, and the New-Class 'Thesis.'" In *Intellectuals, Universities, and the State in Western Modern Societies*. Edited by Ron Eyerman, Lennart G. Svensson, and Thomas Söderqvist, 50–77. Berkeley, Los Angeles and London: University of California Press.

Ehrenreich, Barbara and John Ehrenreich. "The Professional-Managerial Class" 1978. In *Between Labor and Capital*. Edited by Pat Walker, 5–48. Montreal: Black Rose Books.

Eyerman, Ron, Lennart G. Svensson, and Thomas Söderqvist, eds. 1987. *Intellectuals, Universities, and the State in Western Modern Societies*. Berkeley, London: University of California Press.

Freidson, Eliot. 1986. *Professional Powers: A Study in the Institutionalization of Formal Knowledge*. Chicago and London: University of Chicago Press.

Giddens, Anthony. 1973. *The Class Structure of the Advanced Societies*. London: Hutchinson.

Gouldner, Alvin. 1979. *The Future of Intellectuals and the Rise of the New Class*. New York: Seabury Press.

Habermas, Jürgen. 1975. *Legitimation Crisis*. Trans. Thomas McCarthy. Boston: Beacon.

Holzner, Burkat and John H. Marx, eds. 1979. *Knowledge Application: The Knowledge System in Society*. Boston: Allyn and Bacon.

Hurn, Christopher Y. 1985. *The Limits and Possibilities of Schooling: An Introduction to the Sociology of Education,* 2nd ed. Newton, MA: Allyn and Bacon.

Illich, Ivan. 1971. *Deschooling Society.* New York: Harper and Row.

———. 1973. *Tools for Conviviality.* New York: Harper and Row.

Laclau, Ernesto and Chantal Mouffe. 1985. *Hegemony and Socialist Strategy: Towards a Radical Democratic Politics.* Trans. Winston Moore and Paul Cammack. London: Verso.

Larson, Magali Sarfatti. 1977. *The Rise of Professionalism: A Sociological Analysis.* Berkeley, and London: University of California Press.

Lash, Scott and John Urry. 1987. *The End of Organized Capitalism.* Madison: University of Wisconsin Press.

Liston, Daniel P. 1988. *Capitalist Schools: Explanation and Ethics in Radical Studies of Schooling.* New York and London: Routledge and Kegan Paul.

Martin, Bill and Ivan Szelé nyi. 1987. "Beyond Cultural Capital: Toward a Theory of Symbolic Domination." In *Intellectuals, Universities and the State in Western Modern Societies.* Edited by Ron Eyerman, Lennart G. Svesnsson and Thomas Söderqvist, 16–49. Berkeley, and London: University of California Press.

Miller, Peter. 1987. *Domination and Power.* London and New York: Routledge and Kegan Paul.

Mills, C. Wright. 1951. *White Collar.* London, Oxford, and New York: Oxford University Press.

Misgeld, Dieter. 1985. "Education and Cultural Invasion: Critical Social Theory, Education as Instruction, and the 'Pedagogy of the Oppressed.' " In *Critical Theory and Public Life.* Edited by John Forester, 77–118. Cambridge, MA: MIT Press.

Morrow, Raymond A. "Social Closure Theory as Critical Theory: An Agenda for Reconciliation." *Canadian Journal of Sociology.* Forthcoming.

Morrow, Raymond and Carlos Alberto Torres. 1990. "Ivan Illich and the De-Schooling Thesis Twenty Years After." *New Education* 12:3–17.

Müller, Detlef K., Fritz Ringer, and Brian Simon, eds. 1987. *The Rise of the Modern Educational System: Structural Change and Social Reproduction 1870–1920.* Cambridge, England: Cambridge University Press.

Murphy, Raymond. 1988. *Social Closure: The Theory of Monopolization and Exclusion.* Oxford: Clarendon Press.

Offe, Claus. 1984. *Contradictions of the Welfare State*. Ed. John Keane. London: Hutchinson.

Parkin, Frank. 1979. *Marxism and Class Theory: A Bourgeois Critique*. New York: Columbia University Press.

Parsons, Talcott and Gerald M. Platt. 1973. *The American University*. Cambridge, MA: Harvard University Press.

Porat, Marc Uri. 1978. "Global Implications of the Information Society." *Journal of Communication* 28:70–80.

Ringer, Fritz. 1987. "Introduction." In *The Rise of the Modern Educational System*. Edited by Detlef Müller, Fritz Ringer and Brian Simon, 1–14. Cambridge: Cambridge University Press.

Rouse, Joseph. 1987. *Knowledge and Power: Toward a Political Philosophy of Science*. Ithaca and London: Cornell University Press.

Walker, Pat ed. 1978. *Between Labor and Capital*. Montréal: Black Rose Books.

Wright, Erik Ohlin. 1978. *Class, Crisis and the State*. London: Verso.

———. 1985. *Classes*. London: Verso.

6

Critical Pedagogy as Performative Practice: Memories of Whiteness

❑

Henry A. Giroux

While critical educators and performance artists have tradition-ally occupied separate spaces and have addressed vastly different audiences, the pedagogical and political nature of their work over-laps and continues to leak into each other. At the risk of overgener-alizing, both cultural studies theorists and critical educators engage in forms of cultural work that locate politics in the relations that ar-ticulate among symbolic representations, everyday life, and the ma-chineries of power; both engage cultural politics as an experience of sociality and learning as the outcome of diverse struggles rather than a passive reception of information; both critical traditions have emphasized what theorists such as Lawrence Grossberg and Paul Gilroy call the act of doing, being in transit,[1] and the importance of understanding theory as the grounded basis for "intervening into contexts and power. . . . in order to enable people to act more strate-gically in ways that many change their context for the better."[2] Moreover, theorists working in both fields have argued for the pri-macy of the political by calling for and struggling to produce critical public spaces, regardless of how fleeting they may be, in which "pop-ular cultural resistance is explored as a form of political resistance."[3] But while both groups share certain pedagogical and ideological practices, they rarely are in dialogue with each other due in part to the disciplinary boundaries and institutional borders that atomize, insulate, and prevent diverse cultural workers from collaborating across such boundaries.

I want to analyze how the intersection of the pedagogical and the performative might provide artists and educators alike with an opportunity to address the importance of pedagogical practices that are not only interdisciplinary, transgressive, and oppositional, but also fundamental to enacting a broader political project aimed at increasing the scope of racial, economic, and social justice in a time of diminishing hope. But first, I want to explore the interrelationship between what I will call the pedagogical as performative and a performative pedagogy.

A performative practice in its more orthodox register largely focuses on events as cultural texts that link the politics of meaning to deconstructive strategies of engagement. Such a pedagogy in Judith Butler's terms focuses on representations and "discourses that bring into being that which they name."[4] Within this form of pedagogical practice there is a great deal of emphasis on texts and how they are "presented, 'licensed,' or made 'excessive'."[5] There is a growing tendency within literary studies and cultural studies, especially in its North American versions, of "privileging cultural texts over practice as the site of the social and political."[6] The exclusive emphasis on texts, however, runs the risk of reproducing processes of reification and isolation as when the performative is framed outside of the context of history, power, and politics. In this instance, texts occupy a formalistic space that might disavow a universalistic aesthetic yet views issues such as one's commitments to the other, the ethical duty to decide between what is better and what is worse and, by extension, human rights as either meaningless, irrelevant or leftovers from a bygone age. In its most reductive moment, Lewis Gordon argues that performativity as a pedagogical practice often falls prey to a "focus on politics as rhetoric . . . [in which] the political dimension of the political is rendered invisible by virtue of being regarded as purely performative-or, as in more Foucauldian/Nietzchean articulations of this drama, purely manifestations of will to power. What one performs is rendered immaterial. Whatever 'is' is simply a performance."[7] Progressive artists and cultural studies theorists recognize that the complex terms of cultural engagement are produced performatively, but unlike Gordon, many believe that the issue is still open regarding how the performative can have some purchase either in terms of social action, or contribute to producing new forms of identity and politics while simultaneously developing a political and ethical vocabulary for making connections and struggling to create multiple public cultures.

I want to frame the relevance of a politically progressive notion of the performative within a present marked by the rise of right-wing politics, a resurgent racism, and ongoing punitive attacks on the poor, urban youth, and people of color. The invocation of a broader political context is not meant to suggest that such work be dismissed but be analyzed more critically in light of a cultural politics in which power is addressed primarily through the display of texts, bodies, and representations. A critical pedagogy of the performative might begin with Raymond Williams's insight that the "deepest impulse (informing cultural politics) is the desire to make learning part of the process of social change itself."[8] For Williams, a cultural pedagogy signals a form of permanent education which acknowledges "the educational force of our whole social and cultural experience . . . [as an apparatus of institutions and relationships that] actively and profoundly teaches."[9] Education as a cultural pedagogical practice takes place across multiple sites and signals how within diverse contexts, education makes us both subjects of and subject to relations of power.

As a performative practice, the pedagogical opens up a narrative space that affirms the contextual and the specific while simultaneously recognizing the ways in which such spaces are shot through with issues of power. Central to this referencing of the ethical and political is a pedagogical practice that refuses closure, insists on combining theoretical rigor and social relevance, and embraces commitment as a point of temporary attachment in order to take a position without standing still. The pedagogical as performative also draws upon an important legacy of artistic production in which memory work becomes a marker for recognizing one own shifting, unstable, and often contradictory location as a place from which to begin's one's work as a public intellectual.[10]

Rooted in ongoing cultural exchanges, translations, and border engagements, the pedagogical as performative rejects any rendering of the performative that conveniently edits out the difficulties and struggles posed by institutional constraints, historical processes, competing social identities, and the expansive reach of transnational capitalism. Similarly, the pedagogical as performative practice acknowledges the full range of multiple, shifting and overlapping sites of learning that, in part, produce, mediate, legitimate, and challenge those forces that are waging an assault on democratic public life in the United States. In this instance, the political becomes more pedagogical as diverse cultural workers recognize the need to work together to create/perform/construct those spaces in which desire, memory, knowledge, and the body reconfigure the possibility of speaking otherwise in order to act otherwise in diverse public cultures and terrains.

Seizing upon the role that artists and educators might play as part of a broader oppositional strategy of engagement, cultural critics such as Suzanne Lacy, Mary Jane Jacob, Coco Fusco, Stanley Aronowitz, and Carol Becker have attempted to create a new language through which people can understand and produce culture within democratic and shared structures and spaces of power. Rejecting the well-policed distinctions that pit form against content, beauty against politics, and subjective experience against objective representations, many critical educators and progressive artists have endeavored in different ways to break down the rigid boundaries and binary oppositions between art and politics, ethics and power, high and low culture, margins and center, and so on. Rather than taking up the notion of public intellectual as academic fashion plate ready for instant consumption by the *New York Times*, a number of artists (particularly performance artists and practitioners of the "new public art"), such as Barbara Kruger, Tim Miller, Guillermo Gomez-Pena, and others have reconstituted themselves within the ambivalencies and contradictions of their own distinct personal histories while simultaneously recognizing and presenting themselves through their role as artists, social critics, and public intellectuals.

Of course, few of these cultural workers define themselves self-consciously as public intellectuals. And, yet, what is so remarkable about their work is the way in which they render the political visible through pedagogical practices that attempt to make a difference in the world rather than simply reflect it. The pedagogical as performative takes on a dimension in this work that allows audiences to grapple with new questions and as Peggy Phelan, puts it ways of mis/understanding that address and critically engage the central and most urgent social problems of our time. For instance, the pedagogical as performative does not merely provide a set of representations/texts that imparts knowledge to others, it also becomes a form of cultural production in which one's own identity is constantly being rewritten. Moreover, cultural politics and the authority to which it makes a claim are always rendered suspect and provisional—not to elude the burden of judgment, meaning or commitment but to enable cultural workers to challenge forms of disciplinary knowledge and social relations that promote material and symbolic violence. The authority that artists and educators legitimate in any pedagogical site, in this instance, becomes both an object of auto critique and a critical referent for expressing a more "fundamental dispute with authority itself."[11]

I want to extend the relationship between critical pedagogy and the performative through what Jacques Derrida calls "performative interpretation . . . [that is,] "an interpretation that transforms the very thing it interprets."[12] As a pedagogical practice, "performative interpretation" suggests that how we understand and come to know ourselves and others cannot be separated from how we represent and imagine ourselves. This is not merely an attempt to reassert the pedagogical/political significance of storytelling as a performative practice as much it is to reaffirm such narratives as an integral component of memory-work and the need for people to speak affirmatively and critically out of their own histories, traditions, and personal experiences. Refusing to reduce politics to the discursive or representational, performative interpretation suggests reclaiming the political as a pedagogical intervention that links cultural texts to the institutional contexts in which they are read, the material grounding of power to the historical conditions that give meaning to the places we inhabit and the futures we desire. Within this notion of pedagogical practice, the performative becomes a site of memory, a location and critical enactment of the stories we tell to assume our role as public intellectuals willing to make visible and challenge the grotesque inequalities and intolerable oppressions of the present moment.

In what follows, I want to be more specific about how we can think politics in terms of a pedagogy of performance. In doing so, I want to switch frames by once again invoking Derrida's notion of "performative interpretation" in order to address how particular traumatic events relate to the wider disjunctions of racial politics presently at work in shaping public memory. More specifically, I want to engage an event in my own youth in which I had to cross and negotiate the fixed racial boundaries of the white working-class neighborhood that I grew up in the fifties and early sixties. The pedagogical practice at work here attempts to engage a form of memory-work that addresses whiteness both as a signifier of racial privilege to be unlearned and as an identity in transit offering the possibilities for opposition and resistance.

In my white working-class neighborhood, race and class were performative categories defined in terms of events, actions, and the outcomes of struggles we engaged in as we watched, listened, and fought with kids whose histories, languages, styles, and racial identities appeared foreign and hostile to us. Race and class were not merely nouns we used to narrate ourselves, they were verbs that governed how we interacted and performed in the midst of "others," whether they were middle-class kids or Black youths. Most of the interactions we had with "others" were violent, fraught with anger and hatred. We viewed kids who were Black or privileged from within the spaces and enclaves of a neighborhood ethos that was nourished by a legacy of racism, a dominant culture that condoned class and racial hatred, and a popular culture that rarely allowed Blacks and Whites to view each other as equals. Everywhere we looked segregation was the order of the day. Community was defined within racial and class differences and functioned largely as spaces of exclusion, spaces that more often than not pitted racial and ethnic groups against one another. Solidarity was mostly based on the principles of exclusion, and race and class identities closed down the promise of difference as central to any notion of democratic community.

When college students walked through my Smith Hill neighborhood from Providence College to reach the downtown section of the city, we taunted them, mugged them on occasion, and made it clear to them that their presence violated our territorial and class boundaries. We viewed these kids as rich, spoiled, and privileged. We hated their arrogance, and despised their music. Generally, we had no contact with middle-class and ruling-class kids until we went to high school. Hope High School (ironically named) in the 1960s was a mix of mostly poor black and white kids, on the one hand, and a small group of white, wealthy kids on the other. The school did everything to make sure that the only space we shared was the cafeteria during lunch hour. Black and working-class white kids were generally warehoused and segregated in that school. Tracked into dead-end courses, school became a form of dead-time for most of us—a place in which our bodies, thoughts, and emotions were regulated and subject to either ridicule or swift disciplinary action if we broke any of the rules. We moved within these spaces of hierarchy and segregation deeply resentful of how we were treated, but with little understanding, and no vocabulary to connect our rage to viable forms of political resistance. We were trapped in a legacy of commonsensical understandings that made us complicitous with our own oppression. In the face of injustice, we learned to be aggressive and destructive, but we learned little about what it might mean to unlearn our prejudices and join in alliances with those diverse others who were oppressed.

Rather, the everyday practices that shaped our lives were often organized around rituals of regulation and humiliation. For instance, the working-class black and White kids from my section of town entered Hope through the back door of the building while the rich White kids entered through the main door in the front of the school. We didn't miss the point, and we did everything we could to let the teachers know how we felt about it. We were loud and unruly in classes, we shook the rich kids down and took their money after school, we cheated whenever possible, but more than anything, we stayed away from school until we were threatened with being expelled. While class registered its difference through a range of segregated spaces, race was more problematic as a register of difference. Along with the Black kids in the school, our bodies rather than our minds were taken up as a privileged form of cultural capital. Both working-class Whites and Blacks resented those students who studied, talked in the elaborated code, and appeared to live outside of their bodies and desires. Both groups fought, desired, moved, and pushed our bodies to extremes, especially in those public spheres open to us, that is, the football field, basketball court, and the baseball diamond.

As a working-class White kid, I found myself in classes with Black kids, played basketball with them, and listened mostly to Black music. But we rarely socialized outside of school. Whiteness in my neighborhood was a signifier of pride, a marker of racial identity experienced through a dislike of Blacks. Unlike the current generation of many working-class kids, we defined ourselves in opposition to Blacks, and while listening to their music did not appropriate their styles. Racism ran deep in that neighborhood, and no one was left untouched by it. But identities are always in transit, mutate, change, and often become more complicated as a result of chance encounters, traumatic events, or unexpected collisions. The foundation of my White racial identity was shaken while I was in the ninth grade in the last year of junior high school.

I was on the junior high basketball team along with a number of other White and Black kids. The coach had received some tickets to a Providence College game. Providence College's basketball team had begun to receive extensive public attention because it had won a National Invitation Basketball tournament; moreover, the team roster included a number of famous players such as Lenny Wilkens. We loved the way in which these guys played; we tried to emulate their every move into our own playing styles. Getting tickets to see them play was a like a dream come true for us. Having only two tickets to give away, the coach held a contest after school in the gym to decide who would go to the game. He decided to give the tickets to the two players who made the most consecutive foul shots. The air was tense as we started to compete for the tickets. I ended up with two other players in a three-way tie; we had one chance to break it. As I approached the foul line, Brother Hardy, a large Black kid started taunting me as I began to shoot. We exchanged some insults and suddenly we were on each other, fists flying. Suddenly I was on the floor, blood gushing out of my nose; the fight was over as quickly as it started. The coach made us continue the match, and, ironically, Brother Hardy and I won the tickets, shook hands, and went to the game together. The fight bridged us together in a kind of mutual esteem we didn't quite understand but respected. Soon afterwards, we starting hanging out together and became friends. After graduating from junior high school, we parted and I didn't see him again until the following September when I discovered he was also attending Hope High school.

I made the varsity my sophomore year, Brother Hardy never bothered to try out. We talked once in awhile in the school halls but the racial boundaries in the school did not allow us to socialize much with each other. But that soon changed. The second month into the school year, I noticed that during lunch hour everyday a number of Black kids would cut in front of White kids in the food line, shake them down, and take their lunch money. I was waiting for it to happen to me, but it never did. In fact, the same Blacks who did the shaking down would often greet me with a nod or "hey, man, how you doin?" as they walked by me in the corridors as well as the cafeteria. I later learned that Brother Hardy was considered the toughest Black in the school; he had put out the word to his friends to leave me alone.

During the week, I played basketball at night at the Benefit Street Club, situated in the Black section of the city. I was one of the few Whites allowed to play in the gym. The games were fast and furious, and you had to be good to continue. I started hanging out with Brother Hardy and on weekends went to the blues clubs along with him and his friends. We drank, played basketball, and rarely talked to each other about race. Soon some of my friends and myself were crossing a racial boundary by attending parties with some of our black teammates.

I couldn't articulate how my crossing the racial divide gradually served to challenge the white racism to which my body had grown accustomed, but it slowly became clear to me in those formative years that I had to redefine the modalities of my whiteness as I moved within and across a number of racially defined spheres. I had no intention of becoming a Black wannabee, even if such an option existed in the neighborhood in which I grew up and, of course it didn't. But at the same time, I began to hate the racism that shaped my own identity and the identities of my White friends. My crossing the racial divide was met at best with ridicule, and at worst with disdain. Crossing this border was never an option for Brother Hardy and his friends; if they had crossed the racial border to come into my neighborhood, they would have been met with racial epitaphs and racist violence. Even in the early sixties, it became clear to me that such border crossings were restricted and only took place with a passport stamped with the legacy of racial privilege. My body was relearning about race and identity because I was beginning to unlearn the racist ideologies that I took for granted for so long. But I had no language to engage how I felt nor did I understand how to reject the notion that to be a working-class White kid meant one had to be a racist by default.

The language I inherited as a kid came from my family, friends, school, and the larger popular culture. Rarely did I encounter a vocabulary in any of these spheres that ruptured or challenged the material relations of racism or the stereotypes and prejudices that reinforced race and class divisions. It was only later as I entered the sixties that I discovered in the midst of the Civil Rights and anti-war movement languages of dissent and possibility that helped me to rethink my own memories of youth, racism, and class discrimination.

My sense of what it meant to be a White male emerged performatively through my interactions with peers, the media, and the broader culture. The act of listening and watching various media provided an intersection of knowledge and drama that legitimated the social roles we occupied as kids as well as the range of possibilities by which we could imagine something beyond the world in which we lived. The trauma I associated with negotiating between the solidarity I felt with Brother Hardy and my White working-class friends suggests that education works best when those experiences that shape and penetrate one's lived reality are jolted, unsettled, and made the object of critical analysis. In looking back on my experience, moving through the contested terrains of race, gender, and class, it is clear to me that power is never exerted only through economic control, but also through what might be called a form of "cultural pedagogy." Racism and class hatred are a learned activity, and as a kid I found myself in a society that was all too ready to teach it.

I have tried to illustrate how memory-work as a pedagogical dimension of the performative turns biography into a social text, how such a text might challenge our understanding of the present, our relationship to others, and what it might mean to use such texts as part of a broader struggle for radical democracy and racial justice.

I want to finish by suggesting that pedagogy as a performative and political practice become a defining principle among artists, media workers, social workers, teachers, and other cultural workers who work in diverse sites and public spheres. It is crucial that the relevancies that inform such cultural work provide a vision and space, a language of critique and possibility, for addressing what the responsibilities defining the role of the artist/cultural worker and critic might be within and across national and transnational terrains.

In part, this suggests the necessity for cultural workers to develop collective projects in which traditional binarisms of margin/ center, unity/difference, local/national, public/private can be reconstituted through more complex representations of identification, belonging, and community. This implies a fundamental redefinition of the meaning of artists as public intellectuals. As public intellectuals, we must define ourselves not merely as marginal, avant-garde figures, professionals, or academics acting alone, but as cultural workers whose collective knowledge and actions presuppose insurgent visions of public life, community, and moral accountability. What is crucial is a conception of the political that is open yet committed, respects specificity without erasing global considerations, and provides new spaces for collaborative work engaged in productive social change.

Artists, educators, and other cultural workers need to rethink how cultural work in the arts, schools, and other sites can be expressed through an "integrative critical language through which values, ethics, and social responsibility"[13] are fundamental to creating shared critical public spaces that engage, translate, and transform those vexing social problems that mark the current historical period. The time has come for artists, educators, and other cultural workers to join together to defend and construct those cultural sites and public spheres that are essential for a viable democracy. Under these conditions, art would be unsettling without being elitist, and politics would not mean as Edward Said has pointed out, that the artists or cultural worker had fully arrived, but that one could never go home again.[14]

Notes

1. See bell hooks, "Performance Practice as a Site of Opposition," in *Let's Get It On*, edited by Catherine Ugwu, (Seattle: Bay Press, 1996), pp. 210–221; Paul Gilroy, " '. . . To Be Real' The Dissident forms of Black Expressive Culture," in *Let's Get It On*, edited by Catherine Ugwu (Seattle: Bay Press, 1996), pp. 12–33.

2. Lawrence Grossberg, "Toward a Genealogy of the State of Cultural Studies," in *Disciplinarity and Dissent in Cultural Studies*, edited by Cary

Nelson and Dilip Parameshwar Gaonkar, (New York: Routledge and Kegan Paul, 1996), p. 143.

3. David Bailey and Stuart Hall, "The Vertigo of Displacement," *Ten 8*, 2:3 ((1992): 19.

4. Peter Osborne and Lynne Segal, "Gender as Performance: An Interview with Judith Butler," *Radical Philosophy*, no. 67 (Summer 1994): 33.

5. Simon Frith, *Performance Rites* (Cambridge: Harvard University Press, 1996), p. 204.

6. Herman Gray, "Is Cultural Studies Inflated?" in *Disciplinarity and Dissent in Cultural Studies*, edited by Cary Nelson and Dilip Parameshway Goankar (New York: Routledge and Kegan Paul, 1996), p. 211.

7. Cited in Joy James, *Transcending the Talented Tenth: Black Leaders and American Intellectuals* (New York: Routledge and Kegan Paul, 1997), p. 175.

8. Raymond Williams, "Adult Education and Social Change," in *What I Came to Say* (London: Hutchinson-Radus, 1989), p. 158.

9. Raymond Williams, *Communications* (New York: Barnes and Noble, 1967), p. 15.

10. bell hooks, "Performance as a Site of Opposition," in *Let's Get It On*, edited by Catherine Ugwu (Seattle: Bay Press, 1995).

11. R. Radhakrishnan. "Canonicity and Theory: Toward a Poststructuralist Pedagogy." in *Theory / Pedagogy / Politics*, edited by Donald Morton and Mas'ud Zavarzadeh, (Urbana: University of Illinois Press, 1991), pp. 112–135.

12. Jacques Derrida, *Specters of Marx* (New York: Routledge and Kegan Paul, 1994), p. 51.

13. Both of these quotes are taken from Suzanne Lacy, "Introduction: Cultural Pilgrimages and Metaphoric Journeys," in *Mapping the Terrain: New Genre Public Art*, edited by Suzanne Lacy (Seattle: Bay State Press, 1995), pp. 20, 43.

14. Edward Said, *Representations of the Intellectual* (New York: Pantheon, 1994).

7

Tracking, Detracking, and the Politics of Educational Reform: A Sociological Perspective

❑

Amy Stuart Wells and Jeannie Oakes

A sociological analysis of schools' efforts to "detrack," or move toward less stratified systems of grouping students for instruction, suggests that reformers must attend to both macro- and micro-dimensions of change and embed their efforts in deep understandings of the culture and history in which these changes take place (Raab 1994). Perhaps the most significant contribution that sociologists of education can make to the study of education policy is contextualizing school-level reforms efforts, such as, detracking within a broader interpretation of the macro-societal expectations of education as a social institution. These societal expectations are shaped iteratively by political and economic developments of the nation or world and the interpretations or redefinition accorded these developments by actors in social institutions (Dale 1994; Hargreaves 1985).

In this chapter, we bring data from our three-year study of ten racially mixed secondary school that are detracking into a dialogue with the current political agenda for education reform in the United States—most notably the increasing role of the "market" in the education system and the simultaneous encouragement of decentralization and devolution of educational governance to the school and community level (Dale 1994; Beare 1993; Henig 1994; Torres, in press).

Our attempt to contextualize the change processes of these schools within a broader framework is important because we are studying detracking efforts at a particular moment in history when the dominant political discourse of educational reform calls upon schools to become more efficient and competitive "service delivery systems" designed to meet the specific demands of their most power "clients" (Henig 1994). Virtually absent from this discourse are equity concerns such as providing low-income and minority students—the less politically or economically powerful "clients"—greater educational opportunities.

Detracking reform, on the other hand, challenges the legitimacy of a track structure that creates and perpetuates class- and race-based differences in access to knowledge and the credentials needed for college and successful careers. In this way, detracking is a democratic reform, designed to promote school-level inquiry and dialogue around practices and norms that perpetuate inequality and inhibit interracial respect, understanding, and friendship (see Oakes 1992; CODA 1992). Detracking requires educators, parents, and students to examine the practices of the school as a whole and question how those practices could better meet the educational needs of *all* students. Such an inquiry process runs counter to current political efforts to devolve power and control to market forces and highly individualized consumer-provider relationships between schools and families. By placing detracking efforts in this larger macro-societal context we are able to better understand the political struggles taking place in the ten communities we visited.

Furthermore, we approach this macro-micro analysis of detracking efforts from a critical perspective, and thus we see tracking as one manifestation of prevailing social and power relations (Oakes 1985; Oakes and Wells 1995). Yet, we realize that these power relationships are localized in different schools with their own techniques and tactics, which makes the study of individual school sites relevant to understanding how the prevailing social order came to be and the possibilities for broader social change (Dale 1994; Harvey 1990). While this form of critical sociopolitical study of education has become increasingly popular among sociologists of education in the United Kingdom, education policy studies in the United States have remained far more pragmatic, focused on problem solving within the existing power relations instead of questioning the basis for those relations and its relationship to the failure of educational reform (see Halpin and Troyna 1994; Dale 1994). We hope to inform the study of U.S. educational policy with this more theoretical and critical approach.

Political Context of Detracking Reform

In the last decade, a growing number of educators across the nation have come face-to-face with the pedagogical, moral, and ethical problems associated with tracking or ability grouping. They have been influenced by research showing the harmful effects of tracking on the achievement of low-track students as well as studies demonstrating that race and class play a major role in students' track placements, with low-income, African-American, and Latino children consistently placed in low-level classes regardless of their prior achievement (Oakes 1985; Oakes 1990; Oakes 1995; Oakes and Guiton 1995; Weiner and Oakes 1995). In addition, research on the complex and varied nature of intelligence and its implication that schools and rigid track systems misrecognize and devalue many students' ability and talent has influenced educator's thinking about tracking, as have their own concerns for students who they believe have been labeled incorrectly and their larger frustration with the pedagogical practices that accommodate the track structure (Oakes, Lipton and Jones 1995; Oakes, Wells, Datnow, and Jones 1995). Many such educators have galvanized school- and district-level reform efforts to detrack their schools (see Oakes and Lipton 1992; Wheelock 1992; Ascher 1992).

The frustrations of these educators and their thoughtful questions about how schools detrack led us to embark on a three-year case study of racially mixed secondary schools that were in the process of detracking. More specifically, our research team[1] set out in 1992 to investigate *what happens when* someone with power in a racially mixed secondary school decides to reduce tracking. Thus, rather than look for a simple how-to formula for detracking, we explored the political struggles over detracking at each of ten school sites and how those struggles influenced and were influenced by the normative understandings of educators, parents, and students as well as the technical changes taking place inside the schools (Oakes 1992).

In selecting the ten schools for our study, we sought variation across cases on the racial and social class mix of the student body and surrounding community as well as the geographic locations and characteristics (e.g., region, urbanicity) of the schools and their districts (Oakes and Wells 1995). The ten schools we chose are spread across the country, with one in the Northeast, three in the Midwest, one in the South, two in the Northwest, and three in various regions of California. Six are high schools, ranging in size from 1,400 to

3,000 students, and four are middle schools with between 550 and 1,300 students. The racial and ethnic composition as well as the socioeconomic status of students within the schools varies widely. Different schools include significant mixes of White, African American, Latino, American Indian/Alaska Native, and/or Asian students. We visited each of the ten schools three times and conducted in-depth, semi-structured interviews; observed campuses, classrooms, and meetings; and collected pertinent documents.

The overarching purpose of our study was to uncover the dynamics of detracking reform in the context of the schools and communities where it is taking place and to understand what such reform means to those participating in it (Oakes and Wells 1995). Thus, we set out to tell the stories of real people in real schools in order to inform not only practitioners but also state and federal policymakers of the barriers and possibilities of detracking reform. The policy relevance of our study was grounded in the broad political support for detracking from conservative and liberal policymakers alike in the late 1980s and early 1990s.

For instance, detracking in the form of eliminating remedial or bottom-track classes has been, in the recent past, touted by politicians on the right as consistent with the "educational excellence" movement of the 1980s and states' efforts to raise standards and tighten graduation requirements. On the left, detracking has been perceived as a Civil Rights issue, an attack on within-school racial segregation and unequal educational opportunity based on race and class. Thus, in the last decade support for detracking has come from a wide range of organizations, including the NAACP Legal Defense and Educational Fund, the ACLU, the Children's Defense Fund, the College Board, the Carnegie Corporation, and the National Education Association (Oakes and Wells 1995).

In 1990, the National Governor's Association proposed eliminating tracking and ability grouping as a strategy to meet the then-new education goal established by President Bush and the governors and described in the Bush Administration's reform proposal, America 2,000 (National Governor's Association 1990). At the same time, and in line with the movement toward higher goals and standards for all students, a number of states targeted tracking in their recent education reforms (e.g., Massachusetts, Kentucky, Texas, and Alabama). At its 1990 national convention, the National Education Association recommended—albeit cautiously—that schools abandon conventional tracking practices.

With a growing number of educators at the local school level, accompanied by policymakers at the national and state levels all calling for less tracking, the movement toward detracking appeared to have broad political support. Yet, a simultaneous shift in educational policymaking was occurring in the 1980s and early 1990s, which, as we learned from our ten schools, has made detracking reform more problematic. This shift is the large political movement toward a more decentralized and deregulated educational system in which practitioners are increasingly forced to respond to market forces rather than public policy in running their schools. In other words, just as more schools are poised to make a commitment to the needs of the least advantaged students by offering them access to higher status courses and curriculum, and just as many policymakers seemed (until very recently) prepared to offer these educators political support for such reforms, the direction of the educational system has become more tightly tied to postmodern demands of the free market and those with the resources to control it. Competitive, market-based reforms designed to decentralize and deregulate education—for example, site-based management, open enrollment, charter schools and tuition vouchers—are changing the dynamics of the educational change process as schools strive to find their niche and powerful "clients" demand educational practices that will assure their children have an advantage in the competitive post-secondary market.

Nearly all of the schools in our study are located in districts that have traditionally been fairly decentralized but have, in the last five years or so, moved toward greater decentralization through site-based management, shared decision-making reforms. Interestingly enough, site-based management reforms were implemented in these districts about the same time that district administrators and boards of education began grappling with their tracking and detracking policies. In this way, decentralization of decision-making became a convenient way to "pass the buck" to educators at the school sites instead of supporting detracking through strong and coherent district policies. In fact, in some districts, policies were designed to dissuade individual schools from detracking students in the top classes.

For instance, at one of the high schools we studied, the district office instructed all the schools that the advanced placement/honors program—the highest track—should not be collapsed into the general college prep track. After ordering schools to leave students in the high end of the spectrum alone, the district office gave schools the following recommendation:

In the spirit of site-based management and decentralized master schedule construction, principals have been asked only to monitor curriculum tracking and ability grouping at their sites. Also, principals have been encouraged to reduce tracking "basic" and "standard" students in subject areas in which departments support this change (Datnow 1995, 11).

And, despite this district's policy of "decentralized master schedule construction," the school board denied the high school's request to change its calendar to better accommodate the schedules, achievement rates, and thus track placement of low-track Latino students.

At one of the middle schools in our study, the district's administrators espouse shared decision-making, but quickly put the brakes on this process if one of the schools goes too far with a reform effort, such as detracking that is unpopular with powerful parents and thus conflicts with the district's goals and philosophy. When asked what he does if educators at one of the schools in the district decide to implement a reform that he does not agree with, the superintendent stated, "If its reasonable—looking at the research and what research tells us about good practice and what needs to be happening—*if it's something that fits the community*, then fine" (Yonezewa 1995, 19; emphasis added).

In the micro-politics of the communities we studied, decentralization of major decision-making from the districts to the schools appears to be highly dependent on two factors: First, whether or not district administrators and board members want to push the responsibility for politically unpopular change, such as detracking, onto educators at the school sites; and second, whether the district officials feel they need to intercede into site-based decisions on behalf of powerful parents or constituents who complain directly to the district office, bypassing the educators at the school. With no powerful state or federal policies mandating detracking or requiring all students to be taught a rich curriculum grounded in high standards, students' opportunities to learn are dependent upon the local political context and the ability of educators to persuade powerful constituents of the need for detracking reform.

The political and philosophical inconsistencies between detracking and decentralization have become more apparent on a macro-policy level as the support for national standards embodied in President Clinton's Goals 2000 legislation (a slightly more liberal successor to Bush's "American 2000" proposal) has plummeted. Passed with bipartisan support in 1994 before the Congressional election, Goals 2000 has been touted as a model of "systemic reform," which calls for centralized accountability and decentralized governance. Schools and districts, under this major piece of federal legislation, are held accountable for students' performance by centralized, "world-class standards." Meanwhile, greater authority is decentralized to the local level, allowing educators, parents, and students to decide how best to meet the standards. More specifically, Goals 2000 offers states funding to develop state curriculum frameworks and complementary assessment programs that would meet or surpass the rigor of the voluntary national standards in twelve subject matter areas. Simultaneously, Goals 2000 has called for states to grant greater autonomy and flexibility to schools as they implement the state frameworks. Theoretically, less government regulation is needed under systemic reform, because schools are held accountable for student outcomes as measured against the standards, frameworks, and tests (O'Day and Smith 1993).

Proponents of this systemic reform strategy of simultaneous centralization and decentralization believe that freeing schools of bureaucratic constraints, while assuring that all students meet the same high standards, will lead to greater equality of opportunities across schools and districts. Yet, when the federal legislation was first proposed, educators, researchers, and advocates argued that efforts to hold all schools accountable based on standards and student outcomes were being cast onto an uneven playing field in which some schools were less able to provide students with the "opportunities to learn" content reflected on the state tests (see for example, Darling-Hammond 1992; Oakes 1994). The final legislation half-heartedly attempted to address these concerns by expanding the bill to include voluntary opportunity-to-learn standards to assess student access to educational resources and high-quality instruction (U.S. Dept. of Education 1994; Lewis 1994).

While the issue of students' varying opportunities to learn remains important in efforts to detrack schools, political developments since the 1994 elections have brought additional equity issues related to decentralization into clearer focus. Republican politicians, once the champions of educational standards, have launched a political assault on the national standards movement. Robert Dole, 1996 presidential candidate and Senate majority leader, attacked the proposed history standards, calling them un-American: "The purpose of the national history standards seems not to be to teach our children certain facts about our history, but to denigrate America's story while sanitizing and glorifying other cultures" (Pitsch 1995[a]).

Overall, Congressional support for the national standards and systemic reform has dissipated, as is illustrated in the House of Representatives' 1995 legislative proposal to fold Goals 2000 and several other federal programs into one large block grant to the states while eliminating the opportunity-to-learn standards. Meanwhile, conservative groups are lobbying Republican members of Congress to end federal involvement in standards setting of any kind (Pitsch 1995[b]; Diegmueller 1995[a] and Diegmueller 1995[b]).

Conservatives have not, however, abandoned the goal of decentralization and deregulation of the educational system as they desert the standards movement. The same 1995 House of Representatives proposal would allow states to use federal block grants for school choice programs that involved private schools, deregulated charter schools, and for-profit private management firms to run public schools (Pitsh 1995[a]).

At the state level, the movement toward centralized standards has also encountered political roadblocks, particularly in California, where the implementation of standards-based systemic reform presaged the national movement by nearly a decade. In 1994, state funding was discontinued for the new state testing system, the California Learning Assessment System (CLAS), designed to test students on the content of the state curriculum frameworks. The demise of CLAS began with a political backlash by conservative religious groups over the content and morality of the test. Recent efforts to revise and reinstate CLAS have failed in the California Assembly (Lindsay 1995). Similar political protests have erupted in other states and districts implementing standards-based or outcomes-based reforms designed to hold schools accountable for student learning in an increasingly decentralized educational system (see for example, "News in Brief" Education Week).

Still, in the state houses as in Congress, the backlash against standards has not lessened the enthusiasm for massive decentralization of decision-making and deregulation of the education system from government equity-based mandates or the infusion of market forces to foster greater competition between schools. And thus we now find ourselves in a era of massive decentralization with fewer policy mechanisms in place to assure that schools are serving all students. Hand in hand with efforts to decentralize is an erosion of political will for equity based reforms and a growing demand for market-based solutions, especially vouchers and private for-profit management of public schools, to educational problems (Torres, in press). Gone is a political climate that could create high-status content standards for all students bolstered by meaningful opportunity-to-learn standards for schools. Such a national reform would be more conducive to detracking at the local school level. Instead, decentralization, deregulation, and market forces are fundamentally changing the relationship between schools and the families they serve, giving more power and voice to those well-served by the existing track structure. At the same time, the promise of higher standards for students relegated to the lowest-track classes is fading from sight.

Decentralization, the Market Metaphor and Detracking Reform

One of the important lessons we have learned from the schools in our detracking study is that many parents of students in high-track classes exude a strong sense of entitlement. According to these parents, their children are entitled to "more"—that is, resources, teacher time, challenging curriculum, and better instructional strategies—because they are more intelligent and talented than other students. Strongly related to this sense of entitlement and its legitimacy is what we have referred to as elsewhere as the social construction of intelligence and cultural biases in favor of White, middle- and upper-middle-class cultural capital inherent in such a construction (see Oakes, Wells, Datnow, and Jones 1995)

Yet, even when these conventional, socially constructed meanings of intelligence, as measured by standardized tests, are employed, high-track students do not always prove to be more meritorious or deserving than low-track students. In fact research on student track placement in racially mixed schools has shown that even when White middle-class and poor African-American students have similar test scores, White students are far more likely to be placed in high-track class than are the African-American or Latino students (Oakes 1995; Oakes and Guiton 1995; Welner and Oakes 1995). And research on students placement in math classes demonstrates the influence that white and middle-class parents have in getting their children into higher-level classes even when their scores and prior achievement is below the cut-off for such courses (Useem 1991).

Thus, we were not surprised to find in our study that powerful, more affluent parents play a significant role in maintaining a hierarchical track structure despite efforts of reform-minded educators to deconstruct the hegemony that supports this system (see Wells and Serna, in press). Yet the educators at the ten schools we visited study have taught us about the salience of the macro-level policy movement toward greater decentralization and the market metaphor for school improvement in the schools' efforts to detrack. This recent trend toward market forces and local control of schools amplifies the power of white and wealthy parents to thwart detracking efforts and maintain a tracking system that benefits their children at the expense of others. Meanwhile, the same postmodern, post-Fordist economic conditions that infuse market solutions into every sphere of public life—increasing concentration of capital in the hands of a small transnational elite, greater dependence of the economy on technology and the information industry, rising un- and underemployment, and the relative weakness of the state vis-à-vis the market—have led to declining fortunes among the middle class and render parents' efforts to pass on their relative economic and social advantage to their children more problematic. Here, at the nexus of the macro-societal changes in expectations of educational institutions and the micro-political practices employed by powerful parents to maintain their market advantage, lie deeper understandings about public education and democracy.

Much of the current political push for decentralization of the educational system and other government run institutions is rooted in the early years of the Reagan presidency. According to Jeffrey Henig 1994), the two broadest unifying themes of the Reagan administration were privatization and "New Federalism." The goals of privatization were to shrink the size of the government at all levels and to increase reliance on market forces, volunteerism, and individual demands to achieve social ends. The goal of New Federalism was to shift power from the national government to the state and ultimately the local level, thus returning greater control to local governments and their constituents while getting big government out of their lives (1994, 84).

Similarly, in his book, *Chain Reaction*, Thomas Byrne Edsall (1991) argues that Reagan's political popularity and success was due in large part to his ability to convince thousands of White working-class voters that the federal government had gone too far in its efforts to protect the rights of minorities, and later working women and gays, becoming far too large, bureaucratic and intrusive in the process. In this way, Reagan's symbolic politics fanned the early flames of a deep resentment toward the federal government and a broader anti-government rhetoric that is evident today in many political actions, from the bombing of the Oklahoma City federal building to the call for ending affirmative action policies. Within this anti-government framework, the dual themes of privatization, which translates into the market metaphor for education, and demand of greater local control go hand-in-hand.[2]

Recent reforms to turn over educational governance to the private sphere, especially tuition voucher plans and the practice of hiring for-profit firms to manage public schools, are direct descendants of Reagan's political advocacy of decentralization and privatization. The United States is not alone in its movement toward education via markets and local control. The educational systems of industrialized English-speaking nations across the globe, including England, Scotland, Australia, and New Zealand, have been shaped by the powerful rhetoric of devolution, deregulation, and parent and community control (Troyna 1994).

According to its critics, this international educational reform movement is part and parcel of an ideological shift in which democracy is framed in terms of individualism, and education is framed in terms of consumerism. The global economic transformation in the post-Fordist, information age and the resulting decline in median and mean incomes of citizens in these relatively wealthy countries has created a political situation in which education is perceived, now more than ever, as an "investment" against declining fortunes. According to Jane Kenway, Chris Bigum and Lindsay Fitzclarence (1993) in their documentation of privatization of education in Australia:

> . . . markets require a shift in focus from the collective and the community to the individual, from public service to private service, and from other people to the self. Clearly, in promoting the marketization of education, policymakers seek to promote and tap into a cult of educational selfishness in the national interest. Educational democracy is redefined as consumer democracy in the educational supermarket. . . . Consumers seek the competitive edge at the expense of others and look for value-added education" (1993, 116).

In a postmodern age in which global markets transcend and dominate political nation states, the substitution of market forces for government run services becomes a "natural" evolution. And thus, the educational system becomes increasingly commodified or reified, which means that social relationships between educators and families become material objects in the sphere of market exchange. The resulting shifts in the educational system lead to market-based solutions such as increased competition, choice, and individualism.

Such shifts, write Kenway et al. (1993), "position education in a consumer-product discourse" (1993, 112).

According to Barry Troyna (1994), the impact of these shifts on the shape and provision of education "has been both fundamental and pervasive," creating a dynamic "where providers are encouraged to compete against one another and consumers are encouraged to express their preferences" (1994, 1).

According to a principal at one suburban school in our study that competes with nearby private schools for White and wealthy students, he cannot consider dropping any of the ten Advanced Placement (AP) courses offered in his school despite the philosophical clash between the school's broader reform effort and the specialized, test-prep curriculum of AP classes. "I guarantee you private schools aren't scrapping AP. I am competing with private schools, and I've got to have those kids."

The increasing reliance on market forces and the shrinking role of the government in providing educational services unquestionably lessens the role that public policy can play in redistributing resources such as educational opportunity, to those who most need it. According to Joel F. Handler (forthcoming) in his book on decentralization, "Privatization shifts power to those who can more readily exercise power in the market" (p. 11). As Kenway et al. note, markets are not premised on the assumption of fairness or equality:

> While their [markets'] proponents make the claim that there is a general benefit from competitive self-interest, they also argue that those who play according to the rules and are best at the game deserve the greatest rewards. Ultimately, markets operate according to the logic of profit, only in certain sets of interests and let the "weak" go to the wall. They work to produce a selfish, individualistic culture in which the main moral imperative is gratification, not the collective good (1993, 120).

Echoing Kenway et al.'s concern, Geoff Whitty (forthcoming) argues that in the last decade in Britain, politicians have come to accept the notion that social affairs are best organized according to the "general principle of a consumer sovereignty." Consistent with this perception, a counselor at one high school in our study noted that parents of the honors students will not even take the time to listen to the teachers or administrators about the pedagogical reasons for doing away with the honors track. She said they are simply "not as concerned with the whole [school] as much as they should be" (Datnow 1995, 63). Similarly, an assistant principal in one of the high schools we studied noted that "many upper class, professional parents hold occupational positions in which they work toward equity and democracy, but expect their children to be given special treatment . . ." (Ray 1995, 2).

The shift in power toward stronger market contenders is readily apparent in the ideology of one high school principal in our study who actively engages in private fund raising activities (as opposed to campaigning for public bond issues) to buy new buildings and equipment for the school. Through this privatization practice, he has become increasingly beholden to wealthy parents in the district:

> You don't let one "A" student go to a private school at all if you can help it. You go to their homes, you recruit them. . . . Because you start losing those people, one of those things those people do is they come out to school, they support schools. Another thing they do is they give their money, they give their money not only to tax . . . we have three or four or five categories, these are the people who give the hundred dollar bill while somebody else is giving ten. You want your ten dollar bills, you don't turn them off, and you're glad for anybody who can give a ten dollar bill, the person who can't give you any bill, you still want them in the public school. But my gosh, we need money just as much as anybody else. You know, we've got a, we've got a funny dichotomy, we are the democratic institution in this nation and yet sometimes we have to recognize that if we don't act a little elite, we're gonna lose the elite and then . . . you can't be just democratic if all you have is the low achievers and the poor people . . . they don't have the money to give their PTO and all that stuff, the extra stuff to raise.

Similarly, according to the principal of one of the middle schools in our study, ". . . as our business manager, superintendent once told me, the power is neither Black nor White; it's green—as in money. And that's where the power is. Rich people have clout. Poor people don't have clout" (see Yonezawa 1995).

Hanging in the political balance above the shift in power away from government control of schools and toward market-based reforms are civil rights and equity issues, such as detracking. The history of U.S. education teaches us that the weaker the role of the federal (and to some extent the state) government in educational policy, the less likelihood that policies to ensure equal access to educational resources will be passed and implemented. Many of the "regulations" and the resultant centralization of educational decision making over the last thirty years—especially federal legislation and court orders—were designed to address the unequal access in locally controlled schools. Similarly, David N. Plank and William L. Boyd (1994) note that intervention on the part of federal authorities or courts has been necessary in nearly all instances to overcome indifference or opposition of local community to the demands of minority members. "The withdrawal of federal or judicial supervision of policies aimed at improving the relative standing of minorities, in these instances, might lead to the reassertion of majority control and the reversal of policies that favor minority interests" (1994, 269).[3]

According to Art E. Wise (1982), the centralization of educational policy in the 1960s and 1970s was designed to address equity issues and overcome problems that the local schools were unwilling or unable to solve, such as segregation or the rights of disadvantaged students. Wise argues that these "equity problems" of access to resources and programs should not be decentralized to the local level because "community control and citizen participation tend to serve the dominant political interests within the community" (1982, 209). It is unlikely, according to Wise, that in a system of decentralized governance that minority student interests will be well served. This historical perspective on the redistributive and regulatory role of the federal government in the name of equity is important to understanding the current political backlash against "big government" and the significance of a critique of complete decentralization and deregulation.

Dan Lewis and Karen Nakagawa (1995), in their research on five cities undergoing various forms of decentralization with no additional resources, found that the reform merely shifts "the appearance of control" to the new participants, while ensuring that "the balance of information and power stays firmly with the traditional elites" (1995, 168). David K. Cohen (1990) argues that White and wealthy parents, who are already politically organized, accustom to community activism and less deferential toward educational professionals, are most ready to fill the local political gaps created by decentralization. To the extent that these activated and involved parents do not see detracking reform as in their best interest, they will prevent it from moving forward. Deregulated schools, responding to the demands of their most powerful, efficacious, and vocal consumers, will be obligated to comply.

Research on parent involvement in education has shown that more affluent, well-educated, wealthy parents frequently use their political power and cultural capital to influence educators to comply with their specific demands (See Lareau 1989; Van Galen 1987). In more deregulated and decentralized educational systems in which schools compete with each other for clients, the demands of these powerful parents could have even greater political and economic consequences for the future of each school.

One of the high school principals in our study is very much guided in his decision making by his interactions with some of the parents, especially the PTO Executive Board, which is a fairly tight knit group of almost all White and middle- to middle-class parents. The Board meets monthly with the principal, mainly to function as his "sounding board" for issues of concern or proposed changes at the school (such as detracking). Each of the fifty PTO board members serves a two-year term; new members are nominated and approved by those currently on the board. This governance structure means that not only is change slow and incremental but it also must not conflict with the perceived best interest of White and wealthy students. Meanwhile, the principal advocates his leadership style and his efforts to include these parents in the decision-making process as an important element in maintaining racial stability (e.g., staving off white flight) in the community.

Similarly, in nearly all the schools in our detracking study, change efforts are thwarted by fear or actual threat of White flight. The superintendent of a district including one of the middle schools in our study discussed the difficulty he encounters when he talks to parents about equity-based reforms in his schools:

> If we're going to start talking about all kinds of other things like equity in schools, how are we going to train the parents to understand what we're even talking about? Because what's going to be perceived is 'You're just trying to give me a bunch of mumbo-jumbo so you can take care of those Black kids'. . . . We're going to upset people and spend a lot of money . . . and what'll happen is the White people will leave the system (Yonezawa, 1995, 15).

In situations such as these, fear of White flight on the part of local educators gives White and wealthy parents greater voice in school governance, which, paradoxically, can work against one of the touted benefits of decentralization—increased autonomy and professionalism of educators. Jane Hannaway's (1993) research on decentralization in two school districts, for example, refutes arguments put forth by proponents of decentralization and deregulation in education that such reforms will provide teachers with greater decision-making power and thus result in improved instruction. Hannaway's notes that teachers, even in centralized and highly regulated districts already have very high levels of discretion. Furthermore, she found in the two decentralized districts that teachers had less, not more discretion. The controls, however, are social controls—that is, political pressure from parents, or "clients," and the community—rather than bureaucratic ones.

High-Track Clients and Detracking Reform

As the prospect of national "world-class" standards fades into the political rhetoric of the 1996 election and states wrestle with the political viability of their own standards and assessment, educators in schools and district offices must answer to anxious parents, particularly White and wealthy parents, who are living in an era of "declining fortunes." In this way, the same macro-societal forces that weaken governments vis-à-vis markets have created an economy in which parents work harder for less and thus demand more of the schools in preparing their children for the future. These parents, who are, in general, better educated and employed in more professional jobs than their fathers were, have learned that they can only match their parents' standard of living—a house, two cars, a yearly vacation, a college-tuition fund, and retirement savings—with two incomes instead of one. They are experiencing economic conditions characterized by lowered wages, higher unemployment and part-time or commissioned employment, inflated real estate values, capital flight, and insecurity (see Apple 1993; Aronowitz and DiFazio 1994; Newman 1993).

Parents are, understandably, concerned about the economic futures of their children. Afraid that their children need even more educational credentials than they have to survive in the emerging information or "new knowledge" age, these parents are placing increasing demands on schools to prepare their children for entry into the most competitive and coveted higher education institutions (Aronowitz and DiFazio 1994). This is the logic of the educational marketplace in which detracking reform is currently situated.

Absent a set of high standards or benchmarks against which these parents can assess their children's learning and progress, they will remain focused on what Pierre Bourdieu (1984) refers to as form over function, or manner over matter. In other words, their anxiety is not allayed much by knowing *what* it is their children are learning in class, but rather *that* their children are getting more than other students. Since the higher education admissions process is based on competitive, comparative system of test scores and class rank, powerful parents will demand greater differentiation between what their children learn and what is offered to other students.

For instance, in two of the high schools in our study students have the option of taking an innovative detracked math sequence, known as the "integrated math program" or IMP. Despite the challenging material covered in the IMP, teachers in both schools have found that, for the most part, honor students are not enrolling in these classes. (Cooper 1995; Datnow 1995). According to one teacher, "the kids who have parents who are saying, 'Well, you're gonna go to a university,' they're looking at what it takes to get into the university. And they know . . . you have to be in AP science and AP math and AP English. And, which is true, if you go through those programs, you're gonna go to a university" (Datnow 1995, 63).

At one of the suburban high schools in our a study, the parent of a student who is in some but not all of the highest track classes said parents at the school talk about Advanced Placement classes all the time:

> I sit and listen to the parents say, "Johnnie and Suzie are taking this and this and this." Of course there is a certain amount of pride that's going on, and I think there is a real feeling among the parents that you have to do this in order to get into the college of your choice. . . . And there's a certain amount of that attitude out there. There certainly is that competitive upper layer there (Wells 1995, 16).

This pressure is salient even in middle schools where differentiation of courses doesn't translate directly into formal credentials that relate to college eligibility. In one of the middle schools, for example, the coordinator of the school's "gifted" program has begun to identify gifted students within the context of heterogeneous classes. As she was confronting and attempting to understand the considerable parent resistance, she lamented to us that, for the most part, parents were not actually interested in to the substance of what she offered; they seemed nearly entirely concerned about the loss of status that being in a separate and different program brought their children (Hirshberg 1995). In still another school, parents of high track students frequently complain about efforts to offer all students advanced curriculum. Generally, they want to know what their children will "get" that other students will not have access to. As one parent put it when a principal announced that the advanced curriculum would be offered to everyone in heterogeneous classes,

"What else is my child going to get? Because if this [the advanced curriculum] is the base, . . . he's supposed to get something extra." Another inquired, "If my kid's in Advanced English next to her kid, what's my kid going to get next, for, my kid is GATE [identified gifted and talented]." In another reforming school, a parent of a high-track student demanded of the principal, "What are you going to offer them that takes them to the cutting edge of education? My kid's gotta be on the cutting edge!"

These quotes illustrate what we call the "demand for differentiation" that we find in all the schools we are studying. These demands most often come from powerful parents who have a great deal of authority in locally controlled schools. Furthermore, this parental resistance to policies aimed at significantly improving opportunities for students in lower-level classes is overlaid with the norms and belief systems that have maintained racial inequality in this country. One middle school teacher we spoke to explained that White parents' resistance to doing away with honors is grounded in norms about race. "Quite frankly, I think the reason we have honors is parental pressure. It's a racial issue. An honors group is a White group." She said their resistance is an example of White parents not wanting their children to mix with African-American students (Yonezawa 1995, 68). Another of our schools that has pushed quite far with reform has done so, in part, by carefully balancing the racial mix of classes so that White parents of high achieving students won't be concerned about a large number of African-American students in their children's detracked classes (Williams 1995).

In an age of so-called declining fortunes, parents are perhaps more panicked than usual about what academic and social advantages their children have over other students. Because poor African-American or Latino students symbolize the bottom of the social structure—a place that downwardly mobile parents do not want to see their children—it may become particularly important that their children have more than those "other" students.

Lessons to Policymakers from the Micro Worlds of Schools

The market image presses educators to meet market demands by designing curriculum for low-track students that is more practical and "realistic" than one driven by a goal of high standards and opportunities for all students. Yet, many educators in our study were convinced that this market-oriented approach runs counter to the purposes and the processes of education. For example, a very charismatic principal at a middle school we studied has overseen the transformation of his school from one that had six different levels of math classes down to just two. While he has fought his share of political battles with district administrators and parent and community members, who strongly oppose his effort to detrack and thus desegregate within his racially mixed school, he remains optimistic that the reform that has taken place within his little school surrounded by corn fields in the Midwest has made a significant impact on student learning and, thus, should inform national policy debates about tracking, detracking, and societal expectations of education as a social institution He argues that schools must operate according to policies that embody a vision of what students and the country can become, rather than conceding to what now may be "Detracking issues are really the salvation of America. I mean, we can't build a high, medium and low America. . . . I mean we really can't say to a kid in second grade. 'You've been elected to low America. We're not going to give you access to learning like we do to everybody else' (Yonezawa 1995, 22). His words suggest the destructive potential of attempting to tailor educational programs to fit various sectors of the market.

In fact, in several instances we found that detracking actually has convinced educators in the schools we studied that low-track students are far more capable of engaging with higher level curriculum and instruction in heterogeneous groups than they had previously thought possible. In other words, they had actually misjudged the market. As one middle school counselor put it, "Heterogeneous grouping has made teachers think differently about all kids. They see more potential in kids; they will work harder with them and their needs." Other educators' comments affirm that this has indeed been the case. For example, one told us, "The program has done amazing things for standard track kids . . ."

Moreover, a number of teachers suggested the mechanisms through which detracking has enabled them to improve the quality of student work in their classrooms. One attributed the change to an atmosphere of higher expectations in heterogeneous classes, "all of sudden somebody says "You can do this!" Another credited the greater access to knowledge in saying, "Heterogeneous grouping helps to stimulate, motivate students because of just the exposure that the students have." Others suggested that heterogeneous grouping makes more salient to teachers the need to employ a broader array of teaching strategies, and the greater opportunities that result enable "low-track" students to achieve. A senior high school English teacher suggested how this greater exposure might take place when she told us, "[the student] who normally wouldn't succeed does succeed because the teacher is using strategies that appeal to various learning modes. Roles change, reverse. More time is spent on concepts, themes, thinking about things, projecting, making predictions, connections between the works read." In a senior high several states away, another teacher echoed this view as she told us how she set up her heterogeneous class to permit a lot of independent student learning, as well as dynamic class discussions that engage students of very different backgrounds and academic strengths. Doing so, this teacher believes she has created a learning environment in which she sees more students looking for what she calls "the genius within them." Her multidimensional classroom, she explains, allows students to develop insight into their own ways of knowing and learning, and when they do that, they become highly motivated "students" in the broader sense of the word, thirsty for a greater understanding of the world around them. Several teachers told us that a more individualized, yet interdependent approach to teaching and learning may be particularly helpful in racially and socioeconomically mixed schools, in which students bring with them to the school setting their different "ways of knowing."

However, it is also clear from these schools' experiences that educators must engage in a critical inquiry into their own practices and the connections between these practices and larger macro-societal forces if they are to detracking and high standards into changed practice in classrooms. For example, a group of teachers at one of the high schools we visited were deconstructing the tracking practices and the process of labeling students by placing them into certain "slots." One of these teachers shared how their dialogue and soul searching related back to the larger macro-societal issues enabled them to press forward;

> We need to start thinking about the students and the parents and the people we serve and in the larger sense of the world. . . . We can see the turmoil and the strife and the process that the world is taking and who better than a group of people who can deal with the academic education . . . who better to create an internal world structure that should be the model for the external world (Datnow 1995, 41).

Clearly detracking is a reform effort that is pushing against the flood of forces going in the other direction. Yet, despite the political shifts away from standards-based reform and towards a more de-centralized and deregulated market system of education, some of the "successes" we've observed in the detracking schools lead us to be-lieve that the micro-school-level change in detracking schools pro-vides a powerful critique of the market metaphor and can inform state and federal policy makers. Taken together, the "successes" of detracking in the schools we studied suggests that a set of enabling policies—policies that create the time and resources for educators to create rich and rigorous curriculum, devise organizational arrange-ments, and acquire teaching strategies to engage diverse groups of students in heterogeneous classrooms—may be far more promising that deregulation, choice, and other market-oriented strategies for pressing schools to bring all students to higher academic standards.

Notes

1. Our three-year study of ten racially mixed secondary schools that are detracking is funded by the Lilly Endowment. Jeannie Oakes and Amy Stuart Wells are the co-principal investigators. Research associates are Robert Cooper, Amanda Datnow, Diane Hirshberg, Martin Lipton, Karen Ray, Irene Serna, Estella Williams, and Susie Yonezawa. Our racially and ethnically diverse team of researchers brought to the detracking study dif-ferent areas of educational expertise—curriculum, policy, and pedagogy—as well as the perspectives of other disciplines, including sociology, political sci-ence, psychology, anthropology, and history.

2. It is important to distinguish between those who call for greater lo-cal control from a Ronald Reagan, New Federalism perspective and the more liberal view of community control as a form of empowerment in the 1960s. The first standpoint is generally taken by those who already have so-cial, economic and political power and are thus resentful of the government's infringement on their right to exercise that power. Those who subscribe to the second view are generally people who have little power to begin with and thus seek public policies that will make local control more meaningful to them through the redistribution of resources.

3. We would like to point out that four school desegregation cases in the past three years have focused specifically on tracking as within school segregation that violates equal protection and/or Title VI provisions (Welner and Oakes 1995). While we see a significant potential role for the judicial system in remedying unconstitutional tracking practices, we are fearful that the large number of conservative federal judges appointed during the Ronald Reagan and George Bush administrations will prevent broad-based reform of the system through the courts. Recent federal, district, the Court of Appeals, and Supreme Court rulings suggest that the tide of the strong,

interventions judiciary on matters of equal educational opportunity is shifting in line with the larger shift toward a smaller government and a more deregulated system. Current federal judges appear more likely to end desegregation court orders than to institute new, more powerful remedies that include detracking. Also, unlike the rapid pace at which school desegregation cases were brought in the late 1960s and 1970s, the detracking movement lacks the strong interventionist role of the U.S. Justice Department in bringing such cases to court, although the U.S. Department of Education's Civil Rights division has targeted tracking practices as an important consideration in determining racially mixed schools' compliance with Title VI requirements for categorical programs.

References

Apple, Michael W. 1993. *Official Knowledge: Democratic Education in an Conservative Age*. New York: Routledge and Kegan Paul.

Aronowitz, Stanley and William DiFazio. 1994. *The Jobless Future*. Minneapolis: University of Minnesota Press.

Ascher, Carol. 1992. "Successful Detracking in Middle and Senior High schools." *ERIC Digest*. New York: ERIC Clearinghouse on Urban Education.

Beare, H. 1993. "Different Ways of Viewing School-Site Councils: Whose Paradigm is in Use Here?" In *Restructuring Schools: An International Perspective on the Movement to Transform the Control and Performance of Schools*. Edited by H. Beare and W. L. Boyd, 220–217. Washington, D.C.: The Falmer Press.

Bourdieu, Pierre. 1984. *Distinction: A Social Critique of the Judgment of Taste*. Cambridge, MA: Harvard University Press.

Clinchy, Evans. 1994. "Higher Education: The Albatross Around the Neck of Our Public Schools." *Phi Delta Kappan* 75, no. 10 (June): 744–.

CODA [Common Destiny Alliance]. 1992. *Realizing Our Nation's Diversity as an Opportunity: Alternatives to Sorting America's Children. A Final Report to the Lilly Endowment, Inc.* Nashville, TN: Vanderbilt University.

Cohen, David K. 1990. "Governance and Instruction: The Promise of Decentralization and Choice." In *Choice and Control in American Education*. Edited by W. H. Clune and J. F. Witte. Vol. 1. New York: The Falmer Press.

Cooper, Robert. 1995. *Liberty High Case Report*. Los Angeles: UCLA Center on Research for Democratic Schools.

Dale, Roger. 1994. "Applied Education Politics or Political Sociology of Education?: Contrasting Approaches to the Study of Recent Education Reform in England and Wales." In *Researching Education Policy: Ethical and Methodological Issues*. Edited by David Halpin and B. Troyna, 31–42. Washington, D.C.: The Falmer Press.

Darling-Hammond, Linda. 1992. *Standards of Practice for Learner-Centered Schools*. New York: National Center for Restructuring Schools and Teaching. Teachers College, Columbia University.

Datnow, Amanda. 1995. *Central High School Case Report*. Los Angeles: UCLA Center on Research for Democratic School Communities.

Delgado-Gaitan, Concha. 1991. "Involving Parents in the Schools: A Process of Empowerment." *American Journal of Education* (November): 20–47.

Diegmueller, K. 1995[a]. "Backlash Puts Standards Work in Harm's Way. "*Education Week* (January 11): 1–12.

———. 1995[b] "Running Out of Steam. Special Report, Struggling for Standards." *Education Week* (April 12): 4–8.

Edsall, T. B. (with Mary Edsall). 1991. *Chain Reaction: The Impact of Race, Rights, and Taxes on American Politics*. New York: N. W. Norton.

Elmore, Richard F. 1993 "School Decentralization: Who Gains? Who Loses?" In *Decentralization and School Improvement: Can We Fulfill the Promise?* Edited by J. Hannaway and M. Carnoy, 33–54. San Francisco: Jossey-Bass Publishers.

Fine, M. Summer. 1993. "[Ap]parent Involvement: Reflections on Parents, Power, and Urban Public Schools." *Teachers College Record* 94, no. 4: 682–708.

Gamoran, Adam. 1987. "The Stratification of High School Learning Opportunities." *Sociology of Education* 60: 135–155.

Halpin, David and Troyna, B. 1994. "Introduction." In *Researching Education Policy: Ethical and Methodological Issues*. Edited by D. Halpin and B. Troyna, ix–xiii. Washington, D.C.: The Falmer Press.

Handler, J. F. 1996. *Down from Bureaucracy: The Ambiguity of Privatization and Empowerment*. Princeton, NJ: Princeton University Press.

Hannaway, J. 1993. "Decentralization in Two School Districts: Challenging the Standard Paradigm." In *Decentralization and School Improvement: Can We Fulfill the Promise?* Edited by J. Hannaway and M. Carnoy, 135–162. San Francisco: Jossey-Bass.

Hargreaves, Andy. 1985. "The Micro-Macro Problem in the Sociology of Education." In *Issues in Educational Research*. Edited by R. Burgess, 21–47. Washington D.C.: The Falmer Press.

Harvey, David. 1990. *The Condition of Postmodernity*. Cambridge, MA: Blackwell Publishers.

Henig, J. 1994. *Rethinking School Choice: Limits of the Market Metaphor in Education*. Princeton: Princeton University.

Hirshberg, Diane. 1995. *Explorer Middle School Case Report*. Los Angeles: UCLA Center on Research for Democratic School Communities.

Kenway, J. (with Chris Bigum and Lindsay Fitzclarence). 1993. "Marketing Education in the Postmodern Age." *Journal of Education Policy* 8, no. 2: 105–125.

Lareau, Annette. 1989. *Home Advantage; Social Class and Parental Intervention in Elementary Education*. Washington, D.C.: The Falmer Press.

Lewis, Anne C. 1994. "Winds of Change are Blowing." *Phi Delta Kappan* 75, no. 10 (June): 740–1.

Lewis, D. and K. Nakagawa. 1995. *Race and Educational Reform in the American Metropolis: A Study of School Decentralization*. Albany: State University of New York Press.

Lindsay, D. Panel. 1995. "Puts Brakes on Bill to Rebuild California Testing System." *Education Week* 15, no. 2 (September 13): 15.

National Governor's Association. 1989. *Time for Results*. Washington, D.C.: Author.

Newman, Katherine. S. 1993. *Declining Fortunes: The Withering of the American Dream*. New York: Basic Books.

"News in Brief: A National Roundup." Education Week. www.edweek.org.

Oakes, Jeannie. 1985. *Keeping Track: How Schools Structure Inequality*. New Haven: Yale University Press.

———. 1987. "Tracking in Secondary Schools: A Contextual Perspective." *Educational Psychologist* 22: 129–153).

———. 1990. *Multiplying Inequalities: The Effects of Race, Social Class, and Tracking on Opportunities to Learn Math and Science*. Santa Monica, CA: The RAND Corporation.

———. 1992. "Can Tracking Research Inform Practice? Technical, Normative, and Political Considerations." *Educational Researcher* 21, no. 4: 12–21.

———. 1993. *Opportunity to Learn: Can Standards-Based Reform be Equity-Based Reform?* Paper presented at "Effects of New Standards and Assessment on High Risk Students and Disadvantaged Schools."

Cambridge, MA: A Research Forum of New Standards Project (Harvard University).

Oakes, Jeannie, J.

————. 1995. "Two Cities: Tracking and Resegregation." *Teachers College Record.*

Oakes, Jeannie, and Martin Lipton. 1992. "Detracking Schools: Early Lessons from the Field," *Phi Delta Kappan.*

Oakes, J and G. Guiton. 1995. "Matchmaking: The Dynamics of High School Tracking Decisions." *American Educational Research Journal* 32, no. 1: 3–33.

Oakes, Jeannie, M. Lipton, and M. Jones. 1995. *Changing Minds: Deconstructing Intelligence in Detracking Schools.* Paper presented at the annual meeting of the American Educational Research Association, San Francisco.

Oakes, Jeannie and A. S. Wells. 1995. *Understanding the Meaning of Detracking in Racially Mixed Schools: Overview of Study Methods and Conceptual Framework.* Paper presented at the Annual Meeting of the American Educational Research Association, San Francisco.

Oakes, Jeannie, A. S. Wells, A. Datnow, and M. Jones, M. 1995. *Detracking: The Social Construction of Ability, Cultural Politics and Resistance to Reform.* Paper presented at the annual meeting of the American Sociological Association. Washington, D.C.

O'Day, J. and M. Smith. 1993. "Systemic Reform and Educational Opportunity." In *Designing Coherent Education Policy.* Edited by S. H. Fuhrman, 250–312. San Francisco: Jossey-Bass Publishers.

Pitsch, M. 1995[a]. "Dole Decries History Standards for Dwelling on the Negative." *Education Week.* (September 13): 9.

Pitsch, M. 1995[b]. "Bill to Push Block Grant for Education." *Education Week* 14, no. 41 (August): 1, 31.

Plank, D. N. and W. L. Boyd. Antipolitics, Education, and Institutional Choice: The Flight from Democracy. *American Educational Research Journal* 31, no. 2 (summer): 263–281.

Raab, Charles. D. 1994. "Where Are We Now: Reflections on the Sociology of Education Policy." In *Researching Education Policy: Ethical and Methodological Issues.* Edited by D. Halpin and B. Troyna, 17–30. Washington, D.C.: The Falmer Press.

Ray, Karen. 1995. *Grant High School Case Report.* Los Angeles: UCLA Center for Research for Democratic School Communities.

Torres, Carlos A. 1996. "State and Education Revidited: Why Educational Researchers Should Think Politically About Education." *Review of Research in Education* 21: 225–331.

Troyna, B. 1994. "Reforms, Research and Being Reflexive About Being Reflexive." In *Researching Education Policy: Ethical and Methodological Issues*. Edited by D. Halpin and B. Troyna, 1–15. Washington, D.C.: The Falmer Press.

U. S. Department of Education. 1994. *Goals 2000: Educate American Act: Making American Education Great Again*. Washington, D.C.: Author.

Useem, Elizabeth L. 1991. "Student Selection into Course Sequences in Mathematics: The Impact of Parental Involvement and School Policies." *Journal of Research on Adolescence* 1, no. 3: 231.

Van Galen, Jane. 1987. "Maintaining Control: The Structuring of Parent Involvement." In *Schooling in Social Context: Qualitative Studies*. Edited by G. W. Noblit and W. T. Pink. Norwood, NJ: Ablex Publishing.

Wells, A. S. 1995. *Plainview High School Case Report*. Los Angeles: UCLA Center on Research for Democratic School Communities.

Wells, A. S. and I. Serna. *The Politics of Culture: Understanding Local Political Resistance to Detracking Reform in Racially Mixed Schools*. Cambridge, MA: Harvard Educational Review. In press.

Welner, Kevin G. and Jeannie Oakes. 1996. "(Li)Ability Grouping: The New Susceptibility of School Tracking Systems to Legal Challenges." *Harvard Educational Review. 66* (3) pp. 451–470.

Wheelock, A. 1992. *Crossing the Tracks*. New York: The Free Press.

Whitty, G. "Citizens or Consumers? Continuity and Changes in Contemporary Educational Policy." In *Critical Educational Theory in Unsettling Times*. Edited by D. Carlson and M. Apple. Minneapolis, MN: University of Minnesota Press.

William, E. Stella. 1995. *Rollinghills Middle School Case Report*. Los Angeles: UCLA Center on Research for Democratic School Communities.

Wise, A. E. 1982. *Legislated Learning: The Bureaucratization of the American Classroom*. 2nd Ed. Berkeley: University of California Press.

Yonesawa, Susan. 1995. *Bearfield Middle School Case Report*. Los Angeles: UCLA Center on Research for Democratic School Communities.

8

Structuring College Opportunities: A Cross-Case Analysis of Organizational Cultures, Climates, and Habiti

❏

Patricia M. McDonough

One thriving tradition in the sociology of education is the analysis of the role of achievement, aptitude, and expectations, as well as race, gender, and socioeconomic status in influencing individual educational attainment. However, existing attainment studies emphasize individual attributes as the key determinants of inequalities, largely neglecting the role of educational organizations.

In contrast, the school effects literature posits organizational contexts as critical to understanding the empirical patterns of individual educational outcomes and analyzes schools' organizational structures, resources, constraints, and contingencies (Coleman 1987; Oakes 1989) in order to document how different school environments produce different curricula, administrative supports, and student outcomes. Building on the empirical and conceptual insights of organizational culture and climate research (Martin 1992; Ouchi and Wilkins 1985; and Schein 1990), school culture analysts have established a strand of this research which identifies the symbolic elements of schools that affect organizational performance and goal attainment.

Finally, cultural theorists have brought new concepts, theories, and methodologies to the study of educational attainment. In particular, Pierre Bourdieu's (1977a; 1977b; 1984) work has focused on the role of schools in reproducing class structures and analyzing the internal dynamics of educational systems. His class reproduction research examines specific forms of consciousness and culture which support and codetermine structures, including educational structures. He suggests looking at the interaction between social structures and a group's habitus (habitus is a class-based system of beliefs about the social world). Sociologists of U.S. education have used this framework to explain the use of class advantage for educational mobility (DiMaggio 1982; Lareau 1989).

However, each of these intellectual traditions still have unresolved problematics which define future research agendas. From the perspective of organizational theory we need to: detail the differences between, as well as locate similarities across, cultures and organizations (Smircich 1983); provide explanations for variations in organizational climates and norms (Schein 1990); and move away from descriptive analyses to an examination of the relationship between an organization's internal culture and it's larger socioeconomic environment (Ouchi and Wilkins 1985). Educational researchers are focused on identifying the specific causal processes of educational attainment—how the web of opportunities, structural arrangements, contingencies and timing work together to shape families' and students' interactions with, and movements through, schools (Hearn 1987). Finally, some critics (MacLeod 1987) have mistakenly accused Bourdieu of having a static class reproduction model because of an underdeveloped explanation of the dynamics of individual and structure interaction, while other critics have rightly criticized Bourdieu's under-specification of the link between individual agency and social structures, particularly schools.

This chapter will meet these research imperatives and speak to this intersection of cultural, organizational, and educational research through an examination of how high schools, which serve different socioeconomic status populations, shape their students' college choice decision-making and thereby affect their students' postsecondary educational attainment. I will offer (1) an explanation of how organizational cultures are linked to wider socioeconomic status cultures; (2) an analysis of how social class operates through educational organizations to shape students' perceptions of appropriate college choices thereby affecting patterns of educational attainment; and (3) an extension of Bourdieu's habitus to organizational contexts and a demonstration of how individuals and schools mutually shape and reshape each other. Moreover, organizational habitus will be shown to be a powerful analytic tool for understanding schools' roles in reproducing social inequalities.

Theoretical Framework

Bourdieu, Social Class, and College Choices

This research blends together Bourdieuian and organizational culture theories in a new way of viewing the social-class based cultures of schools as enabling or constraining students' educational and occupational mobility. Status groups are social collectives that generate or appropriate distinctive cultural traits and styles as a means to monopolize scarce social and economic resources (Weber 1978). Elite status groups have appropriated educational credentials for the intergenerational transmission of social status and power (Bernstein 1977). Cultural capital is a symbolic good which is most useful when it is converted into economic capital. Although all classes have their own forms of cultural capital, the most socially and economically valued forms are those possessed by the middle and upper classes, which are transmitted to their offspring as a supplement to economic capital in order to maintain class status and privilege across generations (Bourdieu 1977a and b). Middle- and upper-class families highly value a college education and advanced degrees as a means of ensuring continuing economic security.

Cultural capital is precisely the knowledge which elites value yet schools do not formally teach. With the complexity of college choices in the U.S. system, a college education is a status resource or symbolic good and high school students' college-choice processes are influenced by their social, cultural, and organizational contexts. Students high in cultural capital have clear strategies of how much and what kind of schooling they should have and this disposition is important because to maximize or conserve cultural capital you must be willing to consent to the investments in time, effort, and money that higher education requires. Parents transmit cultural capital by informing offspring of the value and the process for securing a college education, and its potential for conversion in the occupational attainment contest. The cultural capital useful to a college-bound senior is knowledge of what college is, why attainment of a college degree is important, what the diversity of institutions and the conversion capacity of various degrees are, and the admissions process.

Cultural capital mediates the relationship between family background and school outcomes and may have its greatest impact on educational attainment through affecting the quality of college attended (DiMaggio 1982). Thus, cultural capital provides advantages to students in their interactions with educational institutions (Lareau 1989) and it confers advantages on those making the transitions between educational institutions (McDonough 1992).

Bourdieu also uses the concept of habitus to refer to a deeply internalized, permanent system of outlooks, experiences, and beliefs about the social world that an individual gets from her immediate environment. Habitus is a common set of subjective perceptions held by all members of the same group or class that shapes an individual's expectations, attitudes, and aspirations. Those aspirations are both subjective assessments of the chances for mobility and objective probabilities. They are not rational analyses, but rather are the ways that people from different classes make "sensible" or "reasonable" choices for their own aspirations (MacLeod 1987). They do so by looking at the people who surround them and observing what is considered "good" or "appropriate" across a variety of dimensions. Habitus exerts an influence on individual decision-making in organizational contexts by creating a common set expectations of appropriate college choices that limits the universe of possible colleges into a smaller range of manageable considerations. I view schools as the mediator of a social class community's collective consciousness in regard to the processes and outcomes of college choice.

Families and schools are in a mutually influencing process that affects individual student outcomes. Given ability, economic, and value constraints, a student delimits the 3,300 U.S. colleges and universities to a narrow piece of the opportunity structure that she believes is within her grasp. This personal schema is the synthesis of what Bourdieu calls the "objective probabilities" and "subjective assessments" of an individual's chances for mobility, her habitus. However, although an individual develops her own personally synthesized aspirations, college-bound students of relatively the same academic achievement and similar social class backgrounds have roughly similar college choices, which are very different from the choices made by relatively equal ability students from different social-class backgrounds.

This relatively similar aspirational schemata is not a coincidence. The patterns of students' aspirations are shaped by the class context of the communities, families, and schools in which these students live their daily lives. These class-based patterns stand in stark contrast to traditional aspiration or expectation research which assumes an individual-level analysis. Class-based patterns of aspirations are a joint product of family and school influences. Thus, we need to understand the class-based context of high schools as it affects students' college choice decision-making and for that we need to understand organizational culture.

Organizational Culture

According to one leading researcher, existing organizational culture research lacks a common definition of culture and has no shared theoretical paradigm (Martin 1992). Many researchers have attributed the lack of conceptual clarity to different intellectual ancestries in anthropology and sociology for organizational culture (Cameron and Ettington 1989; Ouchi and Wilkins 1985) and organizational climate's intellectual lineage originating in psychology (Schein 1990). This lack of conceptual clarity is further exacerbated by the major misuse and conflation of terms such as culture, climate, and context (Peterson and Spencer 1990).

Nonetheless, organizational culture can legitimately be defined as an organization's underlying values, beliefs, and meanings, while organizational climate refers to the resultant attitudes and behaviors of individuals within the organization. Culture and climate are concepts describing a subset of the internal organizational environment. Culture is deeply held, static, and enduring, while climate is the current, malleable perceptions and attitudes which are the contemporary manifestations of culture. In one particularly instructive analogy for distinguishing between culture and climate, Marvin Peterson and Melinda Spencer suggest that "culture is the meterological zone in which one lives—tropical, temperate, or arctic—and climate is the daily weather patterns (1990, 8).

Currently, the empirical use of organizational culture does not fully capture the complexities of organizational contexts and does not even begin to help us understand the social class similarities of many schools. Moreover, school culture research has been unable to explain why and how schools produce regular patterns of educational attainment measured by outcomes such as college attendance. However, using Bourdieu's (1977 1984) habitus, I will now offer evidence and a theoretical justification for habitus existing not only in families and communities as Bourdieu has suggested, but also in organizational contexts.

James March and Herbert Simon (1958) note that the basic features of organizational structure stem from universal problem-solving needs: because of limited intellectual capacities, people cannot make decisions that involve major cognitive complexity. People require simplified models that capture only the main features of a problem. Moreover, because of time and resource limitations, most decision-making is based on a search for satisfactory alternatives. These constraints are necessary because optimal decision-making requires extremely complex processes. Certainly, developing a more simplified decision-making process than the consideration of the possible 3,300 U.S. college choices would be desirable for most college-bound students.

A student's college choice decision-making is also affected by both the normative expectations that exist among the students, parents, and faculty of a high school, as well as by anticipated consequences, and what alternatives will be considered or ignored. Specifically, a student's perceptions of available alternatives are conditioned by her social status and the environmental evoking mechanism—the guidance process. This combination of social networks and environment is an individual's frame of reference for college planning. If the frame of reference and perceptions are congruent, as in the case of an upper middle-class student seeking to attend a "good" college, then there is no dissonance. But, if in trying to choose a college, a student has a frame of reference that conflicts with her perceptions of what is available to her, she will filter out choices that are too discordant (March and Simon 1958). The example here would be an academically talented student from a low socioeconomic status (SES) background or school who refuses to consider a high prestige college because she feels she would not be "comfortable" there.

The critically important question in evaluating the high school's role in facilitating the transition to college is: What impact does the high school, and specifically the guidance counselor have on enabling or constraining students in securing adequate college preparation and the necessary information on college choice? More importantly, if the school's college counseling does not take into account important status characteristics such as available cultural capital or habitus, then the counseling services will variably impact students from different social classes.

The guidance process impacts students through subtle and unobtrusive controls like assumptions that students are (*a*) familiar with the communication channels for the transmission of college information; (*b*) know the specialized college choice vocabularies; and (*c*) are aware of the necessary deadlines and appropriate timetables. High schools influence students by how they structure the flow and content of information; make explicit expectations that highlight or downplay particular options; limit the search for alternatives; and impose a specific schedule (Perrow 1979). Another important influence could be any assumption the school makes about how familiar students are with basic information and prerequisites. Whatever college choice assistance the guidance office offers enhances or detracts from students' cultural capital.

The guidance counselor is the organizational representative who summarizes her own perceptions of the college opportunity structure and transmits them to the rest of the school, thus becoming the arbiter of the school's college-choice habitus. Bounded rationality frames the analysis of school habitus by looking at the ways that each of these high schools help seniors to limit their search for college choices to a manageable number of considerations. High schools suggest appropriate choices to students, highlight certain goals for college, assume a status background of the majority of students, arrange the physical layout of the guidance operation, and provide environmental stimuli.

Having laid out the theoretical and contextual factors of college choice decision-making, let me now clarify the concepts of a high school's organizational culture, climate, and habitus. In this context, a high school's college-choice *organizational culture* would be its values related to college attendence, and any beliefs as to whether students should attend "any" college or only "better" colleges. Since climate refers to the impact of culture on individual behavior, then a school's college-choice *organizational climate* would be the institution-specific current patterns of college choices and behaviors that are manifested in one school. Finally, since organizational habitus is the impact of a cultural group or social class on an individual's behavior through an intermediate organization, then the college-choice *organizational habitus* would be the specific current patterns of college-choices and behaviors that are manifested in schools with similar socioeconomic status environments.

The specific indices of a school's college-choice organizational culture are whether or not it's mission and curriculum is college preparatory, or is comprehensive and multipurpose. The specific indices of a school's college-choice organizational climate would be how much and what kinds of organizational resources are devoted to the organizational mediation of students' aspirations, especially through:

- availability of college counselor for college-choice guidance as measured by student-to-counselor ratios

- college counseling program features

- assumptions of prior student knowledge built into the counseling systems

- the kinds of material and symbolic resources available

- the networks counselors depend upon for getting up-to-date and insider information and

- the structuring of key tasks such as writing letters of recommendation

Finally, evidence for the existence of a college-choice organizational habitus would be similarities across high schools serving students' from relatively the same social classes.

Data and Findings

This is a cross-case analysis of the college counseling programs of four U.S. high schools: Paloma, Gate of Heaven, University High School (UHS), and Mission Cerrito High School (MCHS).[1] The data for this analysis come from interviews with these schools' counselors, students, and parents, as well as naturalistic observation, and document analysis. All of the schools are located in California. It is not an assessment of each individual counselor's effectiveness or biases but rather an analytic and evaluative description of each school's college counseling program, examining the schools' resources devoted to college preparation, how the counseling effort is structured, the goals and objectives underpinning the college guidance program, and the college planning knowledge assumed of students.

This chapter shows that individual guidance counselors have a direct impact on some students, and more importantly, that the counselor is critical in constructing the broader school climate for college expectations and planning. The counselor is instrumental in implementing the school's organizational response to college planning and, as such, creates an organizational world view that serves to delimit the full universe of possible college choices into a smaller, cognitively manageable range of colleges. The school and the counselor construct this world view in response to their perceptions of the parents' and community's expectations for appropriate college destinations, combined with their own habitus, knowledge, and experience.

Prior studies document little or no positive impact of guidance counselors on students (Hotchkiss and Vetter 1987). Yet, daily, students and counselors experience physical and organizational conditions which influence the frequency and nature of interactions surrounding college planning. Students and counselors at each of this study's schools interpret their needs differently from the needs of students and counselors at the other three schools, and have widely differing ideas about their social class communities. These are local understandings of what it means to go to college and which colleges are "appropriate."

These schools represent four typical schools that are classified on the basis of socioeconomic status culture and organizational support for college guidance. The low-SES/low-guidance school is Mission Cerrito, the low-SES/high-guidance school is Gate of Heaven, the high-SES/low-guidance school is University, and the high-SES/high-guidance is Paloma. The counselors at each of these schools are Mr. Sirotti at Mission Cerrito, Ms. Trent at Gate of Heaven, Mr. Dix at University, and Ms. Ball at Paloma. Paloma's counselor to student ratio of 1:56 is comparable to the U.S. private preparatory school average of 1:65 (Cookson and Persell 1985). Gate of Heaven's ratio of 1:117 is lower than the 1:235 U.S. average for Catholic schools (Coleman, Hoffer, and Kilgore; 1982). The nationwide average for public schools is 1:323, therefore both University High School's ratio of one counselor to 365 students and Mission Cerrito's average of 1:400 is higher than that national public school average (Coleman, Hoffer, and Kilgore 1982).

How much each counselor's effort is devoted to college planning ranges from 50 percent of Mr. Sirotti's total counseling effort to 100

Table 1
Organizational Comparisons

SES / Guidance	Paloma School High / High	Gate of Heaven H.S. Low / High	University H.S. High / Low	Mission Cerrito H.S. Low / Low
Students	210	450	1280	1800
Seniors	56	117	365	400
Counselor	1–Mrs. Ball	1–Ms. Trent	1–Mr. Dix	1–Mr. Sirotti
Percent on Guidance	100%	100%	90%	50%
Avg/Student	10–15 hrs.	1 hr.	45 min.	—

Source: Patricia McDonough, 1997. Choosing Colleges: How Social Class and Schools Structure Opportunity. Albany: State University of New York Press.

percent of Mrs. Ball's effort at Paloma. The range of time that each counselor spends with every senior is just as striking; ranging from no expectation that each senior will be seen by the counselor at Mission Cerrito, to 10 to 15 hours per student for Mrs. Ball at Paloma. Although, Ms. Trent's estimate is only an hour, she does spend considerable time with students individually and in groups all throughout the high school years. What follows is a summary of each school's college counseling culture and climate.

College Choice Organizational Culture

Organizational Mission

The high school guidance office provides a social context that influences individual behavior. This office's structure is a symbolic medium that guides students' thinking about the college decision-making process.

Paloma and Gate of Heaven's college counseling efforts are fully dedicated to college continuation, as are nine out of ten guidance hours at University High School. Everything about these schools' guidance operations conveys the expectation that most, if not all, students should continue on to college, and if possible "good" colleges. This message is evident from Mrs. Ball's individual meetings, to the constant group discussions at Gate of Heaven, to the four-year plans worked out between Mr. Dix and UHS students. Mission Cerrito is in a category of its own: at most, 50 percent of Mr. Sirotti's effort is devoted to assisting the students who are college-bound, approximately 65 percent of seniors.

The professional services of these guidance offices also provide an organizational mechanism for the mutual pursuit of individual and organizational goals. Paloma and University High Schools each keep detailed records of graduates' destinations. These schools use these records both to offer parents evidence that their schools help students reach "appropriate" college destinations, and as networking and insider information for guiding students who may be interested in following in their predecessors footsteps at particular colleges. Gate of Heaven keeps aggregate records of destinations but does not organize an effort to link alumnae with students interested in particular schools. Mission Cerrito does not even keep records of post-high school destinations.

Institutional sagas or cultures develop over time (Clark 1970) and are important because they represent the articulated and formalized values of the institution. Each of the four high schools in this study historically has valued college continuation differently. Paloma is a college preparatory school committed to the highest standards, while University High School claims it has a "national reputation for academic excellence . . . and a strong belief in quality public education." Gate of Heaven has always had a mission to educate women to serve their communities and families and has been sending a good number of young, Catholic women to college for some time. Mission Cerrito is a comprehensive high school for a middle to lower-middle class population where college going is not so much facilitated as expected, primarily in the community college tradition.

Preparatory schools, such as Paloma, are the standard bearers of maximal college planning. The number one mission of a college preparatory school is to enable students to get into the "best" colleges possible. College counseling functions are the centerpiece of Paloma's raison d'être: college preparation. It is the very essence of being at Paloma and, as such, is evident to one degree or another in almost every student-staff interaction.

Curriculum

College destinations are strategic responses to a decision-making process involving two major components: academic preparation (college readiness) and admissions planning and execution (college choice). According to one estimate, 75 percent of American eighteen-year-olds have not taken a strong academic curriculum and therefore do not have the curricular prerequisites for a four-year liberal arts college (Cookson and Persell 1985). Although most U.S. high schools have both a vocational and college-preparatory curriculum, the balance of organizational resources devoted to curricula depends on the historical character of the student population and their eventual destinations.

All of Paloma's students take the necessary curricula to minimally meet the admissions requirements for four-year colleges. Counselors at both UHS and Gate of Heaven try to get information out to students early enough to help them develop a four-year course plan that will ensure that they will be prepared to apply to four-year colleges. As a University High School student describes her curricular preparation:

> you kind of guess at what you're going to take . . . through your senior year. The four-year plan. And those aren't the classes you're necessarily going to take; it's just an outline of the classes you're going to take, and the requirements, and the classes that count for UC [University of California] credit, or the classes that count for State [California State University (CSU)], and whatever.

All the students at Gate of Heaven, Paloma, and University High School spoke positively of their school's curricular advising and those students met the challenge head on and took the requisite courses. Another student found that UHS's course graduation requirements match "the requirements you need to get into most colleges, like State, UC, or you know, private colleges," and although she would not have voluntarily chosen them as her first choices, she is glad she has taken them.

Mission Cerrito students voiced many complaints about inadequate counseling attention and problems resulting from being placed in inappropriate courses. Because of the way Mission Cerrito has designed its advising program, counselors assigned to freshmen, sophomores, and juniors are not familiar with college admissions processes and yet they advise students on their yearly course choices. They, like Mr. Sirotti, are faced with high caseloads (400 students per counselor) and more to the point, are called upon to deal with the whole panorama of student counseling needs: discipline, dropout prevention, personal and family problems. Many students particularly felt that the MCHS college counseling system was poor.

In junior high school, one Mission Cerrito student circled a response on a form indicating that she was planning to go to college. In eighth, ninth, and tenth grades her counselor came into her classes and handed out information sheets on the University of California and CSU admissions requirements.

> I was just pretty much working for State requirements. Well it said biology, and well I had human biology. . . . I was just signing up for what I thought I needed to have. You turn it in and they sign you up for those classes.

With counselor approval, this student signed up for two years of science, one of which was a human biology course. In her junior year, she discovered her two years of science would suffice for graduation requirements but that human biology is not sufficient to meet the CSU requirements. At that point, she made an appointment to see her counselor. The counselor "didn't even realize I was college" bound, which was difficult for her. "The counselor obviously just overlooked it or didn't think . . . I don't know what happened." Because a lot of MCHS advising happens via group sessions or paperwork, problems often get identified too late because "they just talked to everybody in the whole class at once. It wasn't like individual." So, as a senior, our Mission Cerrito student had to take biology again, this time the CSU prerequisite one, surrounded by sophomores where she felt out of place. She hated the whole experience.

Another student offered an example of how she also suffered from inadequate advising. She labelled herself as arriving at MCHS "messed up" because her junior high school counselor had inappropriately informed her of the correct biology course to take. "That was another reason why I was thinking about going to junior college." As was the case with her whole college choice process, this student (on her own), without the help or encouragement of her MCHS counselor, decided to apply to a CSU school and was accepted conditionally: "I have to take biology when I first get there."

She knew that she had no other choice but a community college option because her grades foreclosed anything else.

> I have to go to junior college before I can go to college. There's no way I can get into any college right now. . . . see I never took college preparatory classes. I mean I started out and they were just too hard so I gave up and just went to the easier stuff.

Like most MCHS students, this student does not consider junior college a real college, but it seemed relatively hassle free.

An organization's communication system will be most burdened when concerned with the less structured aspects of its tasks, particularly when explaining problems that are not well-defined. For the student who is the first in her family to go to college, the tasks of preparing and planning for college will be less well-defined than for the individual who has generations of college-going relatives.

The students who fared somewhat better at Mission Cerrito had two things in common: first, all felt that they received good junior high counseling for their high school classes, and second, they all had parents who had gone to four-year colleges and were involved early on with their daughters' college planning. As Rosabeth Moss Kanter (1977) notes, a basic feature of organizational life is a structure of opportunity, which affects the individual's perception of mobility. Opportunity is dynamic and relates a participant's present position to their potential mobility. For the high school student bound for college, placement in the college track is the baseline measure of their opportunity. Students with cultural capital are advantaged by having family members who can explain that there are high-mobility paths within the college track. One of these students got herself placed into the highest tracked math, science, and English courses at MCHS. From junior high school, she was placed in advanced classes: "they just recommend you to be in certain classes . . . I guess you're just put in there. I don't really know how they do that."

The other two students, however, had mixed experiences with Mission Cerrito. Their junior high counselor helped them set up their high school courses. As the first of them put it "they just give you your classes. . . . College just seemed so far away, I didn't even think about it." Although both sets of parents helped their daughters plan their courses, they were not very familiar with the hierarchically tracked nature of the college preparatory courses at MCHS, which offered college preparatory classes in the general or advanced varieties. This first student, who was "in mostly general" courses was keenly aware that the tracked nature of courses was set early on and "always tend to be the same people, like they are ever since elementary school."

Later course advising happened, as she described it, when the counselor came into a class to discuss general college requirements, such as "what you need to get into a college—a four-year, or J.C., or university." However, when senior year began, this student had the feeling that her college choice process had "just snuck up on me." As she sorted through the choosing, applying, and figuring out what she wanted, she felt "kind of like in shock . . . I have to plan my life right now, I don't know what I want to do." She consulted with her counselor, her parents, and looked at the MCHS Senior Guide Book, grappling with "if I wanted to go away or stay around here. I still don't know what I want to do."

In spite of this student's feeling of floundering, her mother had a very positive view of the high school's role in her daughter's college planning. She recalled that the counselor had sent information through the mail in freshman year about required courses that her daughter should take throughout the high school years:

> the high school was very, very good . . . has just been a really major part of helping the family to know what direction to take.

Disgruntled with MCHS for other reasons, the second student felt that the school and counselor played a role in lowering her expectations to a community college even though her parents were encouraging her to go to a four-year college. This second student felt discouraged by Mr. Sirotti, not in a face-to-face individual meeting where he assessed her credentials and opportunities, but through his group presentations. Although Mr. Sirotti spoke generally, the impact was significant for her as an individual:

> Mr. Sirotti said that was probably the best thing. Not just me, but for anybody in general in my class, it's the best way to get used to . . . he generalizes . . . when he told us about the junior college . . . he didn't say it as a form of being kind of a cop-out, he said it in a form of being an excellent idea if you didn't want to go right away into a four-year college.

Senior year this second student did see Mr. Sirotti in a personal interview "before the first quarter ended," which was after she had submitted her four-year college applications. After she informed him of her choices he said, "a really good way to do it is to go two year and transfer to a four year."

She, however, was quite concerned that the junior colleges in the area did not have a good reputation. Although she did not perceive pressure at MCHS to attend four-year colleges, she did notice that "you get a good pat on the back if you say you're going . . . to a university, they go 'Wow,' you know, 'how exciting.' " In the final analysis, both students felt inadequately prepared for college, finally opting to "brush up" at the local community colleges.

College Choice Organizational Climate

College Counseling Program Features

All of Mrs. Ball's efforts are directed at preparing Paloma students for college. Paloma devotes considerable resources to this mission: extensive individual counseling and detailed written guides for students and families on the college decision-making process. Moreover, counselors are in close contact with selective college admissions personnel and engage in and refine the art of writing letters of recommendation (Cookson and Persell 1985). Mrs. Ball does all of these things, while her counterparts at the other three schools do only some of these things, to varying extents.

Mrs. Ball spends a lot of time meeting with students one-on-one. She advises and supports them in developing specific plans including a dream school, a small number of reasonable choices of colleges, and at least one safe admissions bet. Mrs. Ball is acutely aware of the admissions environment and attempts to help students manage their application process, acceptances, and rejections. Assuming that all students intend to pursue college and are familiar with the types and ranges of colleges, Paloma counselors do not begin explicit counseling for specific college choices until midway through the junior year. However, Paloma staff do not leave a student's curricular preparation to chance: all courses are tailored to offer students maximum college choices without unnecessarily narrowing the range of curricular offerings.

Gate of Heaven staff assume that students know very little about college types or requirements and have developed a detailed four-year effort to prepare those young women. Ms. Trent provides increasingly more complex information on options to students over their four years. Gate of Heaven's college-counseling efforts include individualized counseling, group discussions, and teacher involvement, as well as the provision of books and technology for additional support. The college counseling program assumes that students need basic information about college planning, as well as nurturance and support. College guidance at Gate of Heaven begins immediately in the ninth grade and continues throughout a student's high school career.

University High School faces a reality of numbers: the college counselor cannot effectively advise all of the 365 seniors, let alone guide the efforts of every college-bound student. Consequently, the counseling program focuses on helping students set up a four-year curricular plan that meets prerequisites for admissions to most four-year colleges. Then the college counselor informs groups of students how to comply generically with admissions norms.

Mr. Dix primarily helps students with the University of California and California State University systems' processes; he does not try to assist students with the quagmire of specific "feel" of individual campuses, public or private. University High School's college counseling efforts historically have been subject to influence by parental or student demand. The most notable example of this was the establishment of a college advising center and the hiring of an aide (Mrs. Dean) to staff an office that would provide more individual attention to at least some subpopulation of students. University High School's counselor assumes a fixed hierarchy of college oppor-

tunities, and attempts to help students find their place in that hierarchy based on what the counselor assumes to be an immutable
combination of GPA and SAT scores. There is no assumption that
students may be able to manipulate those numbers or that many
private colleges might offer better opportunities. Students at University High School bear the onus of responsibility for college-choice
decision-making: Mr. Dix is unable to provide time for intensive individual counseling or shepherding through the emotions of the admissions process.

Of all of the high schools in this study, Mission Cerrito begins its
college counseling program the latest. Students are not seen or even
addressed in groups about college options until their senior year.
The counselor, Mr. Sirotti, is non-interventionist in individual college decision-making because a large portion of his time is devoted to
dropout prevention. His competing organizational demands nearly
preclude his seeing students individually and he has little or no time
to keep up on specific entrance requirements or information about
different curricula available.

Almost across the board, Mr. Sirotti advocates attending one of
the three local community colleges immediately after graduation. He
does this in groups, written materials, and the rare one-on-one situation. The MCHS college guidance program is reactive, offering minimal information on UC and CSU schools. What little is offered is
often delivered by professionals from those nearby campuses most
frequently attended by MCHS students. Mission Cerrito suffers from
severe resource limitations, with little to offer students in the way of
college guidebooks or commercially available software. MCHS's commitment to college preparation is minimal outside of the counseling
office, although some teachers write letters of recommendation or
may answer a student's occasional question about college.

What do these very different high school contexts enable or con-
strain in terms of students' college planning? The first indicator of
the influence of these diverse school contexts is students' college destinations. Table 8.2 shows how many students go on to college by
type of college. In terms of baseline college continuation, Paloma
sends almost all its students to college, Gate of Heaven and University High School send approximately nine out of ten students; a little over half of Mission Cerrito's students go directly on to college.
However, the aggregate data do not tell the whole story. The types
of colleges these students attend vary quite a bit.

Nearly all Paloma students go to either a University of California or a private four-year college, while just over half of Gate of

Table 2
College Continuation Rates

	Paloma School	*Gate of Heaven H.S.*	*University H.S.*	*Mission Cerrito H.S.*
Percent to College	98	91	89	70
2 Year College	2	32	18	55
4 Year College	96	59	71	15
Private	55	15	31	NA
UC	36	11	39	NA
CSU	0	33	11	NA

Source: Patricia M. McDonough. 1997. Choosing Colleges: How Social Class and Schools Structure Opportunity. Albany: State University of New York Press.

Heaven girls go to four-year colleges. The rest of Gate of Heaven students, 32 percent, go to community colleges. The 59 percent of Gate of Heaven's college-bound students who go to four-year colleges, attend a more heterogeneous mix of schools than Paloma students: 33 percent go to California State Universities 15 percent to private schools, and only 11 percent to University of California schools. Approximately two-thirds of that 11 percent of the Gate of Heaven students who are enrolled at University of California campuses are at campuses that are within 15–50 miles of their homes.

Meanwhile, University High School students resemble their high-SES Paloma counterparts insofar as two-thirds of these students go to four-year schools. Unlike Gate of Heaven girls, they are more evenly distributed between University of California's (39 percent) and private (31 percent) colleges, with only 11 percent at California State University campuses. Mission Cerrito students follow totally different college pathways: 55 percent of them go directly to one of the three junior colleges in their community. Of those students at four-year schools, it is impossible to say how students are distributed among private, University of California, and California State University schools because Mission Cerrito keeps no records of students' destinations. However, Mr. Sirotti did indicate that a small number of students go to the nearby Jesuit University which is in the same town as Mission Cerrito, and a significant portion of students bound for four-year schools end up at the nearby California State University campus. A handful of students, the superstars at Mission Cerrito High School, do go on to University of California campuses or occasionally to prestigious private colleges.

Assumptions of Prior Knowledge

Paloma and University high schools each assume family knowledge of college hierarchies. They base their college counseling programs on this knowledge as well as a certain "taste" (Bourdieu 1984) for colleges higher in the hierarchy. Gate of Heaven and Mission Cerrito make no such assumptions of prior knowledge, yet the differences in resources and outlook on their organizational missions means that Gate of Heaven has constructed a plan to fill in the knowledge gap, while Mission Cerrito has no time to do so nor does Mr. Sirotti or the Mission Cerito High School leadership see it as part of the organizational mission.

However, the high school's assumptions that all students will be able to rely on families to supplement school information leaves a lot to chance for those students whose parents have not gone to college or parents who are relatively uninvolved in their children's choices. A first generation college-bound senior is operating in what for her is uncharted waters and is facing a high degree of uncertainty, both in what college choices to make and how to make appropriate ones. The amount of influence that any counseling operation has on an individual's behavior is related to how much uncertainty it helps the individual absorb.

As we have seen, Mission Cerrito does not have the resources to absorb uncertainty. In fact, Mr. Sirotti's advisement to students to take the community college route seems to have dramatically affected at least some students in adding uncertainty and highlighting that their high school preparations were not adequate. Many students and parents eventually have acted in ways consistent with these assessments and have come to see the community college option as a more suitable first college step. Also, the student, who initially was adamant about not going to a community college, eventually has capitulated to her mother's and Mr. Sirotti's strong preference. Although she finally has agreed to attend the local junior college, the emotional adjustment was very hard on her because she was an integral part of a close circle of nine friends, and everyone else in the group went to a four-year college. She has found watching them go through their application and waiting periods "depressing because I wanted to go so much, but . . . I'll get there."

Gate of Heaven, aware of the uncertainties of college-going for mostly first-generation students, constructed a four-year college counseling program to help students become emotionally accustomed to the notion of college attendance, moving away from home, and separating from friends. In spite of that effort, only approximately one-fifth of Gate of Heaven students went away to college.

All Paloma students easily filled in the advising gap with family knowledge and private counselors. Sometimes the overall climate of expectations of the school will make up for the gap in individual families' knowledge, but this is not a systematic, organizational response to ensure every student's preparation. Individuals who lack college-choice cultural capital are dependent upon the sponsorship of the guidance counselor to help them get insider information and marshall the organizational resources behind their college applications, since they do not have outside sponsorship. In the case of University High School, this stewardship proved to be particularly important.

Beginning her freshman year, one University High School student often found herself dependent on her friends or counselor for developing her college plans. It was when Mr. Dix met with her to develop a four-year plan that she first started thinking about college. She did not know what the SATs were until her counselor "came into our classes" and informed students that the SATs were coming up. Through inquiring she "found out what they were" and discovered that the SATs were required for admissions.

In her junior year, this student's friends started talking about their college choices, she then began to think about her own plan. Even then, her basic lack of knowledge about college planning surprised even her. It was not until she came back from a Southern California campus visit trip that she realized that one school she visited was a private college.

She was quite serious and persistent about her pursuit of assistance from University High School in her college search and frequently visited with either Mr. Dix or Mrs. Dean sometimes consulting with the counselors "three times a week" on a range of items from when to submit transcripts to California State University schools to how to complete financial aid forms.

Individuals make competing claims on an organization's resources, and students like this one without the cultural capital relevant to college choice make more exacting claims. A guidance office not aware of and responsive to the needs of both high- and low-SES students will offer students differential levels of access to their services. University High School appears to be responsive to students if they, like this student, vigilantly ask for assistance, and if they know what to ask for and about. If a student with a class background similar to this student's did not have friends who kept her informed and on schedule, then the University High School counseling operations would have no means of stopping this student from falling through the cracks of their counseling system.

Material Resources

Paloma, Gate of Heaven, and Mission Cerrito each distribute handbooks to assist students in their college choice processes. Although University High School distributes resource materials to students, there is no overview or "how to" guidebook developed or distributed by school.

Mrs. Ball distributes a college handbook to all Paloma students in their junior year. Her explicit purpose is to reach parents about two subjects: not to pressure their daughters to aim for out-of-reach colleges, and to talk to their daughters about how the family's financial condition may affect final college choices. Paloma's guidebook is designed to fine-tune the efforts of a knowledgeable family, resulting not only in a highly organized and efficient college-application process, but also in a very rational and sensitive college planning process. Mrs. Ball also advises students on the time management aspect of college choice. Timetables specify what students should be thinking about and doing in each high school year to enhance their chances of getting into the "right" schools.

Ms. Trent, at Gate of Heaven, distributes not only a college counseling booklet developed by another source, but she also had over fifteen handouts and free advising materials, which she distributed to every student throughout their high school careers, most in the junior and senior years. Ms. Trent had a "College/Career Planning Achievement Award" booklet for juniors and seniors. If students completed at least eight out of ten of the listed steps (for example, visiting with a college representative or visiting a college campus), then they received this achievement award. In addition, Ms. Trent had annual checklists for juniors and seniors to consult all throughout those years in order to stay on track for deadlines. Moreover, the Career Center's resources and college search software each supplemented Ms. Trent's distributed materials.

To get University High School students started, Mr. Dix photocopied pages from Barron's *Profiles of American Colleges* and recommended that students consult Fiske's *Guide to Selective Colleges*. Students consulted those guidebooks and others, and felt comfortable using the publically available guidebooks.

At Mission Cerrito High School, Mr. Sirotti's college planning guidebook for seniors was an effective vehicle for parents to help them help their children find a way through the college maze. Some parents praised the Mission Cerrito High School handbook as an example of how Mr. Sirotti's effort enabled them to become partners with their daughters in the college planning process. One mother was particularly thankful:

> This year specifically they put out a booklet for the seniors about everything that's going to happen during the year and everything. . . . It gave a real good perspective to the seniors.

She was also pleased with the college night meeting Mr. Sirotti arranged for parents to "find out about the junior colleges, about the state program, and the universities." She felt that Mission Cerrito High School helped with applications, deadlines, and counselor availability: "they gave us basic ideas of when things needed to be taken care of . . . they gave a lot of help at school in terms of filling out applications."

Paloma, Gate of Heaven, and University high schools each had extensive information centers located to give easy and open access to students. Mission Cerrito High School had no such facilities. The handful of books and computer software and hardware that was available was located in Mr. Sirotti's personal office and obviously was not very accessible to individual students to use or explore.

Professional Networks

Professional networks are an important source of information. The kinds of affiliations and identifications that individuals have and act upon offer insight into that person's perceptions of his/her appropriate professional worlds. Preparatory school counselors maintain contact with admissions officers through professional networks, ensuring the careful articulation between their schools and the post-secondary institutions where most of their graduates attend.

Mrs. Ball of Paloma is an active member and attends the annual meetings of the National Association of College Admissions Counselors. Through this professional association she puts herself annually in close contact with the admissions officers who will be making decisions about her students. This contact is done in a professional development mode, outside each of their institutional settings. This kind of networking and interaction provides her with insight into what kinds of students fare well at particular institutions and which institution, in any given year, is looking for what particular student characteristics.

Ms. Trent has her own outside consulting business and is connected with other private counselors. She contacts private and public college representatives to come visit Gate of Heaven to advise students of the opportunities available on their college campuses. Also, Ms. Trent took an unpaid leave from Gate of Heaven to do an internship with a local community college in recruitment and admissions.

Mr. Dix did not identify any meaningful professional connections other than the college representatives that came through University High School, and even those visits and connections were cultivated and maintained by Mrs. Dean. Mrs. Dean worked very hard to maintain contact with counselors at particular colleges where University High School graduates frequented; she also had contact with other private counselors.

Mr. Sirotti is grateful for the professional associations he has with University of California and California State University professionals who come to the Mission Cerrito High School campus to inform students about admissions and financial aid procedures for their institutions. He speaks positively about attending local workshops sponsored by the state universities for high school counselors as being a good source of information and insight into admissions prospects at those schools.

In summary, Ms. Trent, Mrs. Dean and Mrs. Ball actively sought contacts and continuing associations with a broad range of public and private college admissions counselors, while Mr. Dix and Mr. Sirotti focused on the University of California and California State University networks and standard seminar formats for updating counselors on admissions information.

Letters of Recommendation

Letters of recommendation highlight an area where organizational competence and resources are critical. For the most competitive colleges, admissions processes favor candidates whose schools write detailed letters of recommendation. Preparatory schools, or any school with highly organized and adequate support for letter writing and other support services, increase their students' admissions options and chances.

Mrs. Ball collects information from classroom teachers to write multipage letters of recommendation that give admissions officers in-depth views of Paloma students. Above and beyond the call of duty, she works on letters for every Paloma senior during summer vacation. Moreover, she has been an admissions officer for thirteen years at a competitive, eastern state university and knows what kinds of information and what level of detail is useful to admissions readers.

Mr. Dix also is aware of the need for University High School students to present good letters of recommendation. He prepares approximately two hundred original letters of recommendation and estimates that he processes six to seven hundred private school applications. He has set aside one of his University High School file drawers to keep track of private school applications and the letters of recommendations he writes for those applicants. He stays current with his letter writing needs by keeping a wall chart of the whole senior class with an "x" next to each student's name for whom he has already written a recommendation.

As we have already seen, Mr. Dix's actual familiarity with students is limited, and before senior year he often sees only those students who are in trouble. To help him write the recommendations, he gives students an information sheet and asks two-to-three teachers to send him comments so that he can become acquainted with the students' academic proficiencies as well as their research and extracurricular interests.

Recommendation letters are not required by California public universities. Since 50 percent of the graduating seniors from University High School go to University of California and California State University campuses, Mr. Dix feels that private school applications require "an inordinate amount of time." He has admitted that with the University of California's and California State University's "it's an easier process for me to deal with." He does not pay attention to these applications unless called upon by students.

Both Ms. Trent of Gate of Heaven and Mr. Sirotti of Mission Cerrito respond to student requests for letters of recommendation but speak of no particular burdens placed on the counseling systems by large numbers of letters needing to be written, nor did they speak of efforts to write or refine in-depth letters on individual students.

Impact of Organizational Habitus

What can we now say about the way that counselors construct an organizational habitus for college choice, and what do each of these schools expect of college-bound students? Table 8.3 summarizes each school's college counseling program. Both of the private schools are proactive in (a) their approach to college counseling, (b) dedicate more counseling resources than their public counterparts, and (c) provide nurturing and supportive services to students, while being specially cognizant of the emotional turmoil involved in college choice. In comparison, the public schools are reactive in providing college counseling, have extremely limited and overtaxed resources, and have little or no time for any additional support services related to college planning.

Counseling begins at each school in very different ways. All Paloma curricular options are designed to be college preparatory and assume that students possess basic familiarity with and have family knowledge of college; counseling begins in the junior year of high school. Mission Cerrito High School, facing limited resources and a burgeoning counselor caseload, begins college counseling in the senior year. Both Gate of Heaven and University High School begin their counseling efforts in the freshman year. For University High School, the "four-year plan" is developed and set into motion to ensure curricular readiness, while Gate of Heaven's approach includes not only a four-year plan, but also slowly introduces students to college types and terms. More importantly, Gate of Heaven begins students' emotional adjustment by having them picture themselves at college.

Each of these four schools makes different assumptions. Paloma leaves little to chance in the way of curricular preparation, offering students a plethora of advanced placement classes within a curriculum designed to guarantee entry into a four-year college. Paloma's college-choice counseling begins in the junior year, assuming that students need assistance from the school in the college choice process but not in a basic orientation to college types and options. At

Table 8.3
College Counseling Summary

	Paloma School	Gate of Heaven H.S	University .H.S.	Mission Cerrito H.S.
Counseling Begins	11th	9th	9th	12th
Support Services	Yes	Yes	No	No
Competing Missions	No	Yes	Yes	Yes
Limited Resources	No	No	Some	Yes

Source: Patricia M. McDonough. 1997. Choosing Colleges: How Social Class and Schools Structure Opportunity. Albany: State University of New York Press.

Paloma there are clear cut and uniform expectations: Nearly 100 percent of the students are going to college, almost all to four-year colleges, with more than half going to private colleges.

Gate of Heaven has an adequate curricular package designed to provide its graduates with a reasonable preparation for a four-year college, with more demanding college preparatory classes available for those students who wish to push themselves. The counseling program, however, begins in the ninth grade and offers students a chance to learn about college for the first time; it adds emotional preparation to their college planning framework. Nearly all Gate of Heaven students go to college, although nearly all go within a 2–15 mile radius. Two-thirds of the students end up at four-year schools, while one-third go to community colleges.

University High School has a full college preparatory curriculum available and a counselor meets with students at the beginning of their high school careers to ensure that they are in suitable classes. Student are not encouraged to deviate from their preordained place in the academic hierarchy, although an academically successful student will be provided with opportunities for enrolling in advanced placement classes at a teacher's behest. Counseling for specific college choices does not begin until junior year and assumes that parental knowledge will be passed on to students about the difference between public and private, California State University versus University of California versus community colleges, and other basic information which frames the range of expected student college choices. Half of University High School students enroll in University of California and California State University schools across the state, with another third of University High School graduates ending up in private four-year colleges all over the country.

Mission Cerrito's curricular advising is loosely coupled (Weick 1976) to its college counseling, with differentiated tracks of college preparatory courses, and some advanced placement classes. Placement in the higher tracks is dependent upon two variables: parental/student knowledge and advocacy, *or*, strong junior high school test scores. College counseling at Mission Cerrito High School assumes very little: Mr. Sirotti's booklet offers basic information on the GED, SAT and ACT exams, as well as on the three public California post-secondary systems most especially on the community college options. Only 15 percent of Mission students focus their aspirations on four-year schools, and that population primarily attends the nearby California State University and/or Jesuit university. The majority of college-bound Mission Cerrito students (55 percent) go to the three local community colleges.

Each of these schools offers four distinct organizational climates for college-choice decision-making in: (a) timing and availability of guidance, (b) curricular options as positioning for two- or four-year colleges, and (c) a network of colleges graduates "usually" attend. Each of these climates presents to the students a particular organizational view of the opportunity structure of American higher education.

Habitus is the system of "durable, transposable dispositions" or subjective perceptions shared by all members of the same social class that frame individual aspirations; they are a combination of the objective probabilities and the subjective assessments of the chances for individual mobility. The evidence in this chapter supports a claim that habitus exists and is transmitted to individuals in organizational climates as well as through families and social-class communities. Habitus can be thought of as generators of strategies which are time and context specific. Habitus may be thought of as "a matrix of perceptions, appreciations, and actions and makes possible the achievement of infinitely diversified tasks" (Bourdieu 1977[a] and [b]).

How is the climate for college-choice decision making in each of these high schools evidence of habitus? Habitus is behavior constrained by practical and strategic considerations as well as by the demands of the moment. Each of the guidance counselors has constructed norms for behavior and expectations for the students he/she advises. Each counselor makes assessments of the objective probabilities of his/her students' chances for admissions, and subjective assessments of those students' chances at happiness or success at various institutions. The counselors offer their assessments to students through handbooks, the array of college representatives they invite to the school, the information packets they keep on hand to pass out to students, and the collective seminars and individual advising sessions.

Individual and community values serve as constraints to any particular habitus and certainly the counselors are aware of and sensitive to parental demands or expectations for "appropriate" colleges or information. But recall that the central role of habitus is in defining and limiting what is seen by an actor and how it is interpreted. In this case, Paloma displays private college options and not community college information; Gate of Heaven focuses attention on the University of California, California State University and community college options in their backyard; University High School highlights University of California and California State University; while Mission Cerrito spotlights the virtues of preparing for the "real thing" by living at home and brushing up at the community college. At the first three schools then, the information and attitudes— the college-choice organizational habitus—conveyed to students results in behavior that predominantly gets students into four-year colleges, while Mission Cerrito's information and expectations channel the majority of students toward two year colleges.

College admissions environments also shape these high school guidance climates and habiti. Paloma and University High Schools are shaped by a national, volatile, competitive college admissions environment, while Mission Cerrito and Gate of Heaven's organizational habiti are shaped by local opportunity structures.

This study has examined how schools structure or affect student decision making and has offered evidence that this is done through curriculum, assumptions of students' prior knowledge of college, use of material resources, counselors' participation in professional networks, and writing letters of recommendation. This study also illuminates the ways in which high school organizational habitus shapes student tastes for particular types of postsecondary institutions.

Note

1. All school names are pseudonyms.

References

Bernstein, Basil. 1977. "Social Class, Language, and Socialization." In *Power and Ideology in Education*. Edited by J. Karabel and A. H. Halsey, 511–534. New York: Oxford University Press.

Bourdieu, Pierre. 1977[a] "Cultural Reproduction and Social Reproduction." In *Power and Ideology in Education*. Edited by J. Karabel and A. H. Halsey, 487–511. New York: Oxford University Press.

———. 1977[b]. *Outline of a Theory of Practice*. Translated by Richard Nice. Cambridge, England: University Press.

———. 1984. *A Social Critique of the Judgement of Taste*. Translated by Richard Nice. Cambridge, MA: Harvard University Press.

Bourdieu, Pierre and Jean-Claude Passeron. 1977. *Reproduction in Education, Society, Culture.* Beverly Hills: Sage.

Cameron, Kim S. and Deborah R. Ettington. 1989. "The Conceptual Foundations of Organizational Culture." In *Higher Education: Handbook of Theory and Research.* Edited by J. C. Smart. Vol. 4:356–396. NY: Agathon Press.

Clark, Burton. 1970. *The Distinctive College.* Chicago: Aldine Publishing Co.

Coleman, James S. 1987. *Public and Private High Schools: The Impact of Communities.* New York: Basic Books.

Coleman, James S., Thomas Hoffer, and Sally B. Kilgore. 1982. *High School Achievement: Public, Catholic, and Private Schools Compared.* New York: Basic.

Cookson, Peter and Caroline Hodges Persell. 1985. *Preparing for Power: America's Elite Boarding Schools.* New York: Basic Books.

DiMaggio, Paul. 1982. "Cultural Capital and School Success: The Impact of Status Culture Participation on the Grades of U.S. High School Students." *American Sociological Review* 47:189–201.

Hearn, James C. 1984. "The Relative Roles of Academic, Ascribed, and Socioeconomic Characteristics in College Destinations." *Sociology of Education* 57:22–30.

———. 1987. "Pathways to Attendance at the Elite Colleges." In *The High Status Track: Studies of Elite Schools and Stratification.* Edited by Paul W. Kingston and Lionel S. Lewis. Albany: State University of New York Press.

———. 1991. "Academic and Nonacademic Influences on the College Destinations of 1980 High School Graduates." *Sociology of Education* 64: 158–71.

Hotchkiss, Lawrence and Louise Vetter. *Outcomes of Career Guidance and Counseling.* Columbus, OH: National Center for Research in Vocational Education.

Kanter, Rosabeth Moss. 1977. *Men and Women of the Corporation.* New York: Basic Books.

Lareau, Annette. 1987. "Social Class and Family-School Relationship: The Importance of Cultural Capital." *Sociology of Education* 56 (April): 73–85.

———. 1989. *Home Advantage: Social Class and Parental Intervention in Elementary Education.* New York: The Falmer Press.

MacLeod, Jay. 1987. *Ain't No Makin It: Leveled Aspirations in a Low-Income Neighborhood*. Boulder, CO: Westview Press.

March, James and Herbert Simon. 1958. *Organizations*. New York: John Wiley.

Martin, Joanne. 1992. *Cultures in Organizations: Three Persepctives*. Oxford, England: Oxford University Press.

McDonough, Patricia M. 1992. *Who Goes Where to College: Social Class and High School Organizational Context Effects on College-Choice Decision-making*. Stanford, CA: Stanford University Dissertation.

McDonough, Patricia M. 1997. *Choosing Colleges: How Social Class and Schools Structure Opportunity*. Albany: State University of New York Press.

Oakes, Jeannie. 1989. "What Educational Indicators? The Case for Assessing the School Context." *Educational Evaluation and Policy Analysis* 11:181–199.

Ouchi, William and A. L. Wilkins. 1985. "Organizational Culture." *Annual Review of Sociology* 11:457–83.

Perrow, Charles. 1979. *Complex Organizations: A Critical Essay*. Chicago, IL: Scott Foresman.

Peterson, Marvin and Melinda Spencer. 1990. "Understanding Academic Culture and Climate." In *Assessing Academic Climate and Cultures*. Edited by William. G. Tierney. San Francisco: Jossey Bass, New Directions for Institutional Research.

Schein, Edgar. 1990. "Organizational Culture." *The American Psychologist* 45(2):109–119.

———. 1991. *Organizational Culture and Leadership*. San Francisco: Jossey Bass.

Smircich, Linda. 1983. "Concepts of Culture and Organizational Analysis." *Administrative Science Quarterly* (September): 339–358.

Steinitz, Victoria A. and Ellen Solomon. 1986. *Starting Out: Class and Community in the Lives of Working Class Youth*. Philadelphia, PA: Temple University Press.

Useem, Michael and Jerome Karabel. 1986. "Pathways to Top Corporate Management." *American Sociological Review* 51:184–200.

Weber, Max. 1978. *Economy and Society* [1920]. Berkeley: University of California Press.

Weick, Karl E. 1976. "Educational Organizations as Loosely Coupled Systems." *Administrative Science Quarterly* 21:1–19.

9

Critical Race Theory, Marginality, and the Experience of Students of Color in Higher Education

❑

Daniel G. Solórzano and Octavio Villalpando

Introduction

Most projections of college enrollments during the next decade show the number of Students of Color[1] increasing throughout the United States (Carter and Wilson 1992, 1994; Kerr 1994; Levine and Associates 1989; U.S. Bureau of the Census 1992). As evidence, these predictions point to current K-12 enrollment patterns and high school graduation rates that result in higher numbers of African American, Asian American, Native American, Chicana/Chicano,[2] and Latina/Latino students on college campuses.

Some current data, however, contend that these trend-based projections may be overestimated (National Center for Educational Statistics 1993). In fact, when we compare each group's college enrollment to their percentage of eighteen- to twenty-four-year-olds or as a percentage of high school graduates African American, Native American, and Latino students are underrepresented. There is a strong consensus on the following point: Within the next ten years, most Students of Color are not expected to improve their proportional college-going or completion rates over current levels (Carter and Wilson 1994; Kerr 1994; Levine and Associates 1989).

Even though the absolute numbers of Students of Color on college campuses will increase during the next decade, it appears that they will continue to have proportionately lower levels of college entrance

211

and graduation rates. This observation was recently acknowledged by the National Education Goals Report when it identified as an objective by the year 2000 to "Eliminate disparities in college entrance rates between white and minority high school graduates who enroll in two- and four-year colleges immediately after graduation . . . (and) . . . in college completion rates . . ." (United States Department of Education 1994, 44).

The suggestion that an increase in the absolute numbers of Students of Color in college will naturally result in an increase in the proportion of college graduates, ignores how educational conditions at each point in the pipeline affect the lives of these students prior to and while in college. Moreover, this simplistic suggestion of absolute increase and proportional graduation rates minimizes the extent to which policies and practices of higher education institutions help define the experiences of Students of Color, and relieves the institutions of any responsibility for influencing students' success. In this article, we will use the framework of critical race theory and the construct of marginality to help us better understand the experiences and conditions of Students of Color in higher education.

Critical Race Theory and Marginality

How can we better understand the persistently low proportions of Students of Color graduating from U.S. colleges and universities? One approach to answering this question is to examine the barriers Students of Color experience on the road to the baccalaureate. One theoretical framework that can be used to identify and explain the obstacles is "critical theory." Indeed, for our purpose, "critical theory" is a framework or set of basic insights, perspectives, methods, and pedagogy that seeks to identify, analyze, and transform those structural and cultural aspects of higher education that maintain the marginal position and subordination of Students of Color (see Tierney 1991, 1993). As this definition asserts, within the framework of critical theory, marginality can be a useful construct in understanding the problem of underrepresentation for Students of Color. For this article, marginality is a complex and contentious location and process whereby People of Color are subordinated because of their race, gender, and class. Moreover, those on society's racial, gender, and class margins do not have the power to define who is at the center and who is at the margin; what is considered privileged or valuable cultural knowledge and experience and what is not; and who has social status and related privilege and who does not.

In a related and recent theoretical development, critical race theory examines how legal doctrine is used to subordinate racial groups (Matsuda, Lawrence, Delgado, and Crenshaw 1993). Critical race theory draws from and extends the broad literature base of critical theory. Critical race theory has at least five elements that form its basic insights, perspectives, research methods, and pedagogy.[3] They are: (1) the centrality and intersectionality of race and racism, (2) the challenge to dominant ideology, (3) the commitment to social justice, (4) the importance of experiential knowledge, and (5) the use of an interdisciplinary perspective. Mari Matsuda (1991) views critical race theory as:

> ". . . the work of progressive legal scholars of color who are attempting to develop a jurisprudence that accounts for the role of racism in American law and that work toward the elimination of racism as part of a larger goal of eliminating all forms of subordination" (1991, 1331).

Therefore, to paraphrase Matsuda, the overall goal of a critical race theory in higher education is to develop a pedagogy, curriculum, and research agenda that accounts for the role of race and racism in U.S. higher education and work toward the elimination of racism as part of a larger goal of eliminating all forms of subordination in higher education.

As a theoretical issue, the type of oppression that is central or takes primacy in one's analysis is an important part of research on Students of Color. Aida Hurtado (1989) addresses this issue in feminist research when she posits that:

> White feminist theory has yet to integrate the facts that for women of color race, class, and gender subordination are experienced simultaneously and that their oppression is not only by members of their own group but by whites of both genders (1989, 839).

Also, Patricia Collins (1986) argues that People of Color can experience race, gender, and class marginality simultaneously and refers to this phenomena as simultaneity of oppression or simultaneous marginality. Moreover, Patricia Zavella (1991) takes the position that:

> Women of color have argued that race, class, and gender—including sexuality—are experienced simultaneously, and to only use a

gender analysis for understanding women's lived experience is reductionist and replicates the silencing and social oppression that women of color experience daily (1991, 73).

Likewise, Marilyn Frye (1992) maintains that one must examine the multiple forms of domination such as race, gender, and class, that immobilize, mold, and oppress the lives of Women and Men of Color, instead of focusing on a single form of oppression. This leads to the following questions: What do those marginal spaces, locations, or processes look like? Moreover, what kinds of questions, analyses, and responses are generated at those intersecting marginal spaces, social locations, and processes? As the preceding theorists note, a critical theory that examines the intersections of race, gender and class can be an important tool for generating issues, questions, histories, art forms, and stories that tell us more about the people and places at the society's margins. Critical race theory suggests that while those on the social margins have less access to opportunities and resources, they also experience different barriers, obstacles, or other forms of individual and societal oppression than those at the center.

In an earlier period, David Riesman (1954) suggested that marginality is a place and condition where one's "intellect is at its best" (1954, 163) and is related to such positive traits as creativity, insight, and self-understanding. More recently, Patricia Collins (1992) maintains that those at the margin can provide a distinctive angle of vision and states, "rather than reject our marginality, Black women intellectuals can use our outsider-within stance as a position of strength" (1992, 36). bell hooks (1990) also contends that while the margin can be a "site of deprivation," it can also be a "site of radical possibility, a space of resistance" (1990, 149). Moreover, hooks (1990) states:

> I am located in the margin. I make a definite distinction between the marginality which is imposed by oppressive structures and that marginality one chooses as site of resistance—as location of radical openness and possibility (1990, 153).

Further, Cornel West (1993) introduces the notion of a critical organic catalyst as a person who stays attuned to what the center has to offer with the critical vision of one from the margin. Also, Gloria Anzaldua (1987) argues that a *mestiza* consciousness provides a unique vantage point for examining individuals, institutions, culture, and society, which in turn can lead to new theories about diversity in U.S. society. Lastly, in utilizing Anzaldua's (1987) work,

Hurtado (1989) notes that, "It is the *mestiza* consciousness that can perceive multiple realities at once" (1989, 855).

Through the process of socialization, those at society's margins have been taught to view themselves and their experiences as negative, to be ashamed of, ignored, or discarded, instead of as a source of strength, knowledge, and pride, to be valued, protected, and shared (Espin 1993). Accordingly, "critical race theory" views race, gender, or class marginality as important social locations and processes, with many positive strengths, and as rich sources of information used to empower or transform those at the social margins. Many of these critical scholars are taking the position that the margins can and should be viewed as both sites of oppression and sites of resistance, empowerment, and transformation. However, hooks (1990) argues that more is known about the margin as site of deprivation or domination and less about the margin as a site of resistance and empowerment. It seems clear that researchers must differentiate between marginality that is imposed and marginality that one accepts as a position of strength.

Centering on the experiences of historically marginalized groups can reveal much about how members of these groups engage in individual and collective acts of resistance to challenge race, gender, and class oppression. Research in the social science and humanities is needed that identifies and analyzes how individuals and groups use different and often unrecognized forms of resistance in response to domination. For instance, do those at the social margins use family and group stories, proverbs, *dichos,* oral histories, music, *corridos,* comedy, and art, as forms of survival, resistance, or transformation? Can these cultural and familial resources be considered a form of cultural resistance to domination, a type of resistant cultural capital of those at society's margins? In a sense, these questions represent a redefinition or recentering of cultural capital since those who resist might be displaying a different form of cultural capital than the one society acknowledges and privileges (West 1993). Indeed, if we frame this concept of resistant cultural capital within the context of higher education, we can provide examples of how marginalized individuals and groups use their status as a source of empowerment.

Marginality and the Experience of Students
of Color in Higher Education

Again, consider the disproportionately low college-going and degree completion rates by Chicana/Chicanos and other Students of Color. Some might argue that Students of Color who graduate from college possess different forms of cultural capital that enabled them to adapt to and comply with the expectations and requirements of the highly competitive college environment. However, while these students may not have been pushed out of higher education like other students, the assumption that they succeed largely because of their ability to conform to the dominant cultural norms of a college environment ignores much of their current and historical experiences in higher education.

Despite their ability to conform, many Students of Color have been and continue to be ascribed a marginal status in higher education. As an example, consider the current prevailing myth that Students of Color continue to be accepted to college based primarily on affirmative action "quotas" and not on their academic abilities (D'Souza 1991). This is a widely held misperception even though there is emerging evidence suggesting that most Students of Color are admitted based on the same criteria and standards as majority students. A recent study of UCLA's Academic Advancement Program, the largest student retention program in the country, discovered that less than 3 percent of Chicana and Chicano students in 1991 had been accepted through "special admission" provisions (Solórzano and Associates 1994). Yet, many of the students who were interviewed as part of the study shared how they felt marginalized, because of the stigma of being perceived by many faculty and students as unfit for college-level work, even though their acceptance to UCLA had been based on regular admission criteria.

One result of this ascribed marginal status is that some Students of Color have developed what we call "critical resistant navigational skills" to succeed in higher education. Many of these skills do not stem from students' conformist or adaptive strategies, but emerge from their resistance to domination and oppression in a system that devalues their ethno- and sociocultural experiences. Moreover, some Students of Color might voluntarily choose to situate themselves on "the margins" as a site of resistance in order to transform the system (see hooks 1990). How can this be? Why would Students of Color choose to be marginalized?

One reason to choose the margins may be that they have reconceptualized the meaning of marginalization. By distinguishing between a dominated marginal status imposed by an oppressive and contradictory higher education system, versus an empowering and self-defined marginal site, Students of Color can incorporate the concept of human agency in determining their experiences on college campuses (Giroux 1983; hooks 1990). Rather than reject and withdraw from the college environment, many Students of Color, who feel stigmatized because of the myth that they are admitted to college to fill affirmative action "quotas," often engage in behavior and activities that refute this "special admission" misperception. For instance, some students assume leadership roles in academic, social, and ethnic student organizations, some do volunteer work as academic tutors, while others work in community-based organizations. Each of these roles would tend to challenge the myth that, in comparison with majority students, these students are academically or socially unprepared for college. Therefore, Students of Color can redefine their marginal location as a place where they can draw strength. They are then able to identify strategies to succeed in a place they perceive to be oppressive. Moreover, in order for Students of Color to complete a degree and accrue other experiential benefits from college, they engage in oppositional behavior by learning and using critical skills to navigate through the system.

What do we mean by oppositional behavior and critical navigational skills? For many, oppositional behavior in higher education conjures images of individual or collective campus protests and demonstrations reminiscent of the 1960s social movement "sit-ins" and "peace marches." It has come to symbolize public or overt forms of expression based on a desire for some type of change. For our purpose, we subscribe to Henry A. Giroux's (1983) suggestion that oppositional behavior must also be based on a liberating, emancipatory, or transformative logic, and not a simplistic reactionary rebellion based on a sense of powerlessness.

While Students of Color have participated in public expressions of oppositional behavior, we believe that they also engage in resistant behavior that is less public, less overt, or not readily observable. This covert resistant behavior and its effect on educational outcomes is difficult to measure using traditional methods of empirical quantitative research. Some would argue that this is part of the reason we know so little about this type of covert oppositional behavior. In contrast, college impact research relying on quantitative methods has consistently found that public oppositional behavior has a positive effect on a range of affective and cognitive outcomes for college students (Astin, Astin, Bayer, and Bisconti 1975; Hurtado 1990; Pascarella and Terenzini 1991). We believe that Students of Color who engage in less public oppositional behavior also achieve many of the same objectives as the more obvious and public oppositional behavior.

As one example of covert oppositional behavior and critical resistant navigational skills on which Students of Color rely, consider the following composite personal account by a Chicana college student we will call Gloria:[4]

> I started as a history major. The lower division classes I had to take in my major were pretty bad. They were supposed to provide an overview of early American history, including the colonization of the West. Chicanas were repeatedly depicted as ignorant and untamed savages in class discussions and readings. Naturally, I was the only Chicana in almost every one of those classes, so every time I opened my mouth to clarify or question an inaccurate statement, I felt dismissed or ignored. I was always getting into arguments with students who said really insensitive and racist things about Mexicans. I argued almost as frequently with professors who couldn't understand how they were also insulting me or might just be plain wrong. I couldn't study for those classes because I felt totally alienated. It was like I was studying and being tested on some things that I knew were wrong. Yet, I was expected to repeat these incorrect "facts" or fail the class. As expected, I had to compromise in every one of those courses and didn't earn any grade higher than a "C" in them. I later found out that some of those professors and students in my department had labeled me as the resident "radical Chicana activist" and "Msssss. Multicultural," even though I really wasn't. I just wanted to help them understand another perspective.
>
> Throughout that entire first year, I talked to some other Chicanos I met through MEChA (Chicana/o student organization) who understood what I was experiencing in my department. They were a lot of help, though they couldn't do anything about my problem. We kind of connected and I realized that many of them were having similar experiences. I also talked regularly about this to one of my *tias* (aunt) who went to a community college. Since neither of my parents went to college, all they could do was listen and encourage me to hang in there. My *tia* suggested that I find Chicana professors and talk to them, but I didn't have much luck there, unfortunately there were only two in the whole college and one of them was in a science department.
>
> Well, because of that experience during my first year, I ended up changing my major to Chicana and Chicano Studies, in part because my GPA declined so much that my undergraduate advisor told me that it would take me about a year-and-a half to raise it in order to be allowed to take any upper division history courses. I decided the hassle wasn't worth it, even though I have liked history since high school. So basically, I lost almost two-thirds of an academic year because I couldn't apply those History classes to any

other requirements, plus my GPA took a serious dive. However, since changing my major I've done very well in all my classes, even though those early bad grades really messed up my overall GPA. I've also decided to continue to graduate school and become a college professor. I want to teach and write about the history of Chicanas. Maybe then at least some people will begin to understand the contributions we've made to the U.S. and the world and stop thinking of us as "dumb Mexicans."

While this composite account might appear as an oversimplistic "success story," it includes many factors that affect the lives of undergraduate Students of Color and depicts a composite of their experiences (Aguirre and Martinez 1993; Olivas 1986; Rendon 1992). By deconstructing Gloria's story, we can operationalize our definitions of oppositional behavior and critical resistant navigational skills.

Gloria obviously had a negative experience with her history classes. She felt alienated and frustrated that her ethnic history was negatively portrayed in readings, lectures, and class discussions. The curricular content of these courses was partly responsible for her deciding to change to a major that she believed presented a more realistic perspective on Chicanas and their history. Changing majors and deciding to pursue a faculty career to teach and write a more accurate history of Chicanas can be interpreted as resistant behavior, primarily because of its transformative objectives (Giroux 1983). Had Gloria acknowledged the problems with her courses but continued as a history major, or chosen to remain silent in classes, her response (or lack of) might not be interpreted as oppositional within a resistance framework because it lacked a transformative purpose.

Gloria shared the fact that one of the consequences of her experience with the history classes was that she never earned a grade higher than a "C." This was because she could not bring herself to repeat "incorrect facts," and therefore was graded poorly. This also had an effect on her ability to continue in the major and influenced her decision to change majors. Later, Gloria admitted that those early grades had a negative impact on her cumulative GPA. Therefore, even after receiving poor grades in her first-year history classes, she persisted in the major at the expense of a declining GPA, but clearly driven by her attempt to correct others' historical misinterpretations of Chicanos. Again, within the resistance framework, this behavior could be considered oppositional because of its transformative nature.

Most of the composite account revolves around Gloria's perceived racist or culturally insensitive attitudes within the institution. Her decisions to: (1) challenge the discourse in the classroom, (2) change to Chicano studies major, and (3) eventually pursue a faculty career, all represent an expression of human agency as a reaction to a perceived racist environment and structure. Her behavior is clearly oppositional and she does not totally conform or adapt to the university environment.

Gloria's use of some critical navigational skills during her first year were reflected in her membership in MEChA and her reliance on its members for support. Her dependence on family members (as depicted through her ongoing conversations with her aunt and parents) for support, and her attempt to identify Chicana faculty also demonstrated the use of navigational skills, which provided much of the basis for her oppositional behavior. Her conscious decision to change her major to Chicano Studies also required the skill to acknowledge that she would not be able to achieve her graduate school objectives unless she changed her major.

This composite account illustrates a way in which a Student of Color has reconceptualized her marginal status. Gloria substituted the marginal status imposed by a perceived oppressive higher education system with an empowering and self-defined marginal site that included the concept of personal agency in order to influence her experiences in college. Her acknowledged identity as a Chicana college student participating in an often hostile environment appeared to provide her with a source of empowerment. Instead of accepting a powerless marginal state, she redefined her location as a place to draw strength and developed critical navigational strategies to succeed. These skills and behaviors can be considered a form of resistant cultural capital.

Conclusion

From a critical race theoretical perspective, higher education reflects the structural and ideological contradictions that exist in the larger society. While colleges and universities have historically been reactionary institutions shaped by dominant social forces, they have also encouraged dissenting ideologies that have produced critical analyses of society. One example of their contradictory nature is illustrated by their discourse on "celebrating" multiculturalism and diversity. While most colleges endorse the importance of multiculturalism and have provided educational opportunities to Students of Color during the last thirty years, as Sylvia Hurtado (1990) observes, they "still remain racially stratified" (1990, 23). Hurtado suggests that higher education may be continuing to reflect a racist ideology, while also challenging this ideology internally.

This contradictory environment provides the context in which Students of Color are not only expected to complete the college degree, but also benefit from their other collegiate experiences—much like the general student body that graduates with high levels of cognitive and affective development after four years of college (Astin 1993; Pascarella and Terenzini 1991). It may be true that some Students of Color will similarly benefit by acquiring the dominant cultural capital and conforming to this oppressive and contradictory environment. However, as we suggest in this chapter, if we recenter the concept of cultural capital by focusing on the oppositional and resistant behavior among Students of Color who do not conform to the ascribed dominant cultural expectations yet demonstrate relative levels of success in college, we may be able to identify some valuable skills they used to navigate through the system. By increasing our focus on these marginalized students who rely on resistant cultural capital to complete a college degree, we can begin to more fully explore how their success is affected by (1) their dependence on other Students and Faculty of Color for support and mentorship, (2) their response to racial intolerance in the curriculum and teaching pedagogy, and (3) university "multicultural" policies and practices.

The questions and framework we pose that use marginality as a site of empowerment and transformation are meant to improve our understanding of the types of skills used by Students of Color to navigate and succeed in higher education.

Notes

1. For this study, Students and Professionals of Color are defined as those persons of African American, Latino, Asian American, and Native American ancestry.

2. For this study, Chicanas and Chicanos are defined as female and male persons of Mexican-origin living in the United States. These terms are also used synonymously with Mexican American. Also, Latinos are defined as persons of Latin American-origin living in the United States.

3. For a comprehensive annotated bibliography on critical race theory see Richard Delgado and Jean Stefancic (1993; 1994).

4. Gloria is a composite character based on information compiled from at least thirty focus groups with students at UCLA. This project, in part, was trying to determine those factors that impact on the retention and graduation of Students of Color (Solorzano and Associates 1994).

References

Aguirre, Adalberto and Ruben Martinez. 1993. *Chicanos in Higher Education: Issues and Dilemmas for the 21st Century.* ASHE/ERIC Higher Education Report No. 3. Washington, DC: George Washington University School of Education and Human Development.

Anzaldua, Gloria. 1987. *Borderlands—La Frontera.* San Francisco, CA: Aunt Lute Press.

Astin, Alexander. 1993. *What Matters in College? Four Critical Years Revisited.* San Francisco, CA: Jossey-Bass.

Astin, Alexander, Helen Astin, Allen Bayer, and Ann Bisconti. 1975. *The Power of Protest.* San Francisco, CA: Jossey-Bass.

Carter, Deborah and Reginald Wilson. 1992. *Minorities in Higher Education: 1991 Tenth Annual Status Report.* Washington, DC: American Council on Education.

Carter, Deborah and Reginald Wilson. 1994. *Minorities in Higher Education: 1993 Twelfth Annual Status Report.* Washington, DC: American Council on Education.

Collins, Patricia Hill. 1986. "Learning From the Outsider Within: The Sociological Significance of Black Feminist Thought." *Social Problems* 33: S14–S32.

Collins, Patricia Hill. 1992. *Black Feminist Thought: Knowledge, Consciousness, and the Politics of Empowerment.* New York: Routledge and Kegan Paul.

Delgado, Richard and Jean Stefancic. 1993. "Critical Race Theory: An Annotated Bibliography." *Virginia Law Review* 79: 461–516.

Delgado, Richard and Jean Stefancic. 1994. "Critical Race Theory: An Annotated Bibliography 1993, A Year of Transition." *University of Colorado Law Review* 66: 159–193.

D'Souza, Dinesh. 1991. *Illiberal Education: The Politics of Race and Sex on Campus.* New York: Free Press.

Espin, Olivia. 1993. "Giving Voice to Silence: The Psychologist as Witness." *American Psychologist* 48: 408–414.

Frye, Marilyn. 1992. "Oppression." In *Race, Class, and Gender: An Anthology*. Edited by Margaret Andersen and Patricia Hill Collins. Belmont, CA: Wadsworth.

Giroux, Henry A. 1983. "Theories of Reproduction and Resistance in the New Sociology of Education: A Critical Analysis." *Harvard Educational Review* 53: 257–293.

hooks, bell. 1990. "Choosing the Margin as a Space of Radical Openness." In *Yearnings: Race, Gender, and Cultural Politics*. By bell hooks. Boston, MA: South End Press.

Hurtado, Aida. 1989. "Relating to Privilege: Seduction and Rejection in the Subordination of White Women and Women of Color." *Signs: Journal of Women in Culture and Society* 14: 833–855.

Hurtado, Sylvia. 1990. "Campus Racial Climates and Educational Outcomes." Ph.D. Diss. Los Angeles: University of California.

Kerr, Clark. 1994. *Troubled Times for American Higher Education: The 1990s and Beyond*. Albany, NY: State University of New York Press.

Levine, Arthur, and Associates, eds. 1989. *Shaping Higher Education's Future: Demographic Realities and Opportunities 1990–2000*. San Francisco, CA: Jossey-Bass.

Matsuda, Mari. 1991. "Voices of America: Accent, Antidiscrimination Law, and a Jurisprudence for the Last Reconstruction." *Yale Law Review* 100: 1329–1407.

Matsuda, Mari, Charles Lawrence, Richard Delgado, and Kimberle Crenshaw, eds. 1993. *Words That Wound: Critical Race Theory, Assaultive Speech, and the First Amendment*. Boulder, CO: Westview Press.

Olivas, Michael. 1986. *Latino College Students*. New York, NY: Teachers College Press.

Pascarella, Ernest and Patrick Terenzini. 1991. *How College Affects Students*. San Francisco: Jossey-Bass.

Rendon, Laura. 1992. "From the Barrio to the Academy: Revelations of a Mexican American 'Scholarship Girl'." *New Directions for Community Colleges* No. 80 (Winter).

Riesman, David. 1954. *Individualism Reconsidered*. New York: Free Press.

Solórzano, Daniel G. and Octavio Villalpando. *Digest of Education Statistics*. Table 181. Washington, DC: National Center for Education Statistics.

Solórzano, Daniel G. and Associates. 1994. *The Design of An Information System for the UCLA Academic Advancement Program*. Los Angeles: A Report to the University of California.

Tierney, William. 1991. "Border Crossings: Critical Theory and the Study of Higher Education." In *Culture and Ideology In Higher Education.* By William Tierney. New York: Praeger.

Tierney, William. 1993. *Building Communities of Difference: Higher Education in the Twenty-First Century.* Westport, CT: Bergin and Garvey.

U.S. Bureau of the Census, Population Projections of the United States, by Age, Sex, Race, and Hispanic Origin 1992–2050." Prepared for Current Population Reports, Series P–25, No. 1092. Washington, D.C., 1992.

U.S. Department of Education. *The National Education Goals Report: Building a Nation of Learners.* (Washington, D.C., 1994).

West, Cornel. 1993. "The New Cultural Politics of Difference." In *Beyond a Dream Deferred: Multicultural Education and the Politics of Excellence.* Edited by Becky Thompson and Sangeeta Tyagi. Minneapolis, MN: University of Minnesota Press.

Zavella, Patricia. 1991. "Reflections on Diversity Among Chicanas." *Frontiers* 12: 73–85.

10

Historical Perspectives on Class and Race in Education: The Case of School Reform in the New South, 1890–1910

❑

Theodore R. Mitchell

Introduction

What follows is an attempt to illuminate the present debates over race and class in the New West through the refracted light of the New South. The issues raised during the era of so-called progressive reform in the South, those of race, class, and social power were not then new nor are they unfamiliar to us today. In fact, the interaction of categories of race and class, mediated by constructs of power, persist as key issues in the understanding of educational policy and practice at the turn of our own century. These issues, including the redrawing of caste lines, the use of schooling as a mechanism for recalibrating the lived experience of race and class, and the use of policy language to reframe relationships of race and class are as important today as they were one hundred years ago. Yet, perhaps nowhere in American history have the issues been more clearly expressed than in the emergent New South. By exploring the lineage of race and class in that setting, we may be better able to understand the more submerged debate of our own era and region.[1]

As we will see, there are both marked similarities and marked differences between the New South of the 1880s and the New West of the 1990s. In both, changes in the state have altered fundamental economic relations, in the South through the elimination of slavery and in the West in the reduction of state sector and state supported defense industries. In both, this economic change has destabilized many of the traditional caste rules that kept class and race aligned. In response, in both settings, some lower-class Whites, feeling a reduction of their relative and historical privilege, have acted independently and self consciously as a class and have sought state support for the repression of people of color. And finally, in both eras, much of the attention and energy around these issues has been focused on education, on access, on content, and on control. As striking as these similarities are, the differences may be even more compelling. As we will see, the central difference between the two eras is the treatment of inclusion and access. Unlike the 1890s, when the state and organized elites sought to create an inclusive set of socializing institutions, a main effort of the New West reformers is to exclude non-white immigrants from education and other services.

Historical sociology, providing this kind of comparison and contrast, creates an opportunity for analytic friction that is unparalleled. Through this kind of analytic contact, students of sociology of education can better view our own time and place, as well as understand the forces that have created the framework for that present. This kind of perspective-making is particularly important in an era dominated by decontextualized thinking and policy talk.

Historical Perspectives on Class and Race in Education:

The Case of School Reform in the New South, 1890–1910

In 1889, as he looked back on three decades of upheaval, Henry Grady reached the conclusion that what the New South needed most was a "white Booker T. Washington" to lead an educational revival on behalf of poor Whites.[2] And while not alone in this sentiment, Grady, as usual, made his point earlier and better than most other harbingers of the New South. What is striking about Grady's remark, and about the subsequent history of educational reform in the South, is how New South reformers did indeed turn to Booker T. Washington and to the examples of industrial training developed at Tuskeegee and Hampton Institutes for models of education appropriate for white tenants, small-hold farmers, and a growing class of industrial workers. In more theoretical terms, what is striking is the confounding of the categories of race and class in the region where both sets of divisions were and continue to be extremely strong.

By the turn of the century, most progressive reformers had come around not only to Grady's way of thinking, but also to an acknowledgment of his implicit plea that reformers borrow from the Tuskeegee model in order to fashion a system of education, socialization, and training, that would build a White as well as Black working class in the New South. That acknowledgment is important in three ways. First, it underscores the importance of developments in Black schooling as templates for the development of educational programs for the White underclass. Second, it highlights a major shift in emphasis among progressive educational reformers away from the construction of a system of education that would address the South's "race problem" exclusively toward the establishment of a system of education directed as well at issues of class. Third, it points to the important difference between class and race as categories of lived experience and those same categories as asserted categories of policy and elite dominated discourse. Together, these three elements allow us to follow efforts by social elites in the New South to create a single category that united, in logic, in treatment and in "policy talk," former slaves and lower class Whites in a single southern working-class. Further, it allows us to see clearly attempts to restructure the experiences of that class in ways consistent with the needs of the emerging industrial and agricultural capitalism in the region.

Representing the shifting priorities of New South reformers, the Conference for Education in the South in 1900 retreated from its earlier focus on Black education by passing a resolution redirecting its efforts to securing a more complete system of education for Whites. The resolution declared, in part, that "the education of the white race in the South is the pressing and imperative need."[3] The following year, the Conference refined its statement of goals, and with a resolution that would have warmed Grady's heart, declared:

> The experience of thirty years has proved conclusively the necessity of giving both to him (Blacks) and the poorer class of southern whites a primary and industrial education. The industrial training now afforded the Negro at Hampton, Tuskeegee, and similar schools . . . indicates the methods which, in our opinion, are best.[4]

The shift in focus from Black to White and the use of Hampton and Tuskeegee as universal models for the education of the southern underclass, an underclass that included some Whites and nearly all Blacks, demonstrates one dimension of the close relationship between developing concepts of race and class within the emergent New South.

In particular, the inclusion of poor Whites in an educational ideology and a framework of educational practice developed to manage the emergence of free Black labor and Black citizenship is suggestive of a complex and changing relationship between race and class within the educational reform movement and within the New South itself.

Within the educational environment, the most important signal of this changing relationship, and the feature most in need of analysis and explanation, was the expansion of categories of subordination, of caste, that once enclosed only Blacks, but were used in new ways to capture certain classes of Whites.

As we will see, when progressive reformers, drawn from a cross section of elite Whites that included planters, merchants, businessmen, and professionals, sought to understand and shape class relations in the New South, they turned quickly and reflexively from that understanding to established patterns of race relations and mechanisms of race subordination, including education.[5]

In some circles, the movement to bring universal schooling to the South was known simply as the Ogden Movement. Robert Ogden was for all of his career the managing partner in Wanamaker's department store chain. He probably would have preferred to be known by a title he conferred upon himself in an article for *Business World*, "a businessman of ideals."[6] Among Ogden's ideals was a commitment to "Negro uplift," a commitment that brought him a lifelong friendship with the young son of Hawaiian missionaries named Samuel C. Armstrong.[7] Along with other leaders of the Southern Education Movement, Ogden began his work as a reformer through Armstrong's experiment at Hampton.

After the Civil War, Armstrong, at age 29 the youngest General in the occupying forces, was stationed at Hampton, Virginia. There, calling often on Ogden's advice and his own missionary upbringing, Armstrong built Hampton Institute as a school to train the "teachers and guides" who would bring to the Black race the complete set of "right instincts and moral strengths."[8]

Hampton was a departure from other efforts at Black education during Reconstruction. The two most powerful models for Black education were, on the one hand, schools established by and for freedmen through subscriptions and, on the other, the missionary institutes established by northern missionary societies and supported by the Freedmen's Bureau.[9] While these "nurseries of treason" emphasized the new legal and political rights of Blacks and sought to teach freedom, Armstrong rejected Black participation in politics and sought to teach duty, responsibility, and Christian virtues, particularly the virtue of hard work.[10] Hampton's task was to train a cadre of teachers who would, in turn, instill these virtues in their own students, along with lessons in industrial and domestic science by which students could, throughout their lifetimes, express their newfound virtue in industrial, agricultural, or domestic labor.[11]

Ogden was taken with the "Hampton Idea," indeed, he was one of the architects responsible for its final design. He remained intimately involved with the affairs of the Institute until his death, serving as President of the Board of Trustees, and watching with some pride as his son-in-law, Alexander Purves, dedicated his professional life to Hampton as its treasurer.

In 1894, a young railroad man named William Baldwin visited Ogden's office. As Ogden later told the story,

> he said he wanted to make me, whom he regarded as a fellow worker, acquainted with a cause that was so dear to his heart.[13]

That cause was the support of Booker T. Washington's Tuskeegee Institute. Baldwin was at that time serving a term as President of the Board of Trustees at Tuskeegee and was even more closely involved in the daily operations there than Ogden was at Hampton.[13] For Baldwin, industrial education for Blacks had particular appeal. According to Charles Dabney, "He went South as a business man whose responsibilities compelled him to take account of the question of Negro labor. He needed the cooperation of thousands of trained Negroes."[14] Securing that cooperation was not just a matter of workplace control; it was a matter of proper education and training.

> As a child who during his period of infancy is kept under careful restraint, and then is turned suddenly out into the world, is inclined to lack the power of self control . . . so the Negro, when his shackles were loosened, aimed to enjoy to the fullest extent freedom from his point of view. . . . He had no outside control, no guidance, no aim. . . . The industrial education of the plantation had stopped.[15]

Without the "industrial education of the plantation," Baldwin feared for the fate of the South, for "the Negro artisan disappeared; the Negro politician took his place." The remedy, though, was at hand. For reformers like Baldwin and Ogden, and that remedy was the Hampton Idea.

Ogden and Baldwin formed a close alliance in their work on behalf of the Hampton-Tuskeegee model of industrial education for Blacks. Ogden joined Baldwin on the Board at Tuskeegee, Baldwin joined the Hampton Board; they served in those capacities together until Baldwin's death in 1905. The two were joined on the Tuskeegee and Hampton Boards by Georgia born and New York raised investment banker and philanthropist, George Foster Peabody. Peabody's interest in Black education began when, at age 16, he was moved by a sermon given by Armstrong in Peabody's Brooklyn church.[16] As the head of his Sunday School Fund, Peabody made sure that the fund contributed generously to Armstrong's efforts at Hampton. Later, through his own gifts and gifts from others, which he directed to Hampton and Tuskeegee, Peabody was able to do much more.[17]

These three men formed the intellectual and organizational nucleus of a movement that brought into its orbit the leading men of affairs in both the North and the South. In its early stages, the movement sought to consolidate the gains made by Armstrong at Hampton and Washington at Tuskeegee and then to spread the Hampton Idea as the new gospel of Black education. It was a gospel that, as Baldwin's remarks demonstrate, rejected politics for the virtue of labor and sought to replace in the mind of every Black the ideal of the "Negro politician" with the image of the "Negro artisan."

In their own terms, the reformers stood "for" Blacks. They opposed lynching, opposed deportation, and opposed suggestions that Blacks be denied all education, all access to public facilities, and all civil rights. As reformer S. C. Mitchell, put it, "(t)he Negro can neither be deported nor repressed, but by a means of the slow and sure forces of education and religion he is becoming capable in industry and moral in society."[18] And although certainly guided in part by a spiritual reckoning, the reform creed was tightly utilitarian.

> In the Negro is the opportunity of the South. . . . The South needs him and cannot spare him; but the South needs him educated to be a suitable citizen. Properly directed he is the best possible laborer to meet the climactic conditions of the South. He will willingly fill the more menial positions, and do the heavy work, at less wages than the American white man. . . . This will permit the Southern white laborer to perform the more expert labor, and to leave the fields, the mines, and the simpler trades for the Negro.[19]

This then was the political meaning of the industrial education movement for Blacks. Embodied by Hampton and Tuskeegee and supported by Northern industrialists and Southern spokesmen for the New South, industrial education attempted to create a Black working class. By virtue (or vice) of their race, Blacks were to be assigned specific roles in the political economy of the New South. By virtue of their training they were to be made able and proficient in those roles. By virtue of the socialization that was a central part of that training, they were to be convinced to celebrate those positions. The task that remained for these reformers to spread the gospel and extend the virtue of Hampton and Tuskeegee in the name of "black uplift," social stability, and economic development.

William Baldwin was invited to speak before the American Social Science Association in 1899 on the topic of "Negro Education." A true prophet, he spoke in transcendent terms. "We know the way," he said, his words rolling like thunder, "Tuskeegee and Hampton have proved it."

> It is the duty of the whole people to take up the burden. Effective organization and carrying out the principles of Hampton and Tuskeegee is the present problem of Negro Education.[20]

Within the circle of disciples of industrial education, Baldwin was more direct. He wrote to Booker T. Washington, "I tell you again that your course is the only one and the work must be organized in other states, and you must do it, and we must get the money."[21] Ogden concurred with the basic argument that "the main hope is in Hampton and Hampton Ideas," and that the instrumental problems were "first, to support the school, and second to make the school ideas national."[22] In this effort, Ogden, Baldwin, and Peabody were to find substantial support in the North and the South.

In 1898, Edward Abbott, a Cambridge Massachusetts clergyman, suggested to friends of Black education that they meet in conference to discuss "the pressing needs of Negro Education."[23] Under Abbott's direction the Conference for Christian Education in the South opened on the grounds of the Capon Springs Hotel in West Virginia on June 29, 1898. Twenty-seven people attended the first Conference, including J. L. M. Curry, scion of the old South and tireless field agent for the Peabody and Slater Funds for Education, John Eaton, former U.S. Commissioner of Education, and Hollis Frissell, Principal at Hampton Institute.[24]

Ogden's interest in the idea of the Conference grew after the fact, and he, Baldwin, and Peabody attended the second Conference in 1899. At the Second Conference Baldwin spoke of the need for a "board composed of competent men" that would be a "channel through which our friends would . . . contribute."

> Now is the accepted time to concentrate with an organization that will be recognized by the whole county as a proper channel through which the Negro industrial education can be reached successfully. The present problem of Negro education is a problem of organiza- tion—of work, not theory.[25]

The subsequent years were indeed years of organization and work . . . and not of theory. Robert Ogden, William Baldwin, George Fos- ter Peabody and southerners J. L. M. Curry, Edwin Alderman, Charles Dabney, and Charles McIver attracted financial support and organizational talent to the task of spreading the gospel of in- dustrial education.

In the Southern Education Board, established by Ogden in 1901, Baldwin's dream of a clearinghouse for donations aimed to- ward industrial education came to fruition. George Dickerman, the Board's Field Agent, matched donors to worthy schools from his home on Cottage Street in New Haven, Connecticut.[26]

In the General Education Board, funded by a million dollar gift from John D. Rockefeller and incorporated a year later by an act of Congress, supporters of industrial education found both security and great hope that the work they had begun would indeed carry on.[27]

But at the same time, pressures within and outside the move- ment acted to direct the attention of the reformers away from African-American education and toward the education of Whites. In facing this new challenge, the Southern Education Board became the centerpiece in a systematic and sustained campaign for univer- sal public schooling in the South, and the General Education Board became, by 1906, the central funding agency of a program in voca- tional training aimed at white farmers. After 1901, the campaign that was begun by Ogden to promote industrial education for Blacks became a campaign that carried the Hampton Idea across the great divide between Black and White.[28]

The southerners on the Board, Charles Dabney, J. L. M.Curry, Edwin Alderman, and most of all, Walter Hines Page, convinced their northern brethren to alter course, to heed Grady's plea, and to begin to address the need for an educational awakening among poor Whites. There were several facets to their call for White education, but each reflected the growing tension between the traditional ideal of race subordination and segregation among Whites. The new political realities were marked by the transition from slavery to freedom for Blacks, and the transition from agriculture into industry for the South as a whole.[29]

Page, the man whom Dabney called "a missionary of the gospel of progress," sounded the first call for White education in a speech he delivered at McIver's North Carolina State Normal College in 1897.[30] He titled the speech "The Forgotten Man," and in it offered a ringing condemnation of the aristocratic and ecclesiastical ideas of education that had dominated the history of southern education and that had left the mass of poor Whites behind, "forgotten and content to be forgotten." The forgotten man "became not only a dead weight but a definite opponent of social progress."[31]

Among the kinds of social progress the poor White opposed was the education, even the industrial education, of Blacks. Ogden's efforts and the efforts of southern reformers played differently in different portions of the South. For elites and reformers, Charles Dabney concluded "the question now was not Shall the Negro be educated but how shall he be trained."[32] But among tenants, smallhold farmers, and the growing number of industrial workers in the region, this was a distinction without a difference. Efforts at increasing the training of African-Americans throughout the 1890s had time and time again run aground upon the reefs of race hatred and race prejudice.[33] In one town, where Edwin Alderman and P. P. Claxton had been preaching the gospel of public education for all and industrial education for Blacks, Alderman overheard one man remark to another "Men who talk like that ought to be lynched."[34]

It was with remarks like that in mind that southern reformers often claimed, with Alderman, that:

> The education of one untaught white man, therefore, to the point that knowledge, and not prejudice will guide his conduct . . . is worth more to the black man himself than the education of ten Negroes.[35]

A somewhat exasperated Curry spoke in similar terms to the Second Conference for Education in the South. "I must be pardoned," he said, "for emphasizing the fact that there is greater need for the education of the other (white) race."[36] While not calling for the extension of the Hampton Ideal to Whites, Alderman and Curry both recognized the need to extend some form of education to Whites, in the first instance, so that their efforts to create a Black working class might proceed.

The movement to shape Black education depended upon the support of White voters and in particular on the mass of poor White voters, who controlled state legislatures, tax levies, and school expenditures. The success of the reformers' efforts to use industrial education to create a new and more complete subordination of Blacks depended at least in part on the ability of White voters to understand the real meaning of Ogden's and Baldwin's arguments. What was crucial to the movement that Alderman and Curry represented was that the mass of White voters comprehend and participate in the creation of mechanisms for the creation and perpetuation of a Black underclass. This, reformers, came quickly to find, was not a simple task and required that they do some basic educating among the Whites themselves.

Whites, particularly poor Whites of the countryside, insisted that Blacks remain a subordinate race and that their subordination remain the subordination of direct repression, restriction, and violence. Reformers, on the other hand, also insisted upon white supremacy and subordination of Blacks, but through what John Kenneth Galbraith calls "condign" rather than coercive power.[37] Training and education were, in the minds of Ogden, Baldwin, and Alderman improvements over the whip and the noose. Yet, the persistence of lynching, night riding, and successful appeals by southern demagogues to race hatred all spoke to the durability of the tradition of coercive race subordination in the political culture of southern Whites. In contrast, the reformers' notion that race subordination could be transformed within the new circumstances of free labor and free men into class subordination made slow headway.

Unscrupulous or uncomprehending editors were quick to label Ogden and his movement "negrophile," and to raise the specter of Black equality and Black domination.[38] The facet of the campaign for White education that dealt directly with the extension of Black industrial training was, then, first and foremost a campaign for public opinion. According to Alderman, "Southern men have shied away from the subject. It has been like touching a sore tooth. We want now to influence public sentiment, to stop being silent, but be wise."[39] Only this wise approach to shaping White public opinion could enable reformers to continue the spread of the industrial gospel across the South.

While these efforts to make White voters "believers" in the gospel of industrial education for Blacks were important, and especially important in the context of the Ogden movement, it became less and less the central concern of reformers interested in the education of poor Whites. As the reformers' exasperation grew, so too grew the restiveness of the White underclass. As it did, elites came to link, rather than differentiate Black and White first in their minds and then in their policy talk. As they did, they turned ever more directly to programs that would treat poor Whites according to the same logic they had been supporting for African-Americans. At the core of that effort lay the same hopes and fears, the same interests and goals, and the same models from which Armstrong and his supporters drew together blueprints for the education of the Black working class.

When the Third Conference for Education in the South resolved the importance of "giving both to him (Blacks) and the poorer class of southern whites a primary and industrial education," the members were not resorting to mere rhetorical flourish. The experience of planters, merchants, professionals with the class of poor Whites over that period was no less destabilizing, no less disturbing, and no less threatening to the emergence of a New South than had been their experience with the freedmen. Page, freed from the necessary trappings and political aims of a more public address, put it bluntly to a reporter. "You will find," he said sourly, "when the woodpile is turned over not a nigger, but a poor White boy."[40]

During the 1890s, the "white boy in the woodpile" had been a populist, arguing loud and long for expanding the money supply, for government ownership of railroads and telegraphs, and for direct election of U.S. Senators. For almost a decade, between 1889 and 1896, the populist insurgency threatened politics and business as usual in the South, demanding greater popular participation in politics and through that participation, control over the economy. Where populist doctrine was most advanced, in Texas and Georgia, for example, leaders repudiated the laissez-faire excesses of the Gilded Age and struggled to redefine the very nature of capitalism.[41]

For Curry, the Populists were "a good many fools."[42] His concept of democracy had no room in it for popular insurgency. "How shall the people rule?" he asked his audience at the Second Conference for Education in the South, "when is their voice authoritative?" Certainly "not by the spontaneous utterance of a promiscuous assembly . . . not unless that voice has been collected and formulated according to prescribed methods and forms."[43] For Page, the improper and inadequate education offered to poor Whites made them, during the 1890s "the prey of small agitations. See how," he continued, they lie bound by the straw of the Farmers' Alliance, led by them of the long beards, to whose dominating delusion our greatest public servant (the governor) paid the homage of surrender.[44]

The "surrender" of ordered and stable political relations to the vagaries and uncertainty of popular insurgency was unacceptable to Page and unacceptable to other southern reformers whose intimate and personal association with the upheavals of the 1890s made them particularly attuned to continued unrest among Whites and particularly interested in employing educational means to redirect the political, social, and economic impulses of Whites.[45]

The first years of the twentieth century did little to restore stability to the political environment in the South. The emergence of demagogues across the South, who were willing to whip up race hatred and to pit "the masses against the classes," frightened reformers and threatened their vision of a prosperous and progressive New South. Reformers were aware that the electoral victories of James K. Vardaman in Mississippi, Benjamin Tillman and Col Blease in South Carolina, and Tom Watson in Georgia threatened their dominance and their ability to direct the future development of the region. In order to combat the appeal of the demagogues, reformers sought to redirect and indeed remake the ideology of the poor Whites in order to make of them "the right kind of revolutionists."[46]

It is within this context, the context of class identification and class formation among poor Whites and continued insurgencies that the Second Conference for Education in the South resolved in 1899:

> That in the development of industrial education upon lines now well established by noteworthy models, the conference recognizes . . . a hopeful means toward the better working out of existing social, economic, and racial problems.[47]

Reformers placed upon education for Whites the same mandate they had earlier placed on schools for Blacks: to educate along vocational lines, to inculcate the virtues of hard work, and most significantly, to elevate the satisfaction of poor Whites with their existing class position. "Schools such as these," remarked one industrialist, "say whether they (poor Whites) shall be mob-leaders and night riders or leaders in civil and religious righteousness."[48] For J. L. M. Curry, the matter was even more straightforward. "Such an education," he remarked to the legislature in South Carolina, "will not only benefit its recipients, but contribute to material prosperity and to social quiet."[49]

The social quiet the reformers sought was layered through several levels. Most clearly, reformers sought the development of sets of class relations that would be harmonious and hospitable to the development of industrial and agricultural capitalism in the region. This was the "material prosperity" they referred to again and again. Underneath that, and motivating much of the policy transformation under consideration, were attempts to first create harmonious relationships within traditional race categories in the South. Thus, reformers had sought first to excite the paternalistic attitudes of Whites toward ex-slaves. When, as we have seen, this not only did not work, but also gave rise to self-conscious class formation among lower-class Whites, reformers had to develop new ways of constructing the relationships they felt would produce "social quiet." Finally, and at the base of this was a focus on the individuation of responsibility, accountability, and opportunity. In matters of both race and class, reformers discouraged collective identity and sought to identify possibility only with the individual.[50]

One of the most significant converts to the doctrine of white industrial education was Frederick Gates, John D. Rockefeller's personal assistant and later Secretary of the General Education Board. With Gates' leadership, the Board threw its considerable influence behind the project of creating among Whites a kind of education that would:

> Not try to make these people or any of their children into philosophers or men of learning or of science . . . nor will we cherish even the humble ambition to raise up from among them lawyers or doctors, for the task that we set before ourselves is a very simple as well as a very beautiful one . . . to train these people as we find them for a perfectly ideal life just where they are.[51]

Early on in its discussions, the Board resolved to focus its attention on agricultural education and on the development of vocational training programs for farmers. The Board's mode of reform, summarized by Gates, was to fashion programs that rationalized and beautified rural life, and that made that life bearable if not hospitable to a class of people whose lot it was to remain "as we find them." The plan had three main virtues. First, it brought vocational training to the mass of poor Whites who still lived and worked in rural areas. It literally met Gates' requirement to "educate them where they are." Second, emphasis on agricultural education served to appropriate the traditions and myths that lay behind the popular insurgencies of the 1890s. By arguing, as they did, that vocational agriculture would bring farmers higher incomes and more power in the marketplace, reformers were able to claim at least some of the populist heritage as their own. Finally, the rural focus of vocational agriculture enabled reformers to ally themselves with deeply rooted cultural myths of agrarian virtue. This, in turn could be neatly contrasted to the industrial focus of Black education. Thus, in this last instance at least, the transformation from industrial to agricultural education enabled poor Whites to continue to assert their racial superiority over Blacks while, in fact, being trained and socialized as members of a working class with both agricultural and industrial components. The stability and order so sought after by New South reformers demanded the settling of the agrarian question as much as the settling of the race question and the reconciliation of farmers to their role "just where they are," as producers in a newly industrializing region. More, it demanded that farmers leave politics alone and seek "uplift" through harder work, better husbandry, and more efficient management. This, then, was the translation of the Hampton and Tuskeegee models to White education.

In the years that followed, the General Education Board poured more than $900,000.00 into vocational agriculture programs for White farmers. Seaman Knapp, who directed the Board's Demonstration Program for adults, could rightly claim the mantle Grady held out, the title of the "white Booker T. Washington." Under Knapp, farmers learned that their prosperity depended upon correct application of technical knowledge, not upon political agitation.

Vocational agriculture programs in elementary and high schools replaced the classical curriculum, and were organized around Ogden's "principle that sound constructive work must eliminate the controversial spirit."[52] Reformers supported clubs and organizations for school-age youth that emphasized the social side of agrarian life and that sought to build a spirit of contentment among the rural producers.

"What was best for the emancipated slave," wrote Ogden's biographer in 1924, "has been proved best for the dominant race."[53] Individual farmers and their families might have disagreed. Rates of tenancy rose, increases in farm income were eaten up by increases in prices for manufactured goods. But by Curry's criteria of material prosperity and social quiet, the South, as a whole, did benefit from the wide distribution of vocational training mixed with the ideology of social control. The result of the reforms of the educational crusade was the creation of a new working class, still divided by race, but newly harnessed in service, agricultural or industrial, to the growth of the New South. This, after all, was the Hampton Idea.

In our own pre-millennial age, issues of race, class, and social power have again emerged as central to the construction of educational alternatives and therefore to our own scholarly inquiries. Nowhere has this been clearer than in California, where New West reformers are at work preparing a different region for a different set of transformations. The reform agenda in the New West, and across much of the nation, is to eliminate in state policy the use of race as a category containing independent value and meaning (Affirmative Action) while simultaneously excluding non-citizens, most of whom are people of color, from education and other services. In California, this mixture of exclusion and homogenization of racial categories is the theme that connects recent ballot initiatives (Proposition 187 and the California Civil Rights Initiative), and the decision by the University of California Regents to curtail Affirmative Action in employment and admissions.

In the New West, as in the New South, reformers and their supporters draw strength from a wide spectrum that curs across race and class. Indeed the substantive parallels are striking along at least two dimensions.

First, movements calling for the exclusion of large numbers of children from the educational system on the basis of citizenship status recalls the reformers' struggles with their White audiences in the 1890s.[54] Now, as then, excluding a subordinate caste (Latino immigrants) from education altogether becomes a viable policy alternative, especially among relatively disenfranchised members of the dominant caste. Unlike the experience of the 1890s, today's exclusionists have taken the offensive, and in their offensive they have sought to create a kind of solidarity that reaches across class and even racial lines. Their appeal is flexible, ranging from fiscal responsibility to barely veiled race hatred. Yet, for its flexibility, the theme has a consistent ring: if "they" are included it will threaten "us."

Second, the resurgence of interest in vocational programs, designed to ease the transition from school to work by providing more relevant and often hands-on learning related to industrial and service work recalls much of the language and logic of the New South. Much has been written about such so called school to work programs, and much of that would be familiar and felicitous to Grady, Ogden, and Baldwin. In particular, parallels can be drawn in the programs of both eras that emphasizes individual training and "uplift" over collective action and even collective identity. Now, as then, the policy talk emphasizes the preparation of individuals to play roles in a new economic order, today in a service/information economy. Now, as then, reformers attempt to subordinate issues of race and even class to individualism. And now, as then, we may fairly predict that the results of successful vocational programs will be the recreation of an underclass tracked to differential opportunity, sorted by educational experience, separated from decision-making in the broadest sense, and divided internally by issues of race.

In the end, what is striking is how these two alternatives, exclusion and social control through education and training reemerge and struggle against each other in the various frames of discourse, but in particular in the policy talk of the elite. What is discouraging is that the struggle between these two poles, both now and in Grady's era, seemingly precludes struggle over whether these are the only or the right alternatives. What is demanded, in turn, of a new scholarship of race and class is the creation of new space in the discourse for alternative visions that are not simply about choosing one form of subordination over another.

Indeed, in the theory about race, class, and power, it is a constant that skillful manipulation of these and other categories of subordination (including gender and sexual preference) solidifies the status quo and reifies the logic of control embedded in the social relations of a particular time and place. Typically, we think of this manipulation as attempts to divide and conquer, to pit White against non-White and middle class against lower class. The experience of the New South together with our growing understanding of the New West suggests that the real processes are more complex, enacting a recombination of categories that includes attempts at unification as well as attempts at division.

Within the policy talk about public education, this impoverished discourse becomes a simple case of deciding who loses. The jockeying and recombination of categories of subordination does not enrich the discourse, but instead limits it, and in so doing limits the sense of the possible. In the midst, the struggle for a genuine democratic discourse is too often forgotten.

Democratic education, another lesson learned from the New South, may, in fact, best take place outside the domain of the state, in independent non-formal ways. Insofar as the theory suggests that counter-hegemonic processes are possible, it may be to those examples that we might turn for authentic models of educational thinking not reduced to recategorizing subordination.

Notes

1. Charles Dabney, *Universal Education in the South* (Chapel Hill: University of North Carolina Press, 1939) 2:5. The image of Jefferson is as pervasive as it is self-conscious throughout the "crusade."

2. Henry Grady, quoted in A. D. Mayo, "The Third Estate in the South," *U.S. Bureau of Education Circular of Information* 1890 (Washington, DC: Government Printing Office, 1890), p. 282.

3. William Baldwin, *Second Conference for Education in the South* 1899, p. 9.Proceedings of the Conference for Education in the South. Raleigh, NC: Edwards and Broughtun, 1899.

4. *Third Conference for Education in the South* 1900, pp. 5–6. Proceedings of the Third Capon Springs Conference for Education in the South, 1900. Raleigh, NC: Printing Office, St. Augustine's School, 1900.

5. The question of progressive reform in the South is complex and understudied. Richard Hofstadter's *The Age of Reform: From Bryan to FDR* (New York: Alfred A. Knopf, 1955) set the agenda for several successive scholars of the national progressive movement. Among those who responded to Hofstadter was Robert Wiebe, whose *Search for Order* (New York: Hill and Wang, 1967) established in its title and its argument a useful paradigm that includes both the northern and southern progressive movements. The first attempt to isolate southern progressivism was Arthur Link's, "The Progressive Movement in the South, 1870–1914," *North Carolina Historical Review* 23 (April 1946): 172–195. C. Vann Woodward's classic chapter "Progressivism: For Whites Only," appeared five years later in his *Origins of the New South* (Baton Rouge: Louisiana State University Press, 1951). Both Link and Woodward explored the common themes in northern and southern progressivism while pointing out the unique elements of the southern movement. George Tindall's volume in the History of the South, *The Emergence of the New South* (Baton Rouge: Louisiana State University Press, 1967), carried the theme of progressive politics into the 1920s. Most recently, Dewey Grantham's synthesis, *Southern Progressivism: The Reconciliation of Progress and Tradition* (Knoxville: University of Tennessee Press, 1983) succeeds in placing progressivism into the larger context of southern history. State histories are important in the historiography of progressivism in the South. The question central to most of these is the continuity, or lack thereof, between the old South and the New. Representative of the best of these works are Jonathan Wiener's, *Social Origins of the New South: Alabama, 1860–1885* (Baton Rouge: Louisiana State University Press, 1978), and Dwight Billings, Jr.'s, *Planters and the Making of a "New South": Class, Politics, and Development in North Carolina, 1865–1900* (Chapel Hill: University of North Carolina Press, 1979.). The arguments concerning the use

of education as mechanisms for the socialization and control of Blacks are well made by, W. E. B. Du Bois, *Black Reconstruction in America: An Essay Toward a History of the Part which Black Folk Played in the Attempt to Reconstruct Democracy in America, 1860–1880* (New York: Atheneum, 1983), Horace Mann Bond, *The Education of the Negro in the American Social Order* (New York: Prentice Hall, Inc. 1934) and *Negro Education in Alabama: A Study in Cotton and Steel* (Washington DC: The Associated Publishers, Inc. 1939) and most recently, James Anderson, *The Education of Blacks in the South, 1860–1935* (Chapel Hill: University of North Carolina Press, 1988), esp. ch. 2, 3.

6. Robert Ogden, "Business Idealism," *The Business World* 25, no. 6 (June 1905).

7. None of the several biographies on Robert Ogden is very precise on Ogden's early association with Samuel C. Armstrong, but they appear to have been friendly from Armstrong's college days at Williams. See Philip W. Wilson, *An Unofficial Statesman: Robert C. Ogden* (New York: Doubleday, Page, and Co., 1924), pp. 124–137.

8. Anderson, *Education of Blacks*, p. 39.

9. Ibid., p. 94. Louis R. Harlan, *Separate and Unequal: Public School Campaigns and Racism in the Southern Seaboard States, 1901–1915* (New York: Atheneum, 1968).

10. Elisabeth Joan Doyle, "Nurseries of Treason: Schools in Occupied New Orleans," *Journal of Southern History* 26 (2) 1960, p. 160–171.

11. Anderson, *Education of Blacks*, pp. 36–48.

12. Ogden, quoted in Wilson, *An Official Statesman*, p. 201.

13. John G. Brooks, *An American Citizen: The Life of William Henry Baldwin, Jr.* (Boston and New York: Houghton Mifflin Co., 1910), pp. 230–244. William Baldwin appointed himself Booker T. Washington's editor and speech coach. Baldwin went over each word of Washington's more important addresses, making sure that they would play to White audiences. Baldwin was so nervous before Washington's address at the Atlanta Exposition in 1895 that he was unable to enter the Hall to listen and instead paced the lobby waiting for reports from inside.

14. Dabney *Universal Education*, II: pp. 7–8.

15. Baldwin, *Second Conference for Education in the South* 1899, p. 68.

16. Louise Ware, *George Foster Peabody: Banker, Philanthropist, Publicist* (Athens: University of Georgia Press, 1951), p. 13.

17. George Foster Peabody was only distantly related to the George Peabody who established the Peabody Fund for the development of education in the South.

18. S. C. Mitchell, "The Educational Needs of the South," *Outlook* 76 (February 13, 1904): 416.

19. Baldwin, *Second Conference for Education in the South* 1899, p. 72.

20. Quoted in Brooks, *An American Citizen*, pp. 204–205.

21. Baldwin to Washington, *The Booker T. Washington Papers*, v. 4 (Urbana: University of Illinois Press, 1972) p. 526.

22. Quoted in H. S. Enck, "The Burden Bourne: Northern White Philanthropy and Southern Black Industrial Education, 1900–1915," (Ph.D. Diss., University of Cincinnati, 1970), p. 52. Fellow trustee Collis P. Huntington was at least willing to take some of the burden from Washington, for he wondered "where shall we get another Booker T. Washington for these schools." *The Booker T. Washington Papers*, vol. 4 (Urbana: University of Illinois Press, 1972) p. 499.

23. Dabney *Universal Education,* II: p. 5.

24. J. L. M. Curry was a bridge between the old South and the new. His life is captured by fellow toilers in education work E. A. Alderman and A. C. Gordon in *J. L. M. Curry, A Biography* (New York: Macmillan, 1911); and in Merle Curti's *Social Ideas of American Educators* (Totowa, NJ: Littlefield, Adams, 1959), pp. 261–288. *First Conference for Education in the South,* p. 37.

25. Baldwin, *Second Conference for Education in the South* 1899, p. 75.

26. See *Dickerman Correspondence, Southern Historical Collection* (University of North Carolina, Chapel Hill). Hereafter cited as *SHC*. For an analysis of Dickerman's methods, see Theodore R. Mitchell, *Political Education in the Southern Farmers' Alliance* (Madison: University of Wisconsin Press, 1987), pp. 188, 193.

27. Rockefeller, who, "talking with his son and (Frederick) Gates, thought of setting up a generous trust to stimulate Negro education." Rockefeller talked with fellow Baptist, J. L. M. Curry, and rather than going his own way, decided to investigate Robert Ogden and his "movement." John D. Rockefeller, Jr. joined Ogden's excursion to the Fourth Conference in 1901 and was much impressed with the work he saw at Hampton and Tuskeegee as well as with the kind of thinking that took place under Ogden's direction as President of the Conference. See Allan Nevins, *Study in Power: John D. Rockefeller, Industralist and Philanthropist* (New York: Scribner, 1953) pp. 480–485. Also Frederick Gates, and Dabney, *Universal Education,* II: pp. 123–153.

28. The original members of the Southern Education Board, as appointed by Ogden, were J. L. M. Curry, Charles Dabney, president of the University of Tennessee, Edwin Alderman, president of the University of

North Carolina, Charles D. McIver, president of the North Carolina State Normal and Industrial College, Hollis Frissell, principal of Hampton Institute, George Foster Peabody, and Wallace Buttrick, of Albany, New York. Peabody offered the Board $40,000 operating capital for the first year's work. At its first meeting, the Board expanded its membership, electing William Baldwin, Albert Shaw, editor of the *Review of Reviews*, Walter Hines Page, editor of *The World's Work*, and H. H. Hanna to the Board.

29. Eric Foner, *Politics and Ideology in the Age of the Civil War* (New York: Oxford University Press, 1980).

30. Charles Dabney to Walter Hines Page, *Page Papers* (May 20, 1885). (Houghton Library, Harvard University, hereafter cited as *Page Papers*, Box 9)

31. Walter Hines Page, "Forgotten Man," in *The Rebuilding of Old Commonwealths* (New York: Doubleday, 1902), p. 26. Also Walter Hines Page, *Page Papers*.

32. Dabney *Universal Education,* II: p. 53.

33. See Louis R. Harlan, *Separate and Unequal: Public School Campaigns and Racism in the Southern Seaboard States, 1901–1915* (New York, Atheneum, 1968) ch. 3, Seedtime, North Carolina.

34. Dabney *Universal Education,* I: p 209; Charles Lewis, *Philander Priestley Claxton, Crusader for Public Education* (Knoxville: University of Tennessee Press, 1948), pp. 70–71.

35. E. A. Alderman, "Education in the South," *Outlook* 68 (August 3, 1901): 779.

36. Curry, *Second Conference for Education in the South* 1899, p. 28.

37. John Kenneth Galbraith, within a neo-Marxist framework this shift is one between repressive and ideological control. See Louis Althusser, "Ideology and the Ideological State Apparatus," in *Lenin and Philosophy* (New York: Monthly Review, 1967).

38. See Harlan, *Separate and Unequal*, pp. 97–98; Anderson, *Education of Blacks*, pp. 94–98. Page to Wallace Buttrick (January 19, 1903) in *Page Papers*.

39. Alderman quoted in Harlan, *Separate and Unequal*, p. 97.

40. Page in Columbia, S. C., *State* (April 24, 1903).

41. Populist historiography is massive and only a sampling can be offered here.

42. Curry quoted in Donald Spivey, *Schooling for the New Slavery* (Westport, CT: Greenwood Press, 1978), p. 80.

43. Curry, *Second Conference for Education in the South* 1899, p. 31.

44. Page, "Address at the Inauguration of President Winston of North Carolina" (October 20, 1891), *Page Papers*, Box 9.

45. Edwin Alderman, Charles D. McIver, and J. L. M. Curry all struggled in the trenches during the 1890s. For summaries of their activities, and in particular, of their brushes with the insurgents, see Harlan, *Separate and Unequal,* ch. 3 and Mitchell, *Political Education*, ch. 6.

46. Page to Buttrick (February 10, 1907).

47. Baldwin, *Second Conference for Education in the South*, 1899, p. 8.

48. Nathan Thompson, quoted in Phillip W. Wilson, *An Unofficial Statesman: Robert C. Ogden* (New York: Doubleday, Page and Co. 1924) p. 203.

49. J. L. M. Curry, "Address Before the General Assembly of South Carolina, December 13, 1894," *Curry Papers*, Library of Congress.

50. See Theodore R. Mitchell, *Political Education in the Southern Farmers' Alliance*, ch. 6. Madison, WI: Univ. of Wisconsin Press, 1987.

51. Frederick Gates, "The College and Rural Life" (Confidential Memo to the General Education Board, May, 24, 1912), *G. E. B. Papers*, Rockefeller Archives in Potanico Hills, New York.

52. Wilson, p. 195.

53. Ibid., p. 198.

54. For example, California voters approved a ballot measure that would prohibit undocumented aliens, mostly people of color, from all publicly supported education.

11

From Soweto to the South Bronx:
African Americans and Colonial Education
in the United States

❑

Gloria Ladson-Billings

On June 16 1976, fifteen thousand school children gathered in
Soweto to protest the government's ruling that half of all
classes in secondary schools must be taught in Afrikaans. Students did not want to learn and teachers did not want to teach
in the language of the oppressor.

—Nelson Mandela

The thrust for control over ghetto schools represents a shift in
emphasis by black and poor people from a concern with repli-
cating that which is American to a desire for reshaping it to
include their concerns. There is less concern with social integration than there is with effective education.

—Preston Wilcox, *Alkalimat*

The term "colonial" generally has two references in the United
States context. On one hand it conjures the romantic notions of the
revolutionary spirit of the early European (primarily English) set-
tlers who steadfastly abhorred English taxes and rule without the
benefit of representation. From that notion of colonial we generated
a particular view of history, architecture, city planning, and decor.
The other notion of colonial extant in the United States is the more
sinister, malevolent pattern of conquest and imperialism perpe-
trated by European powers on so-called third world nations in Asia,

247

Africa, and parts of the Americas. This notion, perhaps no less romantic, evokes pictures of black- and brown-skinned men attired in European style military garb, while their children wear school uniforms and study for an English or French designed high school entrance exam.

In this paper, I will attempt to pull together the two disparate notions of colonialism to examine the condition of education for African Americans in the United States. To do this, I will be moving back and forth between the pattern of colonial education in the so-called third world, particularly apartheid South Africa, and U.S. urban schooling. I attempt to develop my argument by using social facts from both contexts. I suggest that the dismal academic achievement of African-American students in the United States is linked to the colonial education they receive in U.S. schools.

My initial conceptualization of African Americans as participants in a colonial education system came as a result of my participation in a *Brown v. Board of Education* conference where an audience member asked the panel, why after forty years of court ordered desegregation, civil rights legislation, affirmative action, and seemingly great strides in equal opportunity have African Americans failed to be successful in public schools? Several panel members posited reasons for this lag, but I suggested that the only explanation for this persistent inequality lies in the structure of public schooling in urban settings. This structure, unlike the structure of education in White middle-class communities is analogous to colonial education elsewhere in the world.

Jonathan Jansen (1990) points out that in apartheid South Africa his students were well aware of the oppressive schooling in which they were forced to participate. He cites a quote from one of his students to illustrate this point:

> THEY decide what we are taught. Our history is written according to their ideas. Biology and physics are taught in our schools but which we cannot apply to our everyday lives. We are not told that most diseases of the workers stem from the fact that they are undernourished and overworked. We are taught biology, but not in the terms of the biology of liberation, where we can tackle the concept of "race" to prove that there is no such thing as "race." We are taught geography but not the geography of liberation. We are not taught that 80% of South Africans are dumped on 13% of the land. . . . We are taught accountancy merely to calculate the profits of the capitalist. (Maurice 1983, cited in Jansen 1990)

Also, on this side of the Atlantic, students show an amazing astuteness about the material conditions of their schools. In his critically acclaimed social commentary on education in the United States, Kozol (1991) provides examples of this awareness:

> If you threw us all into some different place, some ugly land, and put White children in this building in our place, this school would start to shine. No question. The parents would say: "This building sucks. It's ugly. Fix it up." They'd fix it fast—no question. (1991, 104)

But, beyond the material deprivations, there are the continuing psycho-cultural assaults that are apparent as a result of the structural and symbol systems that serve to colonize education in African-American communities. The intransigence of these systems became increasingly evident in the early 1990s when urban communities began to work for more community-based schools.

The African-American community in inner city Milwaukee, Wisconsin grew more frustrated with the lack of educational achievement among its students. Community leaders urged a secession from the Milwaukee Public School District and the creation of a separate African-American school district. After the initial furor of that proposal died down, a subsequent proposal to initiate an African-American male immersion school was presented. This proposal met with greater and wider resistance. Unlike the first proposal, which was considered unlikely to occur, this second proposal could conceivably come to fruition. However, several factors worked to undermine it.

Perhaps it is important to place the Milwaukee situation in its large sociohistorical context. Milwaukee is the largest city in Wisconsin. Located in a state that has a very small African-American population (less than 5 percent), Milwaukee has approximately 195,000 African Americans, representing 25 percent of the city's population (U.S. Census 1990).[1] It is also determined to be (according to housing patterns) the most segregated city in the United States. The city currently has nineteen all African-American schools. Thus, the proposal to institute an African-American male immersion school technically only refers to a call to segregate by gender.

After months of discussions about the legality of such a school, the Milwaukee Public School district agreed to permit, on an experimental basis two coeducational African-American Immersion Schools. The community has accepted this "half a loaf" as a possibility for a more revolutionary educational process.

The Afri-centric Approach to Education

Unfortunately, students are not always aware of the ways in which colonial education works in their lives. Shortly after I began teaching at the University of Wisconsin, a graduate student from Botswana came to talk with me about her thesis on the impact of colonial education. Unfortunately, her adviser had left the university and she was struggling to finish in a timely manner so that she might return home. Our department assigned her another adviser based on the fact that he had spent some time in her country many years previously.

The student had a difficult time communicating with this new adviser. He did not understand what she was trying to do and challenged her on her methodology and data analysis. Desperate to finish her work and return home, the student sought me out and explained her situation. It appeared to me that her ideas were reasonable and all she needed to do was explain them to her adviser. She insisted that she could not approach this (White) man in a way that challenged and contradicted him. Throughout it all she could not see that the very colonial education that she sought to explain had engulfed her in a web of asymmetrical relationships with anyone she perceived as a colonizer. She had grown up in Africa but had not received an African-centered education.

When Molefi Asante (1987) argued that Europocentric constructions of knowledge and truth were not universals and that their systematic representations as such did great psychic damage to African and other non-European peoples, he struck a resonant chord in the African community. African-American educational scholars, practitioners, and community activists had asserted for some time that what was happening to African-American students in schools was linked to growing anti-school and anti-social behaviors.

These behaviors were very evident among African-American males, who as a group, have high school dropout rates (Irvine 1990; Majors and Billson 1992), high school suspension and expulsion rates (Majors and Billson 1992), and high rates of incarceration. Drug and alcohol abuse continues to plague the community. Scholars such as Na'im Akbar (1985), Molefi Asante (1991), Joyce King (1992), and Wade Nobles (1973) have argued persuasively that both the lack of education and the kind of education that African Americans have received about themselves and others play an important role in constructing African-Americans and all things African as deprived, inferior, and pathological. Thus, a need for an Afri-centric or African-centered approach to education is imperative.

The concept of centeredness is not limited to African-Americans. For, by calling into question Europocentric notions of knowledge and truth, all people who have been historically constructed as "other" by virtue of race, ethnicity, language, gender, ability, or sexual orientation have an opportunity to participate in the social construction of knowledge that situates themselves as "subject" rather than "object" of study.

As we look at the ways in which colonial education functions, we can see more clearly why the experience of African-Americans in U.S. schools are parallel to those which existed in apartheid South Africa. The focus of this discussion is on curriculum, pedagogy, administration and governance, and funding:

Curriculum. Curriculum decisions in U.S. public schools are made, allegedly, at the state level, that is, each of the fifty states has its own department of education which oversees curricular decisions. However, the tremendous impact of textbooks (Apple 1986) on the shape of the curriculum means that, in fact, schooling in the United States is standardized. The textbook industry is dependent upon the wishes and whims of the adoption processes in its largest markets—California and Texas. Thus, these two states have inordinate power over the construction and representation of text knowledge. But, even if California and Texas were not the dominant influence in textbook production, the fact that the "market" is constructed as largely White and middle class means that what is considered "official knowledge" (Apple 1993) is that which reifies and valorizes White middle-class history, culture, and values almost to the exclusion of all other forms of knowledge.

This control over knowledge production has profound ramifications for marginalized and oppressed peoples. In apartheid South Africa, the construction of school knowledge meant that the rightful possessors of the land could be reconstructed as savage and inept—not worthy of landownership. And, despite their numerical majority, they could come to see themselves as a minority.[2] Thus, those South-African children who could attend schools learned from a curriculum designed and created for the advancement of White South Africans. Students learn from a curriculum designed to prepare them for passing entrance exams to colleges and universities that they could not attend even if they had enough money or the desire to. To solidify its dominance in the minds of Black students, the government insisted on the use of Afrikaans language. The language mandate represented the breaking point for students of Soweto and precipitated their rebellion.

In U.S. urban schools, the colonial curriculum takes a more subtle, yet pernicious form. The language African-American students bring with them is ignored and ridiculed because, at best, it is seen as a corruption, at worst it is seen as no language. Despite the fact that linguists recognize Black English Vernacular (BEV) as a particular form of English (see for example, Baugh 1994; Dillard 1972; Gee 1989; Smitherman 1986) with lexical and syntactical connections to various West African languages, schools rarely recognize the language as legitimate or that African-American students may be participating in a process of translation as they are being instructed in what is called the "standard form."

An examination of the content of the curriculum demonstrates how marginal African-Americans are to the production of knowledge. In text renderings of U.S. history African Americans make about three appearances—almost always as object, rarely as subject. Their initial appearance comes as slaves arriving to the Americas in 1619, followed by an appearance in the discussion of the plantation system, the Civil War, and Reconstruction, and finally they appear in the 1960s as a part of the discussion of the modern Civil Rights movement.

Even in the so-called multicultural textbooks of the 1990s (King 1992), African Americans make limited and tangential appearances as actors in U.S. history. But, the number of African Americans is not really the issue here. Rather it is the way in which the history is constructed that colonizes the African-American mind. By making textbooks "multicultural," textbook publishers have persuaded schools that they have included the stories of various peoples. But what has actually transpired is that various peoples have been transformed and reconstructed so that their stories "fit" the military/political history that is already in place. For example, U.S. history has been built on a foundation that reifies the Mayflower and the Pilgrims as the paragon of "Americaness."[3] Thus, individuals once staked their claim to American rights as citizens by asserting their ancestral connections to the Mayflower. However, as the mainstream of the U.S. population began to carry an ethnic identity different from White Anglo-Saxon Protestant, the need for a foundational shift in the history was made more apparent.

To "multiculturalize" the history, textbook publishers reconstructed the Mayflower/Pilgrim mythology into an "Immigrant mythology." Thus, everyone who laid claim to America could be categorized as an immigrant. The Europeans from Columbus to the Irish fleeing famine-ridden Ireland were immigrants, the African Americans were called, "involuntary immigrants." The American Indians were now termed, the "first immigrants." The current wave of peoples from the Far East are now the "new immigrants." Historical inaccuracies notwithstanding, this entire immigrant model creates some powerful cultural dislocations (Asante 1987). Since, we are "all immigrants," then the failure of African Americans to rise up the socioeconomic ladder can only be read as an internal failure, that is, something is wrong with them culturally, genetically, psychologically, or socially. The immigrant model allows the dominant group to mute the distinctions of class and gender and galvanize racist sentiment among any who are (or who can) construct themselves as non-Black. This is a similar strategy deployed in apartheid South Africa. By importing labor from India and other parts of Asia, the White government could construct a new category—"coloreds"—to demonstrate the internal inferiority of Blacks.

The writing of a military/political history as both universal and true leaves little or no room for critical analysis. Writing oneself into this history requires that one play a role in a particular military/political construction of oneself. If one's lifework has been that of forging an oppositional culture which is counter to the mainstream, only those seen as "exceptions" can have a place in the currently constructed school histories.

Curricula are not merely designed to say something, they are designed also to *do* something. What is it that the current curricula in U.S. schools is designed to do? Carter G. Woodson (1933) has stated aptly, the power that the curriculum holds over the minds of students, by asserting that there would be no lynching if it had not begun in the classroom. J. King (1992, p. 336) terms this "mental slavery to the dominant intellectual paradigm and school knowledge that promotes assimilation and self-abnegation."

Pedagogy. The second area that demonstrates how education in the United States replicates the colonial model of apartheid South Africa is pedagogy. I am deliberately using this broader notion of pedagogy rather than the term "instruction" to underscore the inclusion of issues such as who the teachers are—their background, training, and so forth—their social interactions—how teachers relate to students and their families—and their teaching styles. All of these constitute pedagogy.

Much of educational literature and, particularly, teacher education literature has been dominated by psychology. This psychologically driven paradigm has rendered pedagogy, or perhaps more accurately, instruction, as a technical undertaking that merely requires that prospective teachers learn the requisite skills in order to be successful. This view of teaching suggests that issues such as culture, class, gender, or race, have little or nothing to contribute to our understanding of teaching. Or, when they do enter the discussion, they appear because they interfere with the performance of technically appropriate instructional strategies.

Work by educational anthropologists suggests that pedagogy is rooted in the cultural beliefs and practices of teachers (see for example, Au and Jordan 1981; Cazden and Leggett 1981; Erickson and Mohatt 1982). Thus, when there is a disjuncture or discontinuity between the culture of the students and that of the teacher, both teaching and learning suffers. My work with successful teachers of African-American students (Ladson-Billings 1994, 1995 in press) looks at instances where teachers either share the same cultural backgrounds as their students, or as a result of a transformative experience that makes visible their own culture (i.e., White culture), come to recognize their students as acting in culturally appropriate ways. Their work becomes what I have termed, "culturally relevant" (Ladson-Billings 1994; 1995 in press).

However, the experience of most African-American students is not in classrooms with culturally relevant teachers. Rather, the teacher, as a functionary of the state, engages in a state approved pedagogy that suggests that learning takes place in narrowly defined ways with the teacher acting always as the authority. In a nation-state whose economic value system is capitalistic, the classroom becomes a place where students compete for scarce resources (e.g., grades, teacher attention, recognition). The teachers as capitalists use their pedagogical practices in ways that reward some and sanction others.

Consider the fact that African-American male students, as a group, enter elementary school performing at or above grade level and within three short years they lag significantly behind their White counterparts (Kunjufu 1984). What happens to precipitate this achievement decline? Of course, one persistent explanation is the inherent cognitive inferiority of African Americans that "catches up" with them by the ages of nine or 10.[4] Another, equally specious argument is the inherent cultural inferiority notion.[5] Rarely considered are the ways in which schools, in general, and teachers, in particular, structure the classroom to reproduce inequitable learning and achievement.

More recently, the psychologists have attempted to reassert themselves in the discussion of the "mismatch" between culture and pedagogy. Thus, preservice and in-service teachers are told that the students' "learning styles" are the reason for their failure to succeed. From my perspective, the learning style literature only serves as a benevolent pathologizing of the students because ultimately, it suggests that somehow the way they learn is not the "normal" way.

In my work, I have called upon teachers to investigate their own "teaching styles" to examine the ways that it might advantage some while disadvantaging others. However, by investigating their teaching styles, I am not asking merely for an inventory of teaching technique, but rather a critical look at the ideology that underlies their beliefs about themselves as well as others, the way they structure social interactions between and among themselves and the students, and their conceptions of knowledge (Ladson-Billings 1995 in press).

Colonial teachers understand that their work is the work of the nation-state. If the state can accommodate only certain people into high prestige work that produces high rewards, then it is the job of teachers to insure that the "right" people are awarded the credentials that lead to this end. In the United States this was originally accomplished much the way it was done in apartheid South Africa. By providing White middle-class students with the best resources, the best trained teachers, and a curriculum that reflects their reality, these students are assured a more than even chance of being credentialed to attend the most prestigious schools and enter the most coveted occupations.

In both cases—apartheid South Africa and the United States—some few Students of Color participate in a "sponsored mobility" that suggests that the system is fair to those who work hard, conform, and demonstrate their ability to fit into the social order. This allows the system to rationalize the high percentage of failure by pointing to the victims as inept, lazy, and undeserving.

Administration and governance. Schools in the United States, unlike schools in most nation-states are the responsibility of the individual localities (states or provinces). Therefore, the administration of schools occurs at the state or local level. School boards are typically elected and make policy decisions at various levels. However, in urban schools serving African-American students, the policymakers are likely to be far removed from the local community.

For example, in the School District of Philadelphia, the school board members are appointed by the mayor. These positions serve to pay off patronage debts. The people who have served the mayor are unlikely to be the people who served the poorest, most disenfranchised members of the community. Students attend schools where the policy decisions are made without their interests being known and/or considered.

This arrangements stands in stark contradiction to the situation that arose in New York in the early 1970s. Parents and community members of the Ocean Hill-Brownsville District (Brooklyn, New York) decided to take control of their schools to insure that the policy and governance issues did reflect what was best for their students. This insistence of community control (not merely community participation) is at the heart of the current debate about Afri-centric or African-centered education.

As previously demonstrated, the White community seems not to be concerned that segregated all African-American schools exist. Rather, the notion that African Americans would make all administrative and policy decisions in these schools seems far more intolerable. So ignorant is the White power structure about what is meant by African-centered education, that former Secretary of Education William Bennett queried, "Well where are they going to live when they finish these schools? Africa?"[6] Do students graduating from Catholic schools move to Southern Ireland or Latin America? Does attending Hebrew school mean you have to live in Israel?

Currently, in both Wisconsin and Minnesota there exist Indian Tribal Schools. The Oneida Tribal School, located near Green Bay, Wisconsin, is a private school financed by the Oneida Indian's gaming profits. Originally the school served students from grades K–8 but after witnessing their steady decline in the local public high school, the tribe agreed to extend its program through high school. Its administrator has won several awards and recognitions (both within the tribe and beyond) for her excellent work. The goal of the school is to prepare its graduates for participation in tribal life and governance—to be able to sustain themselves economically and avoid cultural alienation.

The Indian Magnet School in Minneapolis, Minnesota is a public school with similar aims. Its administrator is known for both his participation in the scholarly community and his effective leadership. He has observed that in order for students from marginalized cultures to be successful in schools, we must "stop trying to put culture in education and start putting education in the culture" (Pewewardy 1994).

In apartheid South Africa many Black teachers worked to subvert the policies of the administration. However, they worked at great personal risk. Their curriculum and teaching was scrutinized and regulated by the government. No matter how successful they were with their students, the structure of the society delimited the role allocation for Blacks.

Funding. Intimately linked to administration and governance is funding. While the complexity of school funding is far beyond the scope of this discussion, some of the central features of funding are relevant here. School funding in apartheid South Africa (and most industrialized nations) is a central government function. The department or ministry of education receives a part of the national budget and allocates monies to various provinces and localities. In apartheid South Africa, there was no pretense of equal budget allocations. White schools were funded at much higher levels than Black ones.

In the United States this funding issue is more complex but equally pernicious. Because of the local province's (state's) role in providing education, the resources from that education emanate from a different source—generally, property taxes. Thus, communities with the most valuable property have the most valuable schools. African Americans, who are disproportionately among the ranks of the poor, either have less valuable property or no property (as renters). Their schools are funded by a smaller property tax base.

Even when school districts purport to share revenues to equalize the funding, the richer school districts have an opportunity to create private foundations to further subsidize their schools. Also, the fact that White schools are likely to be newer and more modern facilities means that despite equal funding, less of their funding has to go toward basic maintenance costs. Poorer Black schools use a higher proportion of their funding to pay for repairing leaky roofs, replacing broken windows, and general upkeep on dilapidated buildings (Kozol, 9).

As more Whites leave the public schools in the United States, public support of the schools declines. Most popular among most gubernatorial candidates is an appeal to the propertied electorate to reduce their property tax burden. This state property tax reduction is paired with continued federal support for tax deductions for property owners and an attempt to cut or abolish the capital gains tax— one of the few taxes that is not leveled against the poor.

The significance of property in the United States cannot be overstated. In the rounding of the nation, the franchise was extended only to White male *property owners*. For all intents and purposes, women, children, and Blacks were considered to be property. Thus, the move of "property" to claim citizenship rights has been one of the more difficult political turns in U.S. civic life (Williams 1991).

In other writings, I (along with Tate 1995) have argued that race continues to be a significant factor in U.S. society, that the United States is based on property rights (not human rights), and the intersection of race and property provides a powerful heuristic for understanding inequality in the society.

School inequality provides a microcosm for the way that inequality functions throughout the society. By proclaiming itself to be meritocratic, the school offers entrance to all students. However, researchers of various theoretical and political persuasions have demonstrated that the school quickly works to sort and separate the students into differential instructional programs leading to differential life chances (see for example, Bowles and Gintis 1976; Rist 1970; Shor 1980). These separations occur along class (Bowles and Gintis 1976), gender (Sadker and Sadker 1986), and racial lines (Kozol 1991).

Some Reasons to Forestall Despair

Despite attempts at court ordered racial desegregation (Tate et al. 1993) and school restructuring (Lipman 1993), schools are ingenious in their ways to re-segregate and reinscribe inequality. However, several moves in African-American communities throughout the nation offer reasons for educational optimism.

The emergence of the African-centered school movement bodes well for the possibility of a "post-colonial" educational experience for African-Americans students. More than merely grouping African-American urban students together—which they experience already—this attempt at reorienting African-American schooling toward core values extant in the African-American community suggests that rather than creating a parallel schooling experience that is bound to reproduce and structure the same inequalities of the current system, this attempt is to free the minds of African-American students from the shackles of oppression and self-hatred.[7]

Mainstream scholars, both conservative and liberal, resent the attempts at African-centered education, albeit for very different reasons. Conservatives endorse the notion of "school choice" because it bolsters their arguments for privatization and federal government support of religious and other independent schools. However, they disparage the principles upon which these schools are rounded because the African-centered education movement argues against the alleged universalism of the mainstream curriculum.

Liberals believe that African-centered education works against the efforts toward equality and integration for which many struggled during the U.S. Civil Rights movement. However, until recently, debate about the "costs" of school desegregation has been absent or subvocal. The tension that liberals experience include the concern for integration and equal access on the one hand, and self-determination and community control on the other.

For the African-American community this debate largely is pragmatic. Most urban African Americans attend segregated, substandard schooling that replicates the European colonial model. The significant people, places, events, and ways of being reflected in the curriculum honor the colonizer. In those schools where there is some integration, whenever the number of African-American students begins to approach some visible representation White students leave (Bissinger 1994).

Increasingly, African Americans have decided that having White students in attendance cannot be the determining factor for quality education. Although the 1960s school desegregation strategy was to have African-American students attend the schools that Whites did because of the belief that "dollars follow White students," that is, resources and supplies are made available in schools that serve White students, the reality of White flight has made that an untenable position. Now, African-American communities realize that they cannot force Whites to stay in communities with them, but they argue that the fact that Whites leave should not (and must not) mean school destruction.

As African-American communities attempt to claim the schools in the schools their children attend, they are insisting that the schooling that occurs in them challenge the existing "regimes of truth" (Foucault 1980). These schools do not downplay the need for students to learn literacy and numeracy skills (Delpit 1986). However, they do insist that students participate in an understanding and self-knowledge that rejects the beliefs of inferiority that permeate the society.

So widespread is this desire for positive self-knowledge that even in communities where African Americans seem satisfied with the school system, there are alternative and Saturday schools emerging to fill the need for affirmation and political awareness.[8] However, many believe that the Saturday school attempts are not a powerful enough "corrective" for the pernicious and devastating effects of the colonial education system.

Just as South Africa stands on the precipice of a new order which will necessarily challenge the colonial structures that defined schooling throughout the apartheid years, so too, must African-

American communities re-invent the schooling experiences of their children. The current system provides no way for African-American students to participate in the highly technological global economy.

Colonial schooling in African-American communities serves to reproduce a social stratification that keeps the masses of African-American students in the same socioeconomic situation of their brothers and sisters in the townships of South Africa, the favelas of Brazil, and the urban centers of Great Britain and Canada—part of a growing permanent underclass where Black children are devalued except for their ability to serve their colonizers.

The paradox of this devaluation is that as I write this paper I sit in a university community in Sweden. Although many in the town speak English, generally I am surrounded by the sites and sounds of Swedish. However, the vast intrusive nature of U.S. cable television means I can receive images from home. Of course, CNN provides the comfort of the English language with a focus on international news. But, the most riveting images come via MTV.

Here, near the Arctic Circle where I have seen (and eaten) reindeer, learned of the struggles of the Lapps, and come to understand better the realities and challenges of democratic socialism, African-American youth point defiant fingers at the power structure. They sing, dance, and rap as an expression of their disaffection and alienation with the present social order. Their music and style mesmerizes the youth of the world. Their compact discs are sold in every music store. They recognize the inherent destructiveness of their colonial education. For some, the answer is to reject education altogether. For those of us who proclaim empathy and solidarity with there cause, we are obligated to work toward the dismantling of colonial schooling wherever it exists.

Notes

1. Even in a state like Wisconsin which has a low African-American population, African-American males constitute 41 percent of the inmate population at Columbia Prison in Portage, WI.

2. It is interesting to note that throughout the rule of Whites in both South Africa and Zimbabwe, Whites were always called, the "White" minority, as if the terms White and minority were not incompatible and needed clarification.

3. This valorization of the Pilgrims is an interesting parallel to the Dutch (Boers) who settled in South Africa. Like the Pilgrims, they fled re-

pression at home and saw themselves as making a new life in an "uninhab-ited," "uncivilized" country which was theirs to do with whatever they chose.

4. This is part of the long-standing argument that Arthur Jensen and others such as William Shockley reintroduced in the 1970s and is currently making a comeback in the work of Herenstein and Murray concerning the heritability of intelligence.

5. This argument became a powerful force behind compensatory edu-cation in the United States. The "cultural deprivation" paradigm suggested that so worthless was the cultural background of certain students (e.g., African-Americans, the poor) that the only hope for their educational sur-vival was early intervention.

Today, while the cultural deprivation language is eschewed, its intent and meaning continues to exist in the term, "at-risk."

6. Interview with William Bennett, "CBS Evening News," March 1992.

7. Scholars such as A. Wade Boykin and Forest Tom (1985), and Na'im Akbar (1985) have written and researched African-American core values. These values often are used as themes in African-American literature.

8. In Madison, Wisconsin where public schools are rated among the best in the nation, African-American parents, educators, and community members have worked together to form an African American Ethnic Acad-emy. This academy meets two Saturdays a month and for a four-week sum-mer session to teach students from kindergarten through grade 12. The academy's curriculum includes African and African-American history and culture, dance, art, music, and basic skills. At the high school level students can avail themselves of tutorials and test-taking skills. This model is not un-like the Freedom Schools that emerged in the 1960s.

Additionally, the national organization, Jack and Jill has redirected its attention to issues of African and African-American culture. A long-standing Black middle-class institution, Jack and Jill had had a tradition of selective membership and inculcating African-American children into bourgeois White society. Thus, members participated in debutante balls, attended symphonies and plays and maintained an obvious distance from working- and lower-class African Americans. Today, parents of Jack and Jill use it as a means to reconnect their largely middle-class students to a cultural her-itage that quickly is slipping away from them.

References

Akbar, N. 1985. "Our Destiny: Authors of a Scientific Revolution." In *Black Children: Social, Educational and Parental Environments*. Edited by H. McAdoo and J. L. McAdoo. Beverly Hills, CA: Sage.

262   *Gloria Ladson-Billings*

Alkalimat, A. 1986. *Introduction to Afro-American Studies.* Chicago: Twenty First Century Books and Publication.

Apple, M. 1986. *Teacher and Texts.* New York: Routledge and Kegan Paul.

Apple, M. 1993.

Asante, M. K. 1987. *The Afrocentric Idea.* Philadelphia: Temple University Press.

———. K. 1991. "The Afrocentric Idea in Education." *The Journal of Negro Education* 60: 170–180.

Au, K. and C. Jordan. 1981. "Teaching Reading to Hawaiian Children: Finding a Culturally Appropriate Solution." In *Culture and the Bilingual Classroom: Studies in Classroom Ethnography.* Edited by H. Trueba, G. Guthrie, and K. Au, 139–152. Rowley, MA: Newbury House.

Baugh, J. 1994. "New and Prevailing Misconceptions of African American English for Logic and Mathematics." In *Teaching Diverse Populations.* Edited by E. Hollins, J. King and W. Hayman, 191–205. Albany: State University of New York Press.

Bissinger, H. L. 1994. "When Whites Flee." *The New York Times Magazine* May 29 1994: 26–33, 43, 50, 53–55.

Bowles, S. and H. Gintis. 1976. *Schooling in Capitalist America.* New York: Basic Books.

Boykin, A. W. and F. Toms. 1985. "Black Child Socialization: A Conceptual Framework." In *Black Children: Social, Educational and Parental Environments.* Edited by H. McAdoo and J. L. McAdoo. Beverly Hills, CA: Sage.

Cazden, C. and Leggett. 1981. "Culturally Responsive Education: Recommendations for Achieving Lau Remedies, II." In *Culture and the Bilingual Classroom: Studies in Classroom Ethnography.* Edited by H. Trueba, G. Guthrie, and K. Au, 69–86. Rowley, MA: Newbury House.

Delpit, L. 1986. "Skills and Other Dilemmas of a Professional Black Educator." *Harvard Educatona Review* 56: 379–385.

Dilliard, J. 1972. *Black English.* New York: Random House.

Erickson, F. and G. Mohatt. 1982. "Cultural Organization and Participation Structures in Two Classrooms of Indian Students." In *Doing the Ethnography of Schooling.* Edited by G. Spindler, 131–174. New York: Holt, Rinehart and Winston.

Focault, M. 1980. *Power/Knowledge: Selected Interviews and Other Writings.* Edited by Colin Gordon and translated by Gordon et al. New York: Pantheon.

Gee, J. 1989. "What is Literacy?" *Journal of Education* 171: 18–25.

Irvine, J. J. 1990. *Black Students and School Failure*. Westport, CT: Greenwood Press.

Jansen, J. 1990. "In Search of Liberation Pedagogy in South Africa." *Journal of Education* 172(2): 62–71.

King, J. 1991. "Unfinished Business: Black Student Alienation and Black Teachers' Emancipatory Pedagogy." In M. Foster, ed., *Readings on Equal Education: Qualitative Investigations into Schools and Schooling*. Edited by M. Foster, 11: 245–271. New York: AMS Press.

———. 1992. "Diaspora Literacy and Consciousness in the Struggle Against Miseducation in the Black Community." *The Journal of Negro Education* 61: 317–340.

Kozel, J. 1991. *Savage Inequalities: Children in America's Schools*. New York: Harper Perennial.

Kunjufu, J. 1984. *Developing Discipline and Positive Self-Images in Black Children*. Chicago: Afro-America Images.

Ladson-Billings, G. 1994. *The Dreamkeepers: Successful Teachers of African American Children*. San Francisco: Jossey Bass.

———. 1995. "Toward a Theory of Culturally Relevant Pedagogy." *American Educational Research Journal*. In press.

Ladson-Billings, G. and W. F. Tate. 1995. "Toward a Critical Race Theory of Education." *Teachers College Record* 97(1): 47–68.

Lipman, P. 1993. *Teacher Attitudes toward African American Student Achievement in Restructured Schools*. Ph.D. diss. University of Wisconsin, Madison, WI.

Majors, R. and J. Billson. 1992. *Cool Pose: The Dilemmas of Black Manhood in America*. New York: Lexington Books.

Mandela, N. 1994. *Long Walk to Freedom*. Boston: Little Brown.

Maurice, E. 1983. "The Curriculum and the Crisis in the Schools." In *Education Curriculum and Development*. Edited by A. P. Hunter, M. J. Ashley, and C. J. Millar, 99–121. Cape Town: University of Cape Town.

Nobles, W. 1973. "Psychological Research and the Black Self-Concept: A Critical Review." *Journal of Social Issues* 29: 11–31.

Pewewardy, C. 1994. "Culturally Responsive Pedagogy in Action: An American Indian Magnet School." In *Teaching Diverse Populations*. Edited by E. Hollins, J. King and W. Hayman, 77–92. Albany: State University of New York Press.

Rist, R. 1970. "Social Class and Teacher Expectations: The Self-Fulfilling Prophecy in Ghetto Education." *Harvard Educational Review* 40: 411–451.

Sadker, M. and D. Sadker. 1986. "Sexism in the Classroom: From Grade School to Graduate School." *Phi Delta Kappan* 68: 512.

Shor, I. 1980. *Critical Teaching and Everyday Life*. Boston: South End Press.

Smitherman, G. 1986. *Talkin' and Testifyin': The Language of Black America*. Detroit: Wayne State University Press.

Tate, W. F., G. Ladson-Billings, and C. Grant. 1993. "The Brow Decision Revisited: Mathematizing Social Problems." *Educational Policy* 7: 255–275.

Williams, P. 1991. *The Alchemy of Race and Rights*. Cambridge, MA: Harvard University Press.

Woodson, Carter G. 1933. *The Miseducation of the Negro*. Washington, DC: Association Press.

Contributors

Michael W. Apple is John Bascom Professor of Education at the University of Wisconsin, Madison. A former elementary and secondary school teacher and past-president of a teachers union, he has worked with educators, unions, dissident groups, and governments throughout the world to democratize educational research, policy, and practice. He has written extensively about the relationship between education and power. Among his most recent books are: *Official Knowledge* (1993), *Education and Power* (1995), and *Cultural Politics and Education* (1996).

Henry A. Giroux is the Waterbury Chair Professor of Secondary Education at Penn State University. He is the author of numerous articles and books including the most recent: *Disturbing Pleasures; Fugitive Cultures; Pedagogy and the Politics of Hope*; and *Channel Surfing: Race Talk and the Destruction of Today's Youth*.

Gloria Ladson-Billings is an Associate Professor in the Department of Curriculum and Instruction at the University of Wisconsin-Madison where she teaches courses in multicultural perspectives on education and culturally relevant pedagogy. She is the author of the critically acclaimed book, *The Dreamkeepers: Successful Teachers of African American Children* and numerous journal articles and book chapters. Her current research interests is critical race theory and its application to education.

Patricia McDonough is an Associate Professor at the Graduate School of Education and Information Studies at the University of California at Los Angeles. Her areas of research include cultural studies, social class stratification especially within education, organizational analysis, and college access. Her book, *Choosing Colleges:*

How Social Class and Schools Structure Opportunity, is being published this year by SUNY Press.

Theodore R. Mitchell is currently serving as Vice Chancellor, Academic Planning and Budget and the University of California, Los Angeles and Dean of the Graduate School of Education and Information Studies at UCLA. His own research has been in examining educational organizations in an historical perspective. His particular interest is in exploring the ways educational organizations in the United States have resisted or embraced change. He is the author of numerous essays and articles, and is currently completing a book entitled *The Republic for Which it Stands: Liberty, Order, and the Development of Public Schools in America*.

Raymond A. Morrow is Professor of Sociology and Adjunct Professor of Educational Policy Studies at the University of Alberta, Edmonton, where he has taught since 1984. A co-author with Carlos A. Torres of *Social Theory and Education* (SUNY, 1995), he has also published extensively in other aspects of social and cultural theory, including a book on *Critical Theory and Methodology* (Sage, 1994) which outlines what is termed an interpretive structuralist research program based in part on the work of Giddens and Habermas.

Jeannie Oakes is Professor of Education and Assistant Dean in the Graduate School of Education and Information Studies at the University of California, Los Angeles where she directs Center X— Where Research and Practice Intersect for Urban School Professionals. Professor Oakes' research and writing target inequalities in the allocation of resources and learning opportunities in U.S. schools, and the progress of equity-minded reform. Much of her work, including *Keeping Track: How Schools Structure Inequality* examines how tracking and grouping students by ability in school affect the classroom experiences of low-income students and students of color. Her recent books include, *Making the Best of Schools*, (1990, Yale University Press) and *Creating New Educational Communities* (1995, University of Chicago Press).

Anita Oliver is a professor at the School of Education at La Sierra University in Riverside, California where she is also Chair of the Department of Curriculum and Instruction. She has done extensive research on the politics of curriculum and textbooks. She is currently finishing a book on textbook conflict in local communities.

Thomas S. Popkewitz is a Professor and Chair of the Department of Curriculum and Instruction, The University of Wisconsin-Madison, and a Visiting Professor of UmeÜ University, Sweden. His interest is in a political sociology of educational knowledge. Current work concerns the changing terrain of social and political theory in education studies, comparative studies of educational reforms, and the social-historical relation of educational research and state governing practices. He is current finishing a manuscript of that focuses on pedagogical discourses as normalizing practices that functions to disqualify certain children from participation.

Daniel G. Solórzano is an Associate Professor and Head in the Division of Social Sciences and Comparative Education at the University of California, Los Angeles Graduate School of Education & Information Studies. His research and teaching interests include the study of the career paths of Scholars of Color using Critical Race Theory and the concept of marginality.

Carlos Alberto Torres is a Professor in the Graduate School of Education and Information Studies, UCLA, and Director of the Latin American Center. He holds a B.A. in Sociology and Teaching Credential from the University de El Salvador, in Buenos Aires, Argentina, an M.A. in Political Science from FLACSO, Mexico City, an M.A. and Ph.D. from Stanford University, and post-doctoral studies in Educational Foundations at the University of Alberta, Canada. Widely published in Spanish, Portuguese, and English, he is the author of more than one hundred research articles and thirty-five books.

Octavio Villalpando is a Post-Doctoral Research Fellow and Interim Director of Institutional Research at California State University, Monterey Bay. His research focuses on Chicanas and Chicanos in higher education, college student development, and the impact of a "multicultural/diverse" environment on Students of Color.

Amy Stuart Wells is an Associate Professor of Educational Policy at UCLA's Graduate School of Education and Information Studies. Her research and writing has focused on the role of race in educational policy making and implementation. More specifically, she studies school desegregation; school choice policy, including charter schools; and detracking in racially mixed schools. She received her Ph.D. from Columbia University in Sociology of Education—a joint program between Teachers College and the Graduate School of Arts and Sciences—in 1991. She is author of several journal articles and books, including *Time to Choose: American at the Crossroads of School Choice Policy* (Hill and Wang, 1993); first author with Irene Serna of "The Politics of Culture: Understanding Local Political Resistance in Detracking in Racially Mixed Schools," (Spring, 1996) Harvard Educational Review; and first author with Robert L. Crain of *Stepping over the Color Line: African American Students in White Suburban Schools* (Yale University Press, in press). In 1995, she began a two-year study of charter schools in ten school districts in California funded by the Ford Foundation and the Annie E. Casey Foundation.

Index

269